AUTHORWARE®
An Introduction to Multimedia

for Use with Authorware 3 and Higher

Simon Hooper

University of Minnesota

PRENTICE HALL Upper Saddle River, NJ 07458

Library of Congress Cataloging-in-Publication Data

Hooper, Simon.
    Authorware : an introduction to multimedia for use with Authorware
  3 and higher / Simon Hooper.
        p.   cm
    Includes index.
    ISBN 0-13-595554-8
    1. Multimedia   2. Macromedia Authorware.
  QA76.575.H68   1997
  006.7'869--dc21   96-49367
                                                              CIP

Editor: *Robert Kern*
Assistant Editors: *Michael Tuminello/Scott Pearlman*
Production Editor: *James Buckley*
Technical Services: *David Moles*
Cover Design: *Joseph Sengotta*
Manufacturing Buyer: *Donna Sullivan*
Page Layout: *Wald Designs*
Production Manager: *Barbara A. Murray*

 ©1997 by Prentice-Hall, Inc.
Simon & Schuster / A Viacom Company
Upper Saddle River, New Jersey 07458

Printed in the United States of America

10 9 8 7 6 5 4 3 2 1

ISBN 0-13-595554-8

Prentice-Hall International (UK) Limited, *London*
Prentice-Hall of Australia Pty. Limited, *Sydney*
Prentice-Hall Canada Inc., *Toronto*
Prentice-Hall Hispanoamericana, S.A., *Mexico*
Prentice-Hall of India Private Limited, *New Delhi*
Prentice-Hall of Japan, Inc., *Tokyo*
Simon & Schuster Asia Pte. Ltd., *Singapore*
Editora Prentice-Hall do Brasil, Ltda., *Rio de Janeiro*

To Kate.

ABOUT THE AUTHOR

Originally from London, England, Simon Hooper moved to the United States in 1978. Currently, he is an Associate Professor in the Instructional Systems and Technology program at the University of Minnesota, where he has taught courses about multimedia design since 1989. Primarily focused on Authorware, Mr. Hooper has been developing computer courseware since the early 1980's. His courseware, as well as his many published articles, have focused primarily on designing materials, Authorware problem solving, and interface design.

CONTENTS

Chapter 3 Creating Presentations   31

Chapter 4 Multimedia   47

Chapter 5 Odds and Ends   59

Chapter 6 The Interaction Icon: Part 1   73

Chapter 7 The Interaction Icon: Part 2   89

PREFACE

WHAT'S AVAILABLE IN THIS TEXT?

Learning to use Authorware can be a demanding task, even for experienced computer users. Although the application is tremendously powerful, it is also sophisticated and takes many months, or even years, to master. Unfortunately, learning Authorware from a manual can be particularly puzzling. Manuals often include detailed information that sometimes cloud critical concepts resulting in confusion and frustration.

My goal has been to develop a different kind of text that will get closer to the experience of learning from a personal tutor. The text uses a multidimensional approach to learning by using three resources to teach, illustrate, and supplement the learning experience.

The first resource is the book. The text differs from a manual is important ways. First, it focuses on Authorware's critical features and ignores detail that can be learned more easily when important fundamental knowledge has been learned. Every chapter includes a brief list of objectives that are intended to steer the reader away from distracting information and to focus on critical ideas. Second, the text includes many follow-along activities that outline important ideas and help you to learn-by-doing in a guided setting. Also, every chapter includes several exercises that are intended to leave you with a rich and working knowledge of the design process.

The second resource is a CD-ROM containing sample files and many instructional videos. Information from each chapter is illustrated using QuickTime videos that will run on Macintosh and PC computers. Ideas that are difficult to understand by reading alone are demonstrated in these videos that play on your computer monitor. The CD-ROM also contains several files that are linked closely to the content in the chapters. Use these files to follow the activities outlined in the text or open and examine the files at your leisure. One way to learn how to use Authorware is to manipulate these files and observe the results of your experimenting.

The third resource is an Internet Web site. You can connect to my Website at :

http://www.prenhall.com/hooper/

The Web site includes three categories of resources: answers to exercises, development tools, teaching updates and discussion of common development problems. Answers to the text exercises will be available in two formats. When appropriate, correct answers to the problems at the end of each chapter will be given. However, where more complex solutions are needed, files are available for you to download to your desktop computer. Separate files are available for Macintosh and PC users.

The development tools are designed to support all multimedia developers and include links to important development software that you can download without charge, connections to Authorware and other multimedia Listserv sites, on-line examples of Authorware and Shockwave files, and opportunities to post questions about development difficulties. Answers to these questions as well as discussions of updates and developing issues will form the foundation of a database of Authorware problem solving tools.

HOW SHOULD YOU USE THIS TEXT?

There is no single best approach to learning to design multimedia using Authorware. However, my experience indicates that there are essentially two classes of Authorware students: Those who have and those who have not previously programmed computers.

One approach, commonly used for computer novices, focuses on learning rudimentary content covered in the early chapters before attempting more complex ideas presented later in the text. This approach "protects" users from the chapters on Variables and Functions that are often challenging for those who have never before programmed a computer.

Another approach, seems to be more effective with users with programming backgrounds. These people may benefit from covering early in the learning process the chapters on Variables and Functions (Chapters 13 and 14). Learning how to integrate Variables and Functions into every phase of the design process is often critical to using Authorware effectively.

A third approach is also popular. This approach teaches Authorware within the context of an Instructional Design course. Instructors who follow this tack may wish to move rapidly through the first few chapters and emphasize the more complex concepts outlined in the chapters on the Interaction icon (Chapters 6-8), Navigate and Framework icons, (Chapters 11 and 12), and Variables and Functions (Chapters 13 and 14). These chapters cover content that is most likely to be the focus of issues concerning human learning and interface design that are often emphasized in design courses.

Features

Text designed for Macintosh and PC students of Authorware!

Authorware; Introduction to Multimedia, incorporates print materials, instructional videos on a CD-ROM, and example files to instruct, model, and demonstrate the skills and concepts needed to use Authorware effectively.

Sixteen chapters systematically lead the user through each component of Authorware:

- Chapter introductions include a brief overview followed by instructional objectives that outline what students will know or be able to do upon completing the chapter.

ACKNOWLEDGMENTS

The world of technology and software moves very quickly. It is difficult to get a textbook developed covering a particular release of an application package before the package has a new release. Good reviewers help us accomplish this. Many thanks to the reviewers below for their thorough and timely efforts!

Mona Hamilton- Tallahassee Community College
Lolita Gilkes— Richland College Community Center
Michael Fimian— Appalachian State College
Derek Redmond— Queens University Film Studies, Canada
Jon Duff— Purdue University
John Sheperd— Duquesne University
Thomas Mueller—Independent
Rik Hall—University of New Brunswick
Janet Bohren—University of Cincinnati
Cecelia Buchanan— Washington University
Mary Emerson— Colin County Community College
Mary Jac Reed—Catholic University of America

- Listings of new and important words and terms used in the chapter.
- Highlights of tips and tricks for dealing with common development problems.
- Detailed procedures outlining steps to complete important tasks.
- Study exercises to test comprehension of important concepts and help readers to apply content to a range of applications.

Developed by Hooper, the accompanying CD-ROM runs on both Macintosh and PC computers and incorporates instructional videos and demonstration files. Instructional videos in QuickTime format on the CD-ROM, which were professionally recorded at the University of Minnesota, model concepts that are difficult to describe in print and illustrate the activities outlined in the chapters. Demonstration files can be opened and inspected to examine how to build files and create routines.

The text is linked to a World Wide Web home page to provide answers to exercises, maintain updated information, and link users with additional educational resources. Macintosh and PC files are available for students to download over the Internet. Users can examine and use these files to check their understanding of important ideas.

Getting Started

CHAPTER OVERVIEW

In this chapter, you will learn the basic structure of Authorware and how Authorware differs from traditional programming languages and other authoring tools. You will also examine the process of creating an Authorware lesson: adding icons to the Course Flow Line; setting options within each icon; and placing lesson content into Display icons.

CHAPTER OBJECTIVES

After completing this chapter you will
- Understand the difference between Authorware and other multimedia development tools.
- Open Authorware and create a new file.
- Learn the basic process of course development in Authorware.
- Navigate between the Presentation Window and the Design Window.

KEY TERMS

Programming language
Authoring language
Course Flow Line
Icons
Display icon
Navigation
Design Window
Presentation Window

SUPPORT MATERIALS

On the CD-ROM disc, run **BEGIN.PKG** if you are a Macintosh user or **BEGIN.APP** if you are using a PC. When the file opens, click once on the title page to begin. Select the button titled **Chapter 1** and run the video to examine how to place icons on the Course Flow Line and to navigate between the Design and Presentation windows.

STUDY TOPICS

A Brief History of Software Development Tools

Before we begin, it may be helpful to understand why Authorware is such a powerful tool for developing educational courseware. The tools used for computer-based lesson design have evolved considerably during the past 20 years. Educational software was originally developed using general-purpose programming languages. Although appropriate in a wide variety of technological, experimental, and industrial settings, these languages were often inappropriate for courseware design because they required developers to possess detailed computer-programming knowledge to create even simple lessons.

The beauty of Authorware is that it permits designers to develop sophisticated lessons without needing to possess the same depth of programming experience or technical knowledge. Authorware is a powerful development tool that accelerates the design process by using icons to represent tasks that are usually created using programming languages.

How Do Programming Languages Work?

Computers understand several different levels of programming languages. At the most basic level, the language that a computer understands is machine code. Machine code is a stream of binary ones and zeros that correspond exactly with the electronic circuits within the computer. For example, the command to double a number might be 01100011. A human analogy involves stimulating specific portions of the brain with electric currents to cause predictable reflex actions.

Writing software in machine code would be an impossibly tedious task. Instead, programmers sometimes use low-level, second-generation, programming languages, such as Assembly, that employ brief commands to replace the streams of ones and zeros that control the machine. Instructions are translated by a tool known as a translator, which converts Assembly language into machine-readable ones and zeros. However, Assembly, too, is a labor-intensive and cryptic programming language that involves learning very precise ways to communicate with the computer and is inappropriate for educational software development.

Many programmers use higher-level, third-generation languages such as Pascal, BASIC, and C to write software. Higher-level languages are generally easier to use than Assembly because they employ programming statements that are closer to human language and programming structures that are somewhat intuitive. Furthermore, programs written in these languages are generally portable. That is, they can be compiled and run on virtually any computer.

Programmers select programming languages to fulfill specific needs. COBOL, for example, a programming language that uses languagelike instructions, was designed to be used by nontechnical users in the business world. COBOL programs are commonly used by direct mail advertisers to manage large databases and to sort and print mailing labels. FORTRAN, a more technical language, was created to be used in scientific environments where processing speed is paramount.

In addition to fulfilling the programming roles for which they were originally designed, most higher-level languages can be used to develop educational materials. In the hands of sophisticated programmers, programming languages are very flexible and allow the designer to include virtually any option that is needed in a lesson. However, such flexibility comes at a price. All functionality must be programmed independently: Answer judging routines must be designed and coded, text placement must be specified precisely, and graphics often must be laboriously defined. Similarly, every complete unit of programming code (known as a subroutine) created for a lesson has to be individually created and tested. The resulting programs produce webs of thousands of lines of interconnected computer code. Updating such programs is always difficult and often impossible when the original programmers are unavailable.

Despite their apparent flexibility, designing materials with traditional programming languages tends to limit design to activities that can be easily programmed and modified. In effect, designers are discouraged from employing the flexibility offered by programming languages because of the expertise and cost associated with implementing such features. Furthermore, most high-level programming languages do not include commands to access peripherals that are often used in educational software design. For example, commands to recognize and interact with a videodisc player are not usually incorporated into high-level programming languages.

What Is Authorware?

Authorware is the state of the art development tool for designing interactive instructional software (which is often called courseware). You can use Authorware to develop any combination of presentations, tutorials, simulations, tests, or educational games. Multimedia software can be used in a variety of educational settings including K–12, postsecondary, community, and corporate education.

What's more, you don't have to be a programmer to develop software with Authorware. Although technical expertise is a definite advantage for some of the more intricate details of the design process, nonprogrammers make excellent Authorware developers. In fact, many of the best developers are those individuals who cannot program, but are able to transfer their educational expertise onto the computer. Authorware encourages nonprogrammers by using a very intuitive environment that is fun and relatively easy to learn.

What Version of Authorware Do I Need?

You may have one of many different versions of Authorware. Over the past decade, Authorware has used several different names: Course of Action; Authorware Academic; Authorware Star; Authorware Working Model; Authorware Professional 2.0; Authorware 3; and now Authorware 3.5. Also, Authorware runs in both Mac and PC environments.

You can use this book to learn how to use many of the different versions of Authorware. The book focuses on Authorware 3.5 for the Macintosh, so many readers may notice differences between both the look of the screens, and the icons and tools that come with the program.

If you are using a PC version of the software, you will find that although some screens look different, the functionality is almost identical on both platforms. This is important because developers often create on one platform and transport their finished products to the other platform for distribution. If you are using an old version of Authorware (i.e., a version lower than 3.0), you may find that quite a few changes have occurred. For example, two new icons called Navigate and Framework have been created to provide greater flexibility. However, the operation of many of the most important features has remained similar across all versions of the program.

Mac or Windows?

Authorware is a cross-platform product designed for both PC and Macintosh users. The bad news (for PC users) is this text describes the Macintosh version of Authorware. All graphic displays, keypress conventions, and other program conventions describe the Macintosh version.

However, the good news is that the two versions are almost identical in functionality. Apart from cosmetic differences, the two versions of Authorware are practically identical. Better still, files written on one platform are directly convertible to the other platform. In other words, if you have both Macintosh and PC editions of the software, you can create a file on a PC, save the file on a disk or a network, and open and run the file on a Macintosh computer (or vice versa).

How Does Authorware Improve Design?

Although other programming languages *can* be used to develop instruction, Authorware has been written specifically to stimulate courseware development. Not only is Authorware much simpler to learn and use, it has been created to include the types of tasks most commonly needed when developing course materials.

One obvious difference between Authorware and other programming languages is that designers do not need to know how to program to use Authorware. Instead, designers use several different icons that have been pre-programmed with built-in functionality. The task for the developer is to learn the role of each icon as well as when each icon should be used and the options that can be employed. However, it should be also noted that previous programming experience does accelerate the learning curve. In particular, learning to use Functions and Variables (which are standard tools in the programmer's repertoire) is greatly facilitated with previous programming experience.

How Do I Get Started With Authorware?

Before you can learn to use Authorware to create instruction, you must know how to open the application, start a new file, save your file, and quit the program. Then you must learn the basic structure of an Authorware lesson. This includes inserting icons on the Course Flow Line, opening icons, and navigating between Presentation and Design windows.

To Open Authorware and Start a File

- Double-click on the Authorware icon to open the application.

- Authorware will start a new file and display its Design window. A Window similar to the following one will appear.

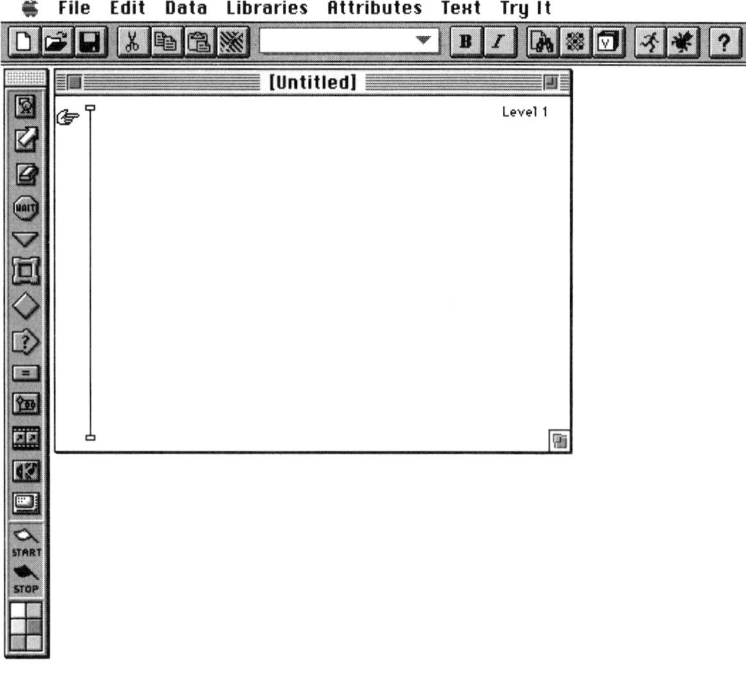

To Save a File

- Remember to save your work regularly. Select Save from the File pulldown menu. (Your program will be saved in the location you identify. If you have saved the program previously, the old program will be overwritten.) Incidentally, in the Authorware manuals, the word "piece" is used instead of file or lesson.

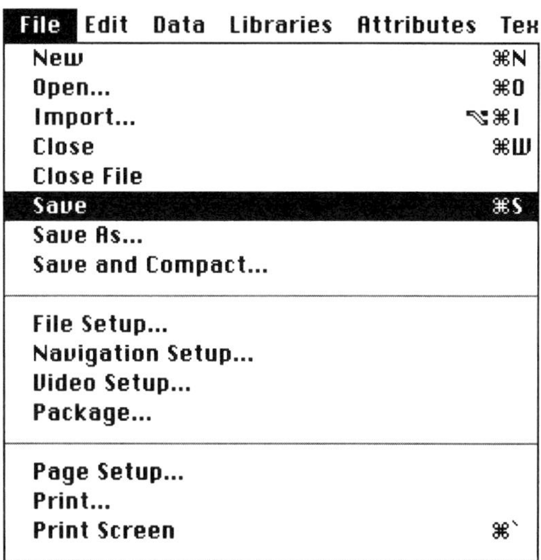

To Quit the Program

- If you want to quit the present file and work on another one, select Close File from the File menu.
- If you want to quit Authorware, select the Quit option from the File menu.

Creating Lessons

The design process involves selecting icons from a palette and placing them on the Course Flow Line (the long vertical line with a finger pointing to it). When the lesson runs, the icons on the flow line are executed sequentially (with exceptions that you will learn later).

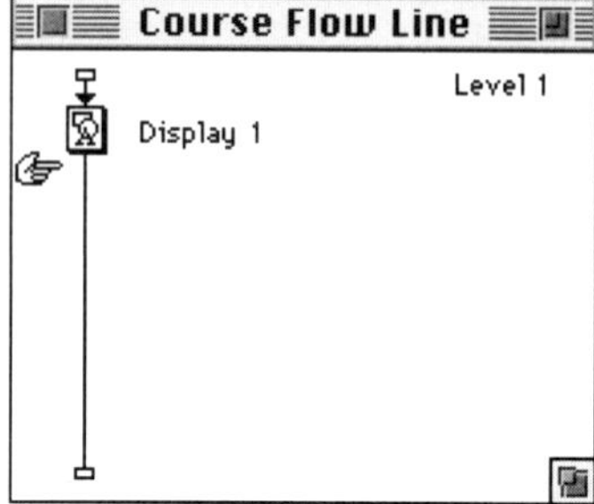

When the design process is complete, the file is converted into a standalone application that can be run on any computer (assuming the computer has the appropriate operating system and processing capabilities). After icons have been placed on the Course Flow Line, the designer must open and set the options for each icon, and place lesson content or instructions in appropriate icons. Placing content into icons requires understanding the differences between Design and Presentation windows.

Design Windows

Authorware lessons are constructed within Design Windows that include a Course Flow Line and a menu of several icons. Descriptions of these follow.

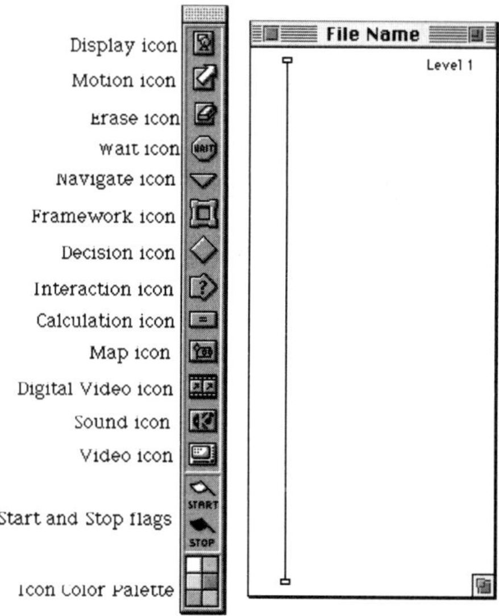

It may help to think of the icons in your lesson in the following way.

- *Display icons* are transparent sheets on which you place objects. These objects can be text or graphics.

- *Motion icons* enable you to move the objects in Display icons in any direction.

- *Erase icons* remove Display icons from the Presentation Window. If you do not remove old displays as you add others, you will soon have text and graphic objects overlaying one another and the screen will be unreadable.

- *Wait icons* control the speed at which information is displayed. Without them, Display icons would be inserted and removed so fast that the user would not have time to read them.

- *Navigate icons* allow users to link to icons attached to a Framework icon. Navigate icons can also be used to create "hypertext."   Hypertext allows the user to navigate by clicking on highlighted words in the lesson.

- *Framework icons* provide organized navigation structures. Framework icons allow the designer to create lesson segments that need not necessarily be completed linearly.

- *Decision icons* control the lesson flow. Icons attached to Decision icons form Paths. These Paths may be executed sequentially, randomly, or may be controlled by using Variables.

- *Interaction icons*, like Display icons, can present text or graphic objects. However, they differ in one important respect: They require the user to respond. The designer can vary the lesson flow according to how the user responds.

- *Calculation icons* both control and monitor conditions. Using Calculation icons is the closest an Authorware designer gets to traditional computer programming. Calculation icons can help you control the order of program presentation, the value of a Variable, and perform a wide variety of other tasks.

- *Map icons* do not change the lesson content, but they help the designer to organize information. In a sense, Map icons are like file folders: they enable you to organize related objects. Map icons are necessary because there is limited room on a flow line.

- *Digital video* icons control the presentation of video files from applications such as Macromind Director and QuickTime.

- *Sound icons* play sound files. Digitized sound files can be easily incorporated into lessons.

- *Video icons* are used to control attached videodisc players and VCRs.

To Insert an Icon onto a Flow Line

- Place the cursor over the icon you want to use and click-hold the mouse.

- With the mouse button held down, drag a Display icon toward the flow line by moving the cursor with the mouse. Place the icon where you want to insert it on the Course Flow Line.

- When the Display icon is in place, deselect the mouse button. (The icon will snap into place on the flow line.)

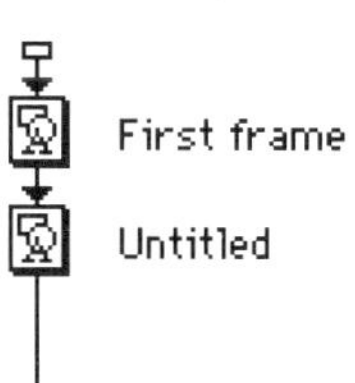

- Notice that when an icon is placed on the Course Flow Line, it is given the default name "Untitled". All icons are initially untitled, but, as will become apparent later, it is important to give every icon a unique name whenever possible. To name an icon, simply type a new name when the default name is highlighted. To highlight an icon's name, select the icon with the mouse (with a single click) or else press the Tab key. Pressing the Tab key highlights successive icons on the Course Flow Line.

- To delete an icon on the Course Flow Line, click on the icon and press the Delete key on the keyboard.

Presentation Windows

Most of the "behind-the-scenes" design work is performed in the Design Window. Here the Authorware designer decides on the lesson logic, how the user will interact with the lesson content, and many other events. However, the end user will never see the Design Window. It is only available to the designer and disappears when the final lesson is created.

The designer enters lesson content into the Presentation Window. The Presentation Window displays the lesson content as the user will see it. Although not identical to the final version, the Presentation Window gives the designer a good idea about how the end product will look and feel.

To Open a Display Icon and Go to Its Presentation Window

- Double-click on the Display icon on the Course Flow Line. (A Presentation window for the icon will open and the Toolbox will be displayed.) You may now enter text and graphics into the Presentation Window.

To Close a Presentation Window and Return to the Design Window

One of Authorware's strengths is its ability to perform tasks in multiple ways. For example, in what follows are three ways to navigate from the Presentation Window to the Design Window.

- Click on the Close box on either the *Presentation Window* or on the *Toolbox*.

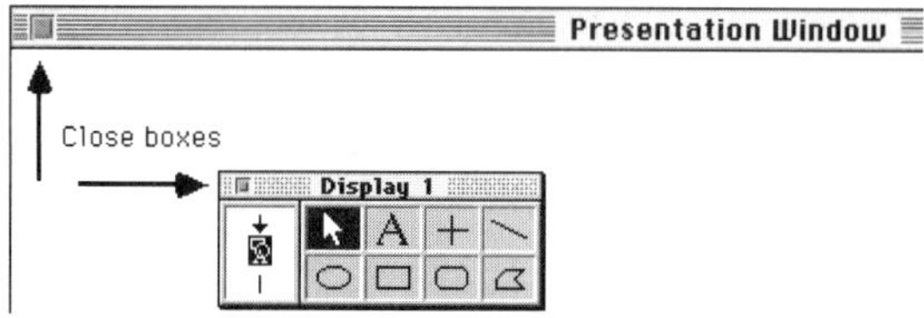

- Select *Show Current* Icon or *Jump to Icons* from the Try It pulldown menu.

- Click once on the Design Window if it is visible behind the Presentation Window.

STUDY EXERCISES

1. Name each of the following icons and briefly describe the role that each plays.

2. What is the difference between the Design and Presentation windows? List at least two different ways to navigate between the two windows.

3. Find someone with computer-programming experience and ask how difficult it would be to create an interactive lesson using a traditional programming language such as FORTRAN, Pascal, or C.

4. Take some time to explore Authorware.

   • Open Authorware and Save a new lesson file.

   • Place some icons on the Course Flow Line.

   • Try to drag the icons to different locations on the Course Flow Line.

   • Double-click on some of the icons on the Course Flow Line and examine the range of options available for each icon.

   • Find two different ways to navigate between the Design and Presentation windows and four ways to navigate back.

Creating Displays 

CHAPTER OVERVIEW

In this chapter, you will learn how to use the Display icon to present text and graphics. You will also learn how to use the Authorware Toolbox to create and manipulate graphic images and several features that facilitate the graphic design process.

CHAPTER OBJECTIVES

After completing this chapter, you will be able to

- Use a Display icon to present text and graphic images.
- Name each tool in the Toolbox.
- Understand the purpose of each tool in the Toolbox.
- Create and modify graphic images using the Toolbox.
- Manipulate text presentations as well as font types and styles.
- Use several special effects to create visually exciting displays.

KEY TERMS

Toolbox
Display options
Select mode, Graphic mode, Text mode
Text fonts and sizes
Lines (thicknesses and fills)
Boxes and ovals (squares and circles)
Overlapping objects
Fills, effects, lines, and modes

SUPPORT MATERIALS

On the CD-ROM disc, run **BEGIN.PKG** if you are a Macintosh user or **BEGIN.APP** if you are using a PC. When the file opens, click once on the title page to begin. Select **Chapter 2** and examine the videos in Part 1 and Part 2 to examine how to use the Authorware toolbox and several important tools available from the Attributes pulldown menu.

The folder on the CD-ROM titled MACDEMOS or PC_DEMOS contains several demonstration files that you can run and examine. The folder contains two versions of each file: a packaged file that you can run, and an unpackaged file containing the icons used to create the file.

Macintosh users: Run the file CHP02.pkg to view its contents.
Open the data file CHP02.A3M to examine how the file was created.

PC users: Run the file CHP02.APP to view its contents.
Open the data file CHP02.A3W to examine how the file was created.

Note: You must have a copy of Authorware on your computer to open the data files.

When you run the data file, you will see eight graphic objects created with the Toolbox. When you press the <u>Continue</u> button an empty Display icon titled You Try!! will open. Try to reproduce each of the objects using only the Authorware tools. If you experience difficulties, examine the Modes, Fills, Line thicknesses, Colors, and other display attributes to help you discover how the objects were created.

STUDY TOPICS

Initially, you will work with just one Display icon on the Course Flow Line. You will focus on the attributes available in the Display icon. The following chapter will explain how to use multiple Display icons to build presentations.

Working with Text and Graphic Objects-Using the Toolbox

When you double-click on a Display icon, the Toolbox opens automatically. To select a tool, single click on its icon with the mouse.

What Does the Toolbox Enable Me to Do?

The Toolbox includes several tools that are used for creating, moving, and editing text and graphics. Although the Toolbox enables you to create many different types of graphic objects, it is not usually used for complex graphic design. In practice, the graphics tools are used for simple tasks, such as drawing boxes, ovals, and lines. More complex graphics are usually created with specialized graphics applications and then imported into Authorware.

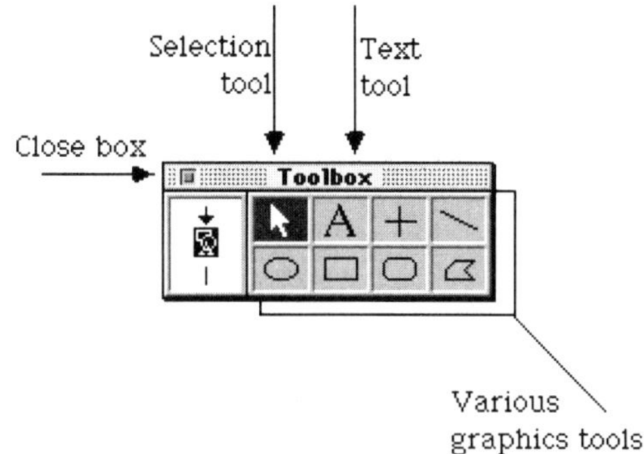

- Click on the Selection tool to enter the Select mode. The Selection tool enables you to select text and graphic objects so you can move them or change their characteristics.
- Click on the Text tool to enter the Text mode. The Text mode enables you to type and edit text objects.
- Click on the Oval, Rectangle, Rounded Rectangle, Polygon, or one of the line options to enter the Graphic mode. The Graphic mode enables you to create or change graphic objects.
- Click on the Close box.
  - If you are *creating* the program, you will return to the Course Flow Line.
  - If you are *running* the program, the toolbox will close.

  The difference between creating and running a lesson will be explained later.

How Can I Control Where and When the Toolbox Is Displayed?

- If you are *creating* the lesson, the Toolbox appears automatically when you open a Display icon: You cannot hide it.
- If you are *running* the lesson and reach a Display icon that you have not developed, the program will stop and the Toolbox will be displayed. After you develop the screen, click on the toolbox's Close box. The Toolbox will disappear and program execution will continue.
- If you are *running* the lesson and see a text or graphic object you want to edit, double-click on the text or graphic object to access the object's Presentation Window. The Toolbox associated with that Display icon will be displayed.
- To move the Toolbox, click-hold on the shaded area above the tools and drag the box to a different location.

How Do I Enter Text?

In this section, we will examine entering text, positioning margins, and setting tabs. The Text tool works like a relatively simple word processor. You can control line length, font type and size, color, and set text and decimal tabs.

To Enter Text

- Single-click on the Text tool (the lesson enters the Text mode).

- Move the cursor off the Toolbox. (Cursor becomes an I-beam.)
- Move the I-beam to where you want to create new text.
- Click once. (A text-width line appears; small boxes identify the margin handles. Clicking and dragging on a margin handle extends or shrinks the length of the text-width line.)

- Type the text. (All text entered becomes a single text object that can be edited.)
- The triangles next to the handles control indentation and word wrap just like the controls on a word processor.

To Control the Width of the Margins

- Move the I-beam (if in the Text mode) or the Pointer (if in the Select mode) to the margin handle you want to move.

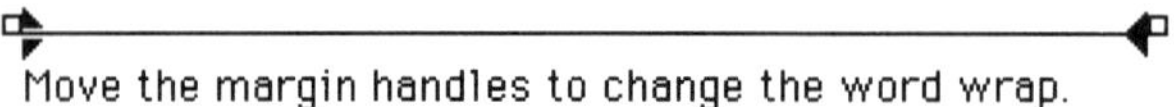

- Click-hold and then drag the margin handle to the desired position.

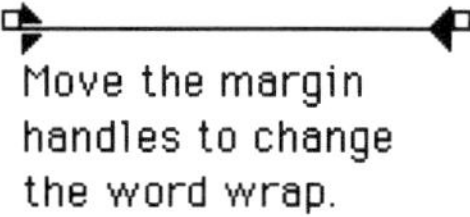

To Set Tabs

- Make sure you are in the Text mode (i.e., the Text tool is highlighted.)
- To insert a tab, click on the text-width line just above the point where you want to add the tab. (A solid triangle will appear at the tab location.)
- If you want to move the tab, drag it horizontally to the new location. (The Tab and its solid triangle are moved to the new location.)

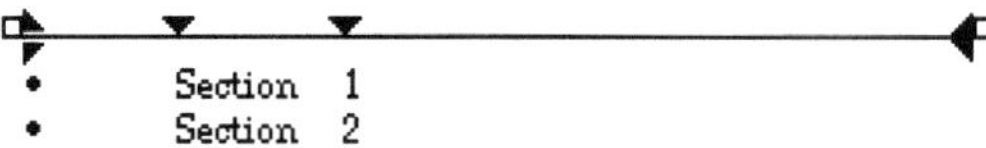

- If you want to create a decimal tab, create a tab at the desired location and then single-click on it. (Tab triangle becomes an arrow.) Remember to type a tab before each word or number that you enter.

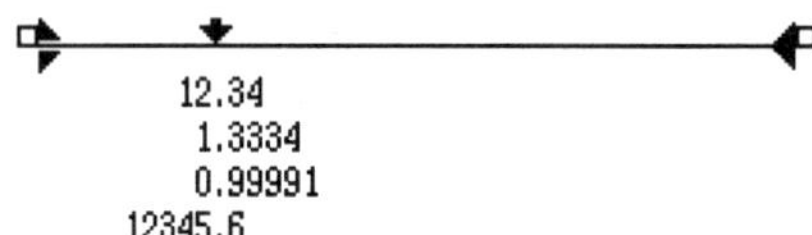

- If you want to remove a tab, drag it to a margin handle and release the mouse.

How Do I Set and Change Text Characteristics?

You can change the characteristics of a text passage at any time-before you enter text, while you are entering text, or after you've entered it. Changing text characteristics before entering text creates new default values. Set or change Text characteristics by selecting options (Font, Size, Style, and Alignment) from the Text pulldown menu.

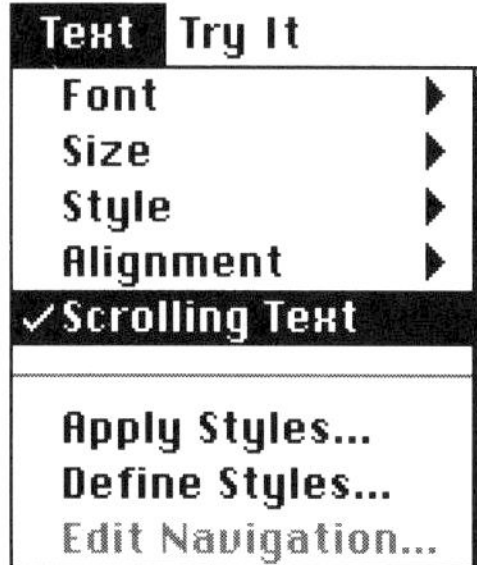

A fifth option, Scrolling Text, creates a scrolling text field that can be used to display more text than is usually possible in a window. Scrolling fields can be modified easily by dragging the text handles and a handle below the text field.

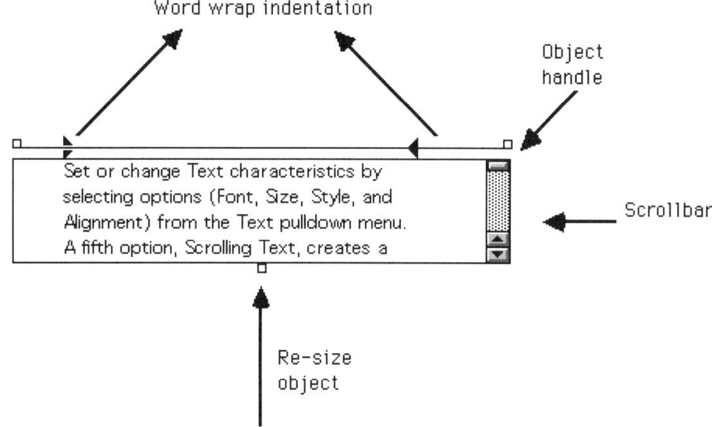

To Select Characteristics Before Entering Text

- Enter the Select mode (click on the Selection tool).

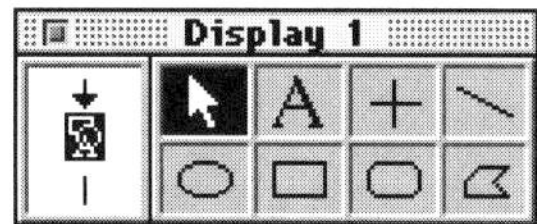

- Pull down the Text menu and select a new characteristic.
- Enter the Text mode and start entering text. This method creates new default values for the Text tool.

To Change Characteristics While Entering Text

- Enter the Text mode.

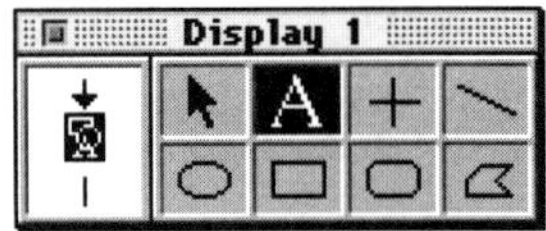

- Pull down the Text menu and select a new characteristic. As you continue typing, subsequent text will have new characteristics. Text entered before the change is not affected.

To Change Characteristics After Entering Text

For the Entire Text Object

- Enter the Select mode.
- Single click on the text object.
- Pull down the text menu and select a new characteristic.

For a Portion of a Text Object

- Enter the Text mode.
- Highlight the text segment you want to change.
- Pull down the Text menu and select a new characteristic.

Text editing generally adheres to practices employed by contemporary word processing and other office utility programs. A summary of these conventions follows.

To Make a Small Change to Text

- Enter the Text mode.
- Move the I-beam to a position immediately to the right of the text you want to change.
- Click once.
- Use the Backspace or Delete key to erase the unwanted text.
- Enter the new text.

To Insert Text

- Enter the Text mode.
- Move the I-beam to the position in which you want to insert text.
- Click once.
- Enter the new text.

To Delete or Change a Single Word

- Enter the Text mode.
- Double-click on the word to be deleted or replaced. (It will be highlighted.)

> Set or change Text `characteristics` by selecting
> options (Font, Size, Style, and Alignment) from the
> Text pulldown menu. A fifth option, Scrolling Text,
> creates a scrolling text field that can be used to
> display more text than is usually possible in a window.
> Scrolling fields can be modified easily by dragging the
> text handles and a handle below the text field.

- To *replace* the word, start typing the new word.
- To *delete* the word, press the Backspace or Delete key.

To Make Large Changes to a Section of Text

- Enter the Text mode.
- Highlight the text you want to change.

> Set or change Text characteristics by selecting
> options (Font, Size, Style, and Alignment) from the
> Text pulldown menu. `A fifth option, Scrolling Text,`
> `creates a scrolling text field that can be used to`
> `display more text than is usually possible in a window.`
> Scrolling fields can be modified easily by dragging the
> text handles and a handle below the text field.

- To *replace* the text, start typing the new text.
- To *delete* the highlighted text, press the Backspace or Delete key.

To Move a Section of Text

- Enter the Text mode.
- Highlight the text to be moved.
- Cut the text.
- Move the I-beam to the new location and Paste the text.

Edit	Data	Libraries	Att
Undo			⌘Z
Cut			⌘X
Copy			**⌘C**
Paste			**⌘U**
Paste As Bitmap			
Clear			
Show Clipboard			

To Duplicate a Section of Text

- Enter the Text mode.
- Highlight the text to be duplicated.
- Copy the text.
- Move the cursor (I-beam) to the location at which you want to insert the copy, and Paste the text.

How Do I Create Graphics?

Several options are available to help you create graphics.

To Create Ovals or Rectangles

- Select the Oval or Rectangle option from the Toolbox.

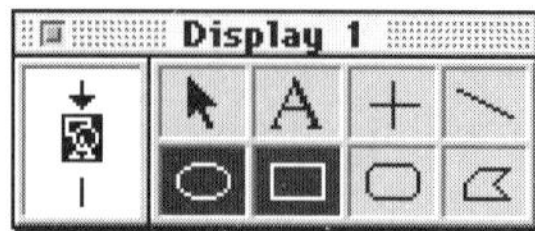

- Place the cursor at one corner of the location where you want the graphic to be placed.
- Click-hold and then drag the mouse diagonally until the object has the desired size and shape.
- Release the mouse key.

Note: If you want a perfect circle or square, hold down the Shift key while you are dragging the mouse to form the graphic object.

To Create Lines in Any Direction

- Select the Diagonal Line tool from the Toolbox.

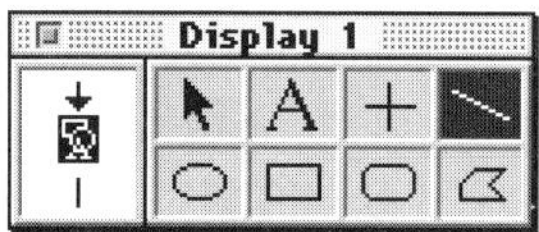

- Place the cursor where you want the line to start.
- Click-hold and then drag the mouse to draw the line.
- Release the mouse key.

To Create Horizontal, Vertical, or 45° Diagonal Lines

- Select the Straight Line tool from the Toolbox.

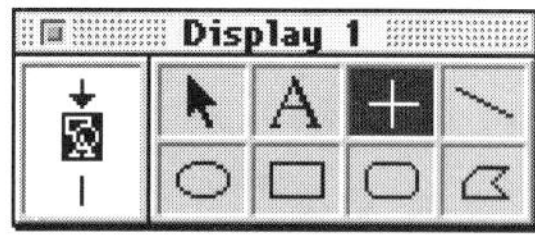

- Place the cursor where you want the line to start.
- Click-hold and then drag the mouse to draw the line.
- Release the mouse key.

Note: You can also create horizontal, vertical, and diagonal lines with the Diagonal Line icon by holding down the Shift key while dragging the line.

Using the Polygon Tool

- Select the Polygon icon from the Toolbox.

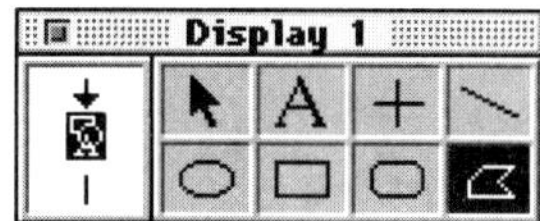

- Place the cursor where you want the polygon to begin.
- Click the mouse to "drop anchor." An invisible anchor will mark the location of the beginning of the first side of the polygon.
- Move the cursor to the point where the first line will end.
- Click the mouse to drop a second anchor.
- Continue moving and clicking the mouse to create the number of anchors needed to create the desired polygon.
- Double-click the mouse on the final anchor to fill the polygon with the currently selected fill color and pattern.

How Do I Change the Size or Shape of Graphics?

You can change the length, direction, and attributes of a line, and you can change the size and shape of an oval or rectangle. To edit any graphic object, first, identify the object that is to be edited by clicking on it with the Selection tool. The object's margin handles will appear when it has been selected, indicating that the object is ready to be edited.

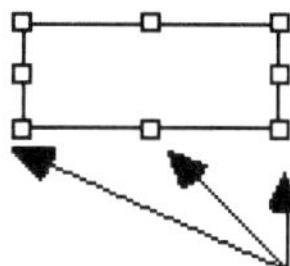

Margin handles

To Change the Length or Direction of an Existing Line

- Enter the Select mode.
- Select the line by clicking on it. (Its margin handles will appear.)

- Place the cursor on a margin handle.
- Click-hold and drag the handle to the new location. (The line will be resized to fit the new margins.)

To Change the Size or Shape of an Oval or Rectangle

- Enter the Select mode.
- Select the oval or rectangle object by clicking on one of its edges. (Its margin handles will appear.)
- To *increase the size* of the oval or rectangle, click-hold the cursor on a corner handle and then drag it to a new location. (The oval will be resized to fit the new margins.)
- To *change the shape* of the oval or rectangle, click-hold the cursor on a side handle and then drag it to a new location. (The shape of the oval will change to fit the new margins.)

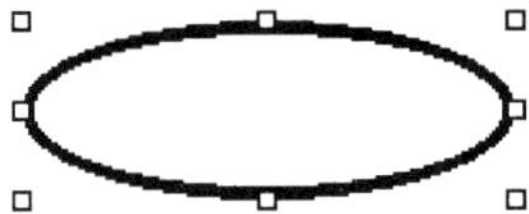

How Do I Change the Attributes of Lines?

Lines have two attributes: thickness and style.

- Line thickness can be invisible (indicated to the designer by a dotted line) or any of four widths.
- Line style can be plain, left arrowhead, right arrowhead, or double arrowheads.

To Change the Attributes of a Line

- If the line is not selected, enter the Select mode and click on the line.
- Display the Line option box by either

  - Double-clicking on one of the line options in the toolbox

    or

  - Selecting the Lines option from the Attributes menu.

- Select the desired line thickness and style from the line palette.

How Do I Fill Rectangles and Ovals?

Rectangles and ovals can be black, white, transparent, or any of 33 patterns. To choose a transparent fill, select the box in the top left corner of the Fills option box.

To Fill in a Rectangle, or Oval

- If the rectangle or oval tool is not selected, enter the Select mode and click on the object.

- Display the Fill Attributes option box by either

    - Double-clicking on the Rectangle or Oval options of the Toolbox

        or

    - Selecting the Fills option from the Attributes menu

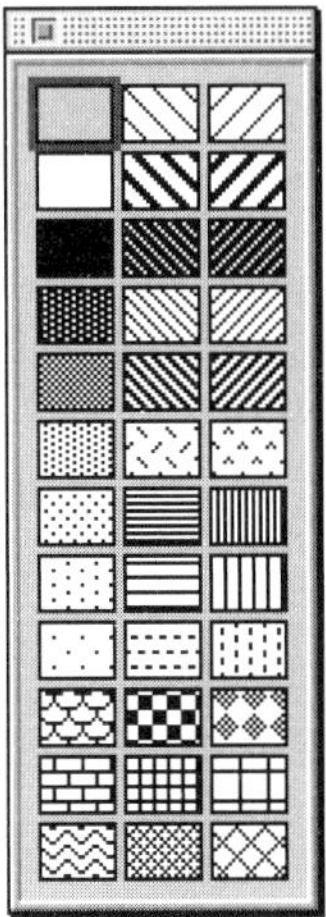

- Click on the desired pattern from the fills palette with the mouse.

How Do I Color Objects?

Objects in Display icons (both graphic objects and text) can be colored using Authorware's color palette. However, the process of coloring objects can be confusing. To understand how to color objects, you need to know that it is possible to color three attributes of an object:

- The border
- The pattern used to fill the object
- The background of the object

To color an object, you must know which of the three attributes you will color. The following box has a thick border, a striped fill, and a solid background.

Authorware's color palette displays all three attributes.

To assign a color:

- Use the selection tool to identify the object to be colored.
- Select the appropriate attribute (i.e., border, foreground, or background).
- Select a color from the color palette.

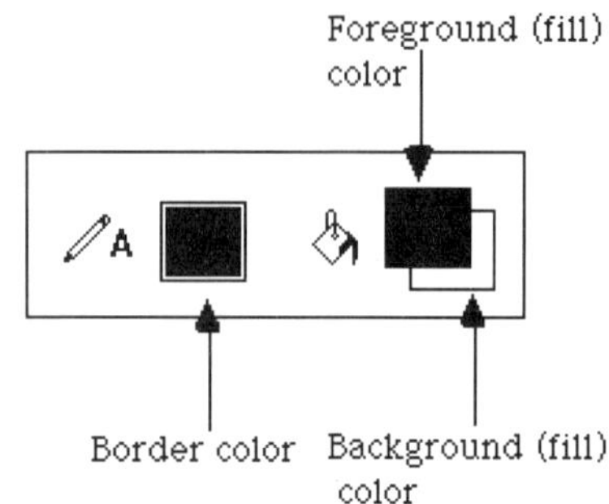

Note: Graphics have three color attributes: Border, Foreground, and Background. However, Text has only two color attributes, Border and Background. Border defines the color of the font. Background defines the Background color. In the following example, the word "Text" has been created with a white border, and a black background color.

How Do I Move Text and Graphic Objects?

To move an object from one location to another, click-hold on the object and drag it with the mouse.

To Move a Text Object

- Enter the Selection mode.
- Place the cursor anywhere within the text object.
- Click-hold on the text.
- Drag the text to the new location.

To Move a Graphic Object

If in the Select Mode

- Select the object by clicking on it with the mouse.
- Drag the object to a new location.

If in the Graphic Mode

- Move the cursor into the object until the cursor changes to a pointer. (Stay away from margin handles.)
- Select the object.
- Drag the object to the new location

Note: If your keyboard has direction arrows, you can move a selected object in very small steps by pressing the ←↑→↓ arrow keys.

Tips for Selecting Objects

The procedure for selecting ovals and rectangles depends on whether the graphic objects are filled or empty.

- If an object is filled with white, black, or a pattern, you can select it by clicking the cursor anywhere inside the object.
- Empty graphic objects are sometimes difficult to move. If an object is empty, you must click the cursor along an edge of the object.

Note: When selecting objects, be careful not to click-hold on a margin handle. If you do, moving the mouse will drag the handle, and instead of moving the selected objects, you will resize them. If this happens, select Undo from the Edit menu (or hold down the Command key while you depress the Z key; hereafter this is indicated as "Command-Z.").

To Move Several Objects at Once

When integrating text and graphics, you may want to move more than one object at a time. If more than one object is selected, moving one object moves all objects. To select multiple objects, press the Shift key while clicking on successive objects with the mouse (using the Selection tool).

- Select the objects you want to move.
- Click-hold inside one of the selected objects.
- Drag the object, along with all other selected objects, to the new location.

How Do I Group Objects?

Sometimes, you will want to treat two or more objects as if they were a single object. Grouped objects are generally easier to manipulate than several individual objects. To do this, you can use the Group command from the edit menu.

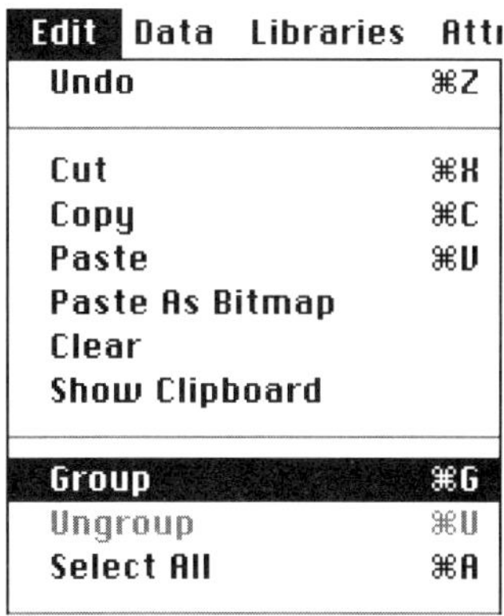

The Group option joins individual objects into one composite object. The objects stay grouped until you ungroup them with the Ungroup command.

To Group Objects into a Composite

- Use the Selection tool and select the objects you want to be part of the group.

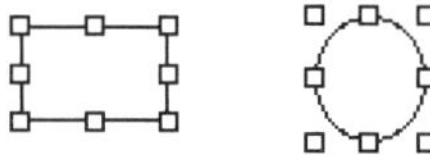

- Select the Group command by either
  - Selecting the Group option of the Edit menu

    or
  - Typing Command-G

All selected objects will be grouped into one composite object.

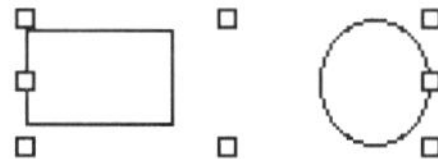

To Ungroup a Composite Object

- Select the composite object you want to ungroup.
- Select the Ungroup command by either
  - Selecting the Ungroup option of the Edit menu

    or
  - Typing Command-U

The composite object is broken into the individual objects that were originally grouped.

How Do I Overlay Text and Graphic Objects?

You can place text and graphic objects anywhere on the screen. Sometimes graphics that are placed close to each other will overlay. In such cases, it may be important to control which objects appear to be on top and which appear to be covered. To control overlay it is important to be aware of three options: overlapping options, mode effects, and object selection.

Overlapping Objects

When objects overlap, they are said to be layered. In the following example, the oval appears to be placed on top of the square. To control the relative position of overlapping objects, use the *Bring to Front* and *Send to Back* options from the Attributes menu.

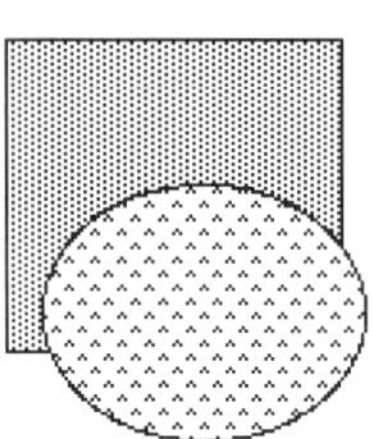

To Bring an Object to the Front

- Using the Selection tool, click on the object. In the following example, the square has been selected

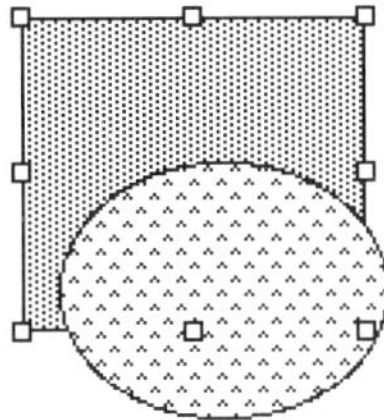

- Select the *Bring to Front* option from the Attributes menu. The object that was originally partially hidden appears dominant over other objects.

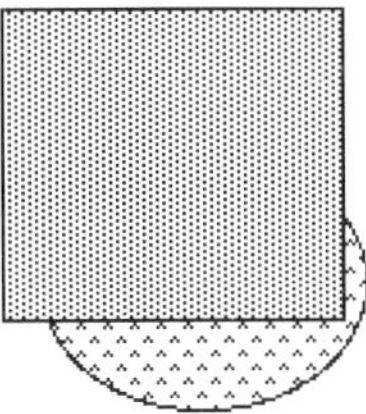

Sending an Object to the Back

- Using the Selection tool, click on the object.
- Select the *Send to Back* option from the Attributes menu.

Mode Effects

An object's mode determines how overlaid objects appear on the screen. Objects may be in the Opaque, Matted, Transparent, Inverse, or Erase mode. By setting the mode of a text or graphic object, you can produce some unusual effects. To use mode effects, select Modes from the Attributes menu.

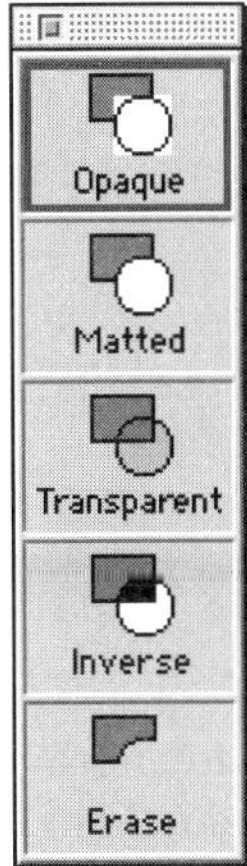

- Opaque objects mask shapes on which they are placed. When overlaid on another graphic, an opaque object covers the lower object. Imported objects often incorporate additional "white space." When the Opaque mode is selected, white space will also obscure objects below. Both of the following objects are opaque.

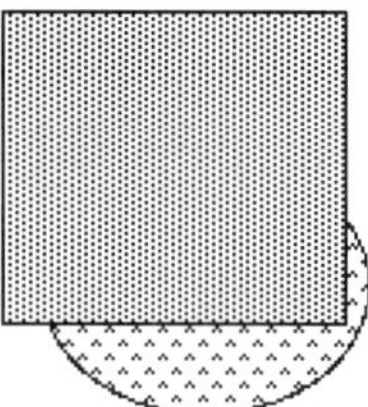

- Matted objects are similar to opaque objects. A major difference is that white space around imported graphics appears transparent when the Matted mode is selected.
- Transparent objects are "see-through." When overlaid on another graphic, the bottom object shows through. The following oval object is set to transparent.

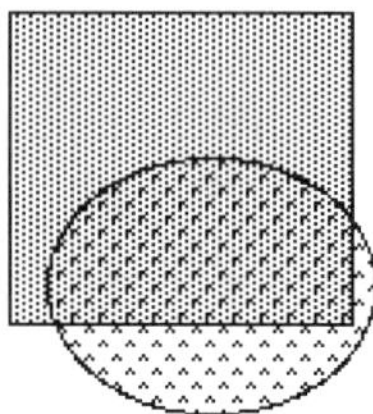

- The Inverse mode often produces unusual effects. White objects appear black when placed onto a white background and white when placed on a black background. The effects of the inverse mode are unpredictable for colored and patterned objects.
- Objects drawn in the Erase mode assume the background color. The Erase mode is useful for masking objects in Display icons.

Selecting Objects

When objects are overlaid, objects in front can restrict access to those behind. To select an object that is behind one or more other objects, you can use either of the following procedures:

Move Aside Obstructing Objects

- Select the object that is in the way.
- Drag the object out of the way.

Move Overlaying Objects to the Back

- Select the object that is in the way.
- Send the object to the back.

How Do I Import Graphics from Another Source?

Graphics created in other applications can be brought into Authorware and used in Display icons by using the Import command, the clipboard, and the scrapbook.

Using the Import Command

The Import command allows you to access graphics to use in Display icons without leaving Authorware.

- Ensure the toolbox is displayed.
- Select Import from the File menu.

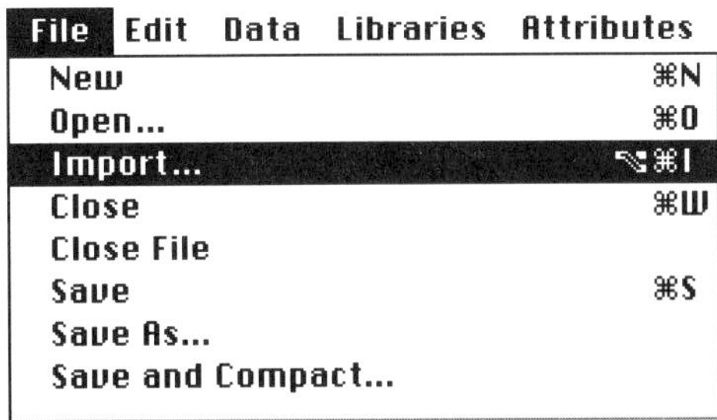

- Open the document that contains the drawing you want to import.

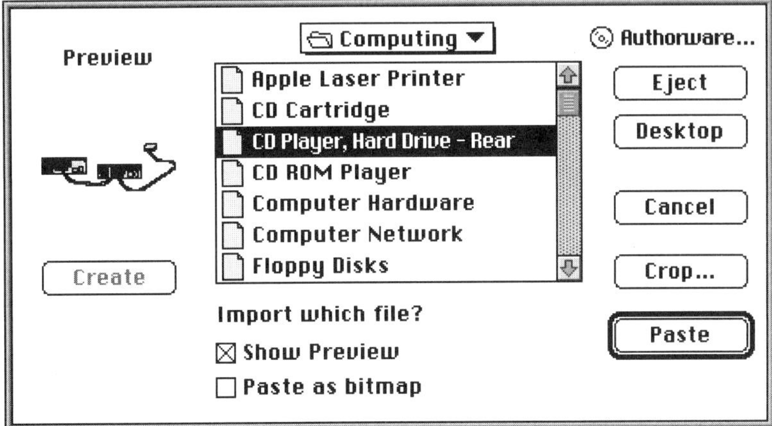

- Paste the entire graphic or select a piece of the drawing by selecting the Crop option. To crop an object, use the mouse to drag across the portion of the graphic that you need.

STUDY EXERCISES

1. Identify each of the following tools in the Toolbox:
   - The selection tool
   - The text tool
   - The rounded-rectangle tool
   - The straight-line tool
   - The polygon tool
2. How do you make the Toolbox disappear and reappear in a Display icon?

   How do you set default values for tools in the Toolbox?

3. Open a Display icon and use the following features to control text layout:
    - Text tabs
    - Decimal tabs
    - Word wrap
    - Text justification

4. Type a paragraph in a Display icon. Change the size, color, and font of the following:
    - A complete sentence
    - A single word in a sentence
    - One character in a word

5. Open a Display icon and create the following:
    - An oval
    - A striped circle
    - A blue rectangle
    - A red square
    - A thick black line
    - A thin yellow line

6. Create a red, a green, and a yellow circle. Use the *Bring to Front* and *Send to Back* options to perform the following:
    - Place the red circle on top of the yellow circle.
    - Place the yellow circle on top of the green circle.
    - Place the green circle on the red circle on the yellow circle.

7. Using the color circles in the previous exercise, experiment with the following options:
    - Effects
    - Modes
    - Color

8. Import graphic images into an Authorware file from one or more of the following sources:
    - Clip art
    - The Internet
    - Scanned images
    - A digital camera
    - A graphics application

9. How do you group several graphic and/or text objects into a single object? How do you reverse the process?

10. Create a game board for a checkers game. Use only the Toolbox to create all the graphics. Make sure the game board contains the following:
    - Sixty-four squares on a regular eight-by-eight grid
    - Twelve checkers on each side of the board
    - Each set of checkers in different colors (or shapes)
    - Alternating colors on successive squares

11. This exercise is intended to encourage you to experiment with the Toolbox. Create a new Authorware file.   Place a Display icon on the Course Flow Line. Title the icon "Practice".

   • Open the display and use the Authorware drawing tools to draw a house.

   • Use arrows to label the door, windows, and other parts of the house.

   • Draw trees with leaves and flowers in a flower bed.

   • Draw a path leading up to the front door.

   • Use a variety of patterns, fills, and line thicknesses throughout your picture.

Save the file on a disk.

Creating Presentations   

CHAPTER OVERVIEW

You have learned how to use the Display icon. In this chapter, you will learn how to create and control presentations using several Display icons in combination with Wait and Erase icons.

CHAPTER OBJECTIVES

Following this chapter, you will be able to
- Use the Wait options and Transition effects.
- Use the Erase options to remove Displays.
- Combine Display, Erase, and Wait icons to create presentations.
- Align objects in Display icons.
- Use Layering to control overlapping objects in different Display icons.

KEY TERMS

Erase icons
Wait icons
Map icons
Erase options
Transitions
Wait options
Layers
Fields
Dialog box

SUPPORT MATERIALS

On the CD-ROM disc, run **BEGIN.PKG** if you are a Macintosh user or **BEGIN.APP** if you are using a PC. When the file opens, click once on the title page to begin. Select **Chapter 3** and run the video to examine how to connect Display, Wait, and Erase icons to create presentations.

The folder on the CD-ROM titled MACDEMOS or PC_DEMOS contains several demonstration files that you can run and examine. The folder contains two versions of each file: a packaged file that you can run and an unpackaged file containing the icons used to create the file. Run the files to see how to create a simple presentation.

Macintosh users:
Run the file CHP03.pkg to view its contents.
Open the data file CHP03.A3M to examine how the file was created.

PC users:
Run the file CHP03.APP to view its contents.
Open the data file CHP03.A3W to examine how the file was created.

Note: You must have a copy of Authorware on your computer to open the data files.

STUDY TOPICS

In Chapter 2, you learned to create screens using a single Display icon. In practice, presentations are created by combining several Display icons. Think of your lesson as a stack of transparent sheets on which you have created text and graphic objects. Each transparent sheet corresponds to a Display icon on the Course Flow Line. As your program develops, these transparent sheets/Display icons are inserted into your lesson to build presentations. Display icons also can be removed to erase parts of the presentation.

You will often want to display or erase text or graphic objects individually. For example, imagine a screen containing two paragraphs and a related graphic. At some point, you may want to remove the graphic and replace it with another picture. Unfortunately, this apparently routine task cannot be completed if all the objects on the screen are placed on the same Display icon.

Wait and Erase Screens

Two Authorware icons help to create presentations: Wait and Erase.
- Wait icons insert pauses into the lesson. Pauses may be either for a set time period or until the learner acts by pressing a key or clicking the mouse button.
- Erase icons remove one or more Display icons and their contents from the screen.

How Do I Use Wait Icons to Pause Between Display Icons?

While a lesson executes, the contents of successive Display icons are displayed in rapid succession. Without pauses, the lesson would execute so quickly that you would not have time to read anything. Therefore, it is necessary to slow the lesson to give the user time to read the screen. The lesson flow can be stopped in two ways:

- By inserting a Wait icon in the program.

- By asking the user to respond with an Interaction icon (see Chapters 6 to 8).

This section will focus on using the Wait icon to temporarily stop the program. When inserted, this icon causes the lesson to pause. The lesson continues when one of the following events occurs.

- A certain amount of time passes

- The user presses any key

- The user clicks on the screen with the mouse

  or

- The user activates a button on the screen

To Use Wait Icon Options

- Place a Wait icon on the flow line at the point where you want the program to pause.

- Double-click on the icon. The Wait Options menu will be displayed.

- Select one or more of the Wait Options; often you will want to select several Wait Options. The Wait Options box in the following figure is set to pause until the learner either presses a key, clicks on the Return button, or waits for 2 seconds.

- Click OK.

Click on the boxes to select the conditions you want to create:

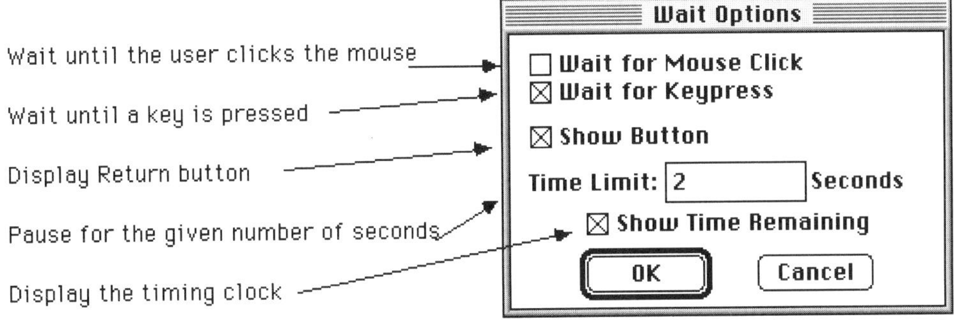

Note: Boxes that display messages or seek input from the designer are named dialog boxes. Many dialog boxes include spaces, known as fields, where designers can type information. For example, the preceding illustration of the Wait icon shows an area where the designer can type the number of seconds that will elapse before the Wait icon ends. It is important to know that many fields in Authorware allow you to enter Variables instead of specific values. This can save many hours when programs need to be modified.

To Move Wait Buttons

Selecting the Show Button option in an Erase icon causes a button (with the default title *Continue*) to appear on the screen.

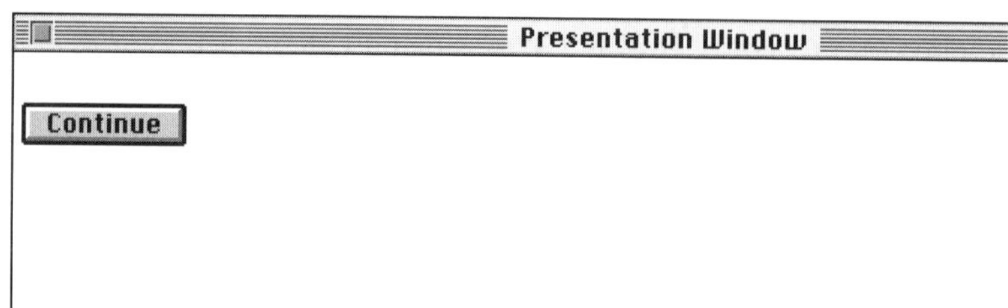

This button is automatically placed at the top left corner of the screen. Many designers move this button to a different screen location. Objects in the top left corner of the screen tend to be over looked by users.

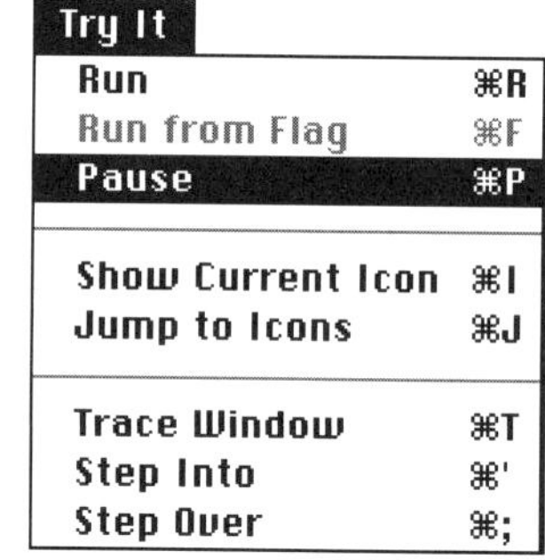

To move the button while running the lesson, it is necessary to first Pause the lesson.

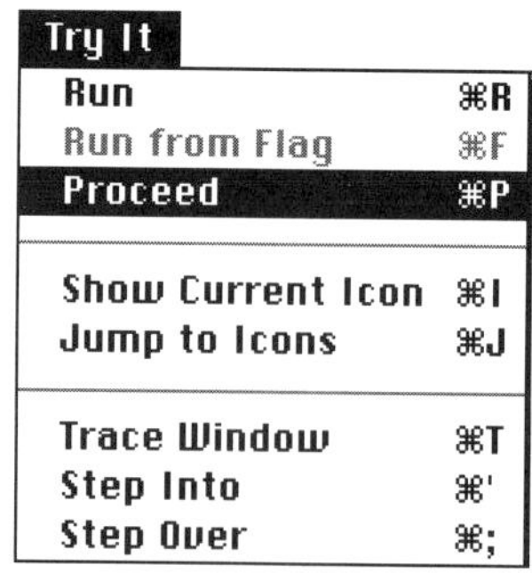

Next, with the mouse, click and drag the button to its desired location. The new location is now the default location for subsequent buttons. Select Proceed from the Try It pulldown menu to resume the lesson.

How Do I Erase Icons?

Remember that Display icons are like transparent sheets that are stacked on top of each other. If Display icons are not removed, the screen will soon become a mass of unreadable text and graphic objects. To prevent this from occurring, you need to remove, or erase, Display icons when you no longer want their contents to appear. An Erase icon can be used to erase one or multiple displays.

It is important to remember that the objects in an icon cannot be displayed or erased separately. During program execution, it is icons, not individual objects, that are displayed and erased. If you want an object to be displayed or erased separately from other objects, you must put that object in a separate Display icon.

To Erase Objects

- Insert an Erase icon on the Course Flow Line where you want one or more icons to be erased.
- Title the Erase icon with a name that hints to the names of the icon(s) to be erased.

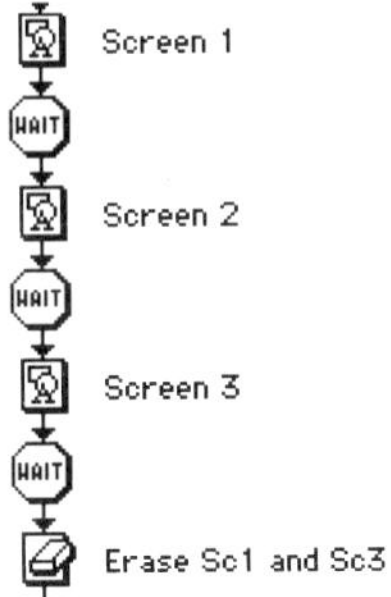

- Double-click on the Erase icon. (All presentation icons that are currently active-that have been displayed but not yet erased-are displayed along with the Erase option box.)
- Select the Display icon that you want to erase. To select an icon, use the mouse to click on an object from its Display icon. Continue to select Display icons if additional objects are to be erased. All selected icons will appear in the Erase icon's options box.

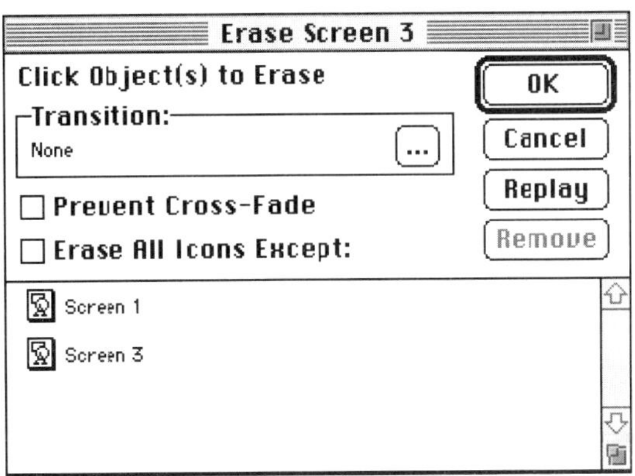

- Select the desired Transition effect and then click on the OK button. If you selected the wrong icon, select and Remove the icon from the list of icons to be erased.

How Do I Display and Erase Objects Using Special Effects?

Authorware provides many options for displaying and erasing objects. These options, known as Transitions, create exciting special effects to present and erase information. If Transitions are not used, objects are displayed and erased from the screen without any special effects.

To Display Objects with Transitions

- Select the icon for which you want a Transition. You can either select the icon on the Course Flow Line (single click on the icon) or open the icon. If you open a Display icon, the icon will open and its contents will be displayed, along with its special effects.

- Access the Transition by

    - Selecting the Transition option from the Attributes menu

        or

    - Entering Shift-Command-E

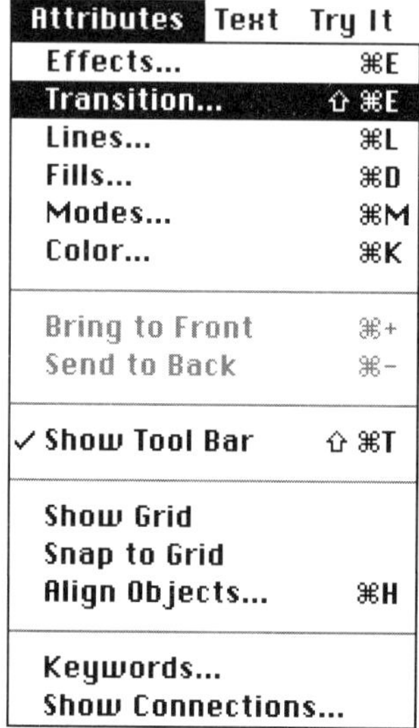

- Select the Transition button.

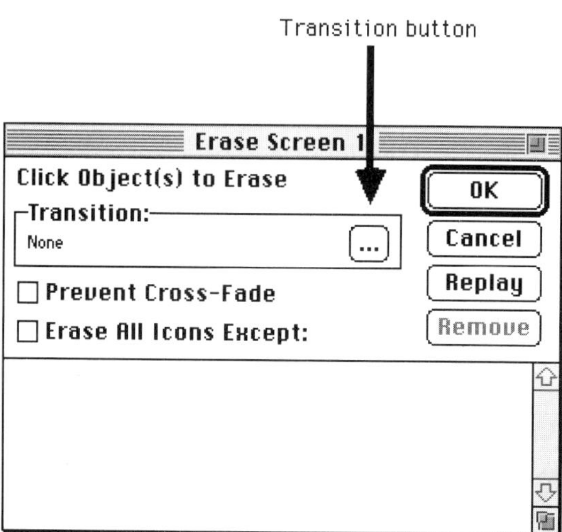

- Select the option you want. Authorware demonstrates each effect as soon as it is chosen.
- If you like the effect, click on the OK button; if not, try another option or click Cancel.

To Erase Icon Objects with Transitions

- Double-click on the Erase icon for which you want to set an erase Transition. (The Erase options will be displayed. This is the same box that appears when you first create and open the Erase icon. You can set Transition effects when you first create the icon or wait until later.)
- Either select the Transition button from the Erase window or pull down the Effects menu and select the Transition option you want. Click the Apply button to view the Transition that you have selected.

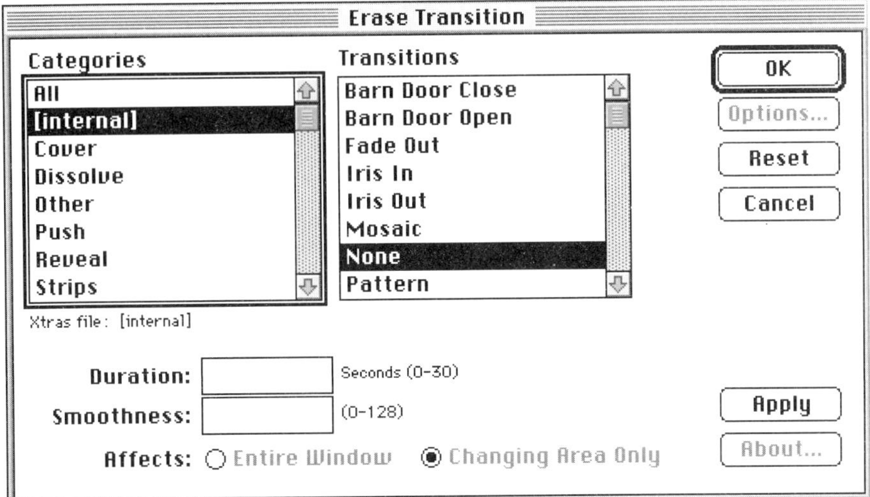

- If you like the effect, click on the OK button; if not, try another option or click *Cancel*. Experiment with Duration and Smoothness options to vary effects and decide whether to apply a Transition to the entire screen or simply the changing information.

Transitions can greatly enhance the impact of your work. For example, using the *Push: Push Down* Transition to remove old and present new information can greatly improve the look of your screens. However, Transitions should be used skillfully and sparingly to gain maximum effect.

How Do I Run My Lesson?

Test your lesson often and early in the development process. Do not create large chunks of your lesson without checking to see that the lesson works properly. It is better to find problems or errors early in the development process before debugging becomes too onerous a task.

Run the lesson from the Try It menu. You can run a lesson at any time. It doesn't matter whether you are in the Design Window or the Presentation Window.

There are four ways that you can run a lesson: from the start to the end of the program, from the start to a point within the program, from a point within the program to the end of the program, and from a point within the program to a later point within the program.

Try It		
Run	⌘R	——Runs program from start
Run from flag	⌘F	——Runs program from flag
Pause	⌘P	——Temporarily stops program run
Proceed	⌘P	——Restarts a paused program
Show Current Icon	⌘I	
Jump to Icons	⌘J	

To Run the Entire Lesson

- Select the Run option from the Try It menu or the Tool Bar

  or

- Type Command R

  Your program will run from first icon to last icon.

To Run from a Point within the Lesson

- Find a point on the Course Flow Line from where you want to begin.
- Drag a Start flag to where you want to begin.   
- Execute the Run from Flag command by

  - Selecting the Run from Flag option from the Try It menu or the Tool Bar

  or

  - Typing Command-F

  Your program will run from the Start flag to the end of the program.

To Run to a Point within the Lesson

- Find a point on the Course Flow Line where you want the lesson to stop.
- Drag a Stop flag to a position immediately after the last icon that you want.

- Execute the Run command by

  - Selecting the Run option from the Try It menu or the Tool Bar

  or

  - Typing Command-R

Your program will run from the beginning to the Stop flag.

To Run between Two Points within the Lesson

- Identify a starting point on the Course Flow Line.
- Drag a Start flag to where you want to begin.
- Identify an ending point.
- Drag a Stop flag to where you want to end.   

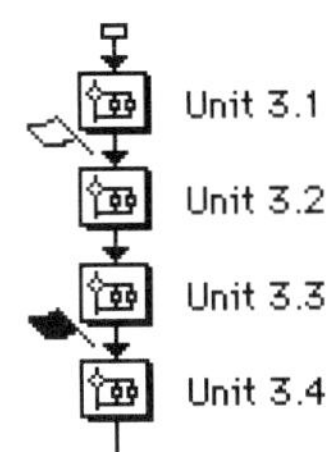

- Execute the Run from Flag command by
  - Selecting Run from Flag from the Try It menu or the Tool Bar

    or

  - Typing Command-F

Your program will run from the Start flag to the Stop flag.

How Do I Temporarily Stop a Running Lesson?

While running a lesson, the file will stop whenever it reaches

- A Wait icon (with user input rather than a time option)
- An Interaction icon that requires a response from the user
- A Stop flag

If you want to stop at any other point in the lesson, you must use the Pause command from the Try It menu. Pausing the lesson allows you to edit or examine the lesson more closely. The lesson will remain stopped until you use the Proceed command.

To Stop a Lesson

- Wait until the program reaches the point at which you want to pause.
- Enter the Pause command by
  - Selecting Pause from the Try It menu

    or

  - Pressing Command-P

To Resume a Lesson

- Enter the Proceed command by
  - Selecting the Proceed option of the Try It menu

    or

  - Pressing Command-P

You can also use the Proceed command to bypass a Stop flag. After the program stops at the flag, enter the Proceed command.

Note: The same key sequence is used for Pause and Proceed (Command-P). If the lesson is running, Command-P stops it. If the lesson is paused, through a pause or a Stop flag, Command-P causes it to continue.

How Do I Edit a Lesson While it Is Running?

One of Authorware's strengths is that you can edit text and graphics "on-the-fly". Your screen layout need not be perfect before you run a lesson; in fact, you don't need to develop any lesson content before you run the lesson.

First, place icons on the Course Flow Line and then run the lesson. The lesson will stop at each empty icon and wait for you to enter text and graphics, or set other options. When you are more familiar with Authorware, you may find this a quick and efficient approach to lesson development.

To Edit Display Icons That Contain at Least One Object

- You must be able to stop the lesson at the point where you want to begin editing. Do so by
  - Inserting a Wait icon after the icon is displayed but before it is erased

    or

  - Inserting a Stop flag after the icon has been displayed, but before it is erased

    or

  - Being ready to execute the Pause command
- Run the program.
- When the program stops, the contents of one or more icons will be displayed.
- Double-click on the object you want to edit. (Margin handles and the Toolbox for the selected icon will be displayed.)
- Check the icon name in the Toolbox to be sure you are working on the correct icon.
- Edit objects in the displays.

To Enter Text into an Empty Display Icon

- Run the program. When the program reaches the empty icon, the program will stop and the Toolbox for the empty icon will be displayed.
- Create desired text and graphic objects.
- Click on the Toolbox's Close box. The Toolbox will disappear and the lesson will resume until the next empty Display icon is reached.

All icons except the Wait icon can be created and their options set during program execution. For Wait icons, settings are predetermined and must be reset for each icon (with the exception of the placement of the Continue button).

Selecting Objects While Running a Lesson

Using the Pause option to interrupt a lesson can cause confusion. Pausing does not cause the Toolbox to appear. Consequently, the handles that are used to move and edit graphic objects also do not appear, making it impossible to edit individual graphics. Instead, handles appear around the perimeter of all the objects in the selected Display icon. For example, in the following figure, three individual rectangles are surrounded by "grey" handles These grey handles indicate that a Display icon has been identified, but the objects cannot be edited yet.

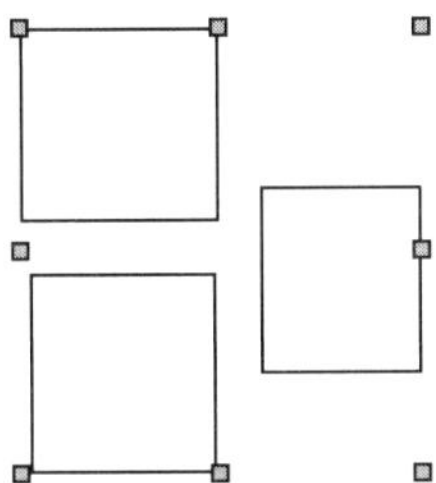

To select an individual object on the Display, double-click on the object to be edited with the mouse to reveal the editing handles. This will reveal the handles for each of the objects in the Display.

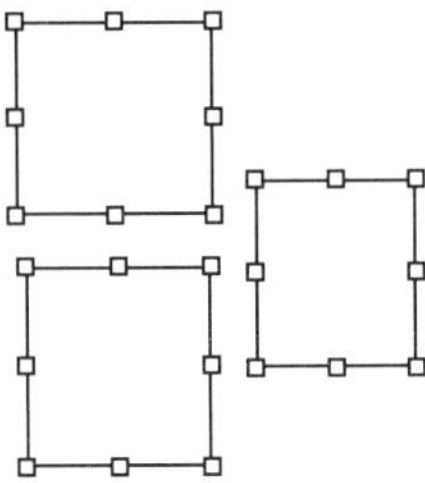

Next, single-click with the mouse on the object you want to edit. The editing handles will appear around the desired object only.

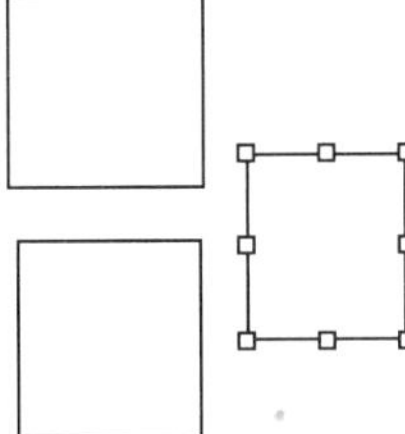

How Do I Duplicate an Icon or an Icon's Name?

When working in the Design Window, you will often want to reproduce an icon that you have used elsewhere. To do so, first copy the icon and then paste it onto the Course Flow Line. To copy the icon, use the selection tool to highlight the icon you want to duplicate, and select Copy from the Edit pulldown menu. To Paste the icon, click on the Course Flow Line at the location where you want to paste the icon. A small hand with a pointing finger will appear, indicating where the icon is to be pasted. Select Paste from the Edit pulldown menu to duplicate the icon.

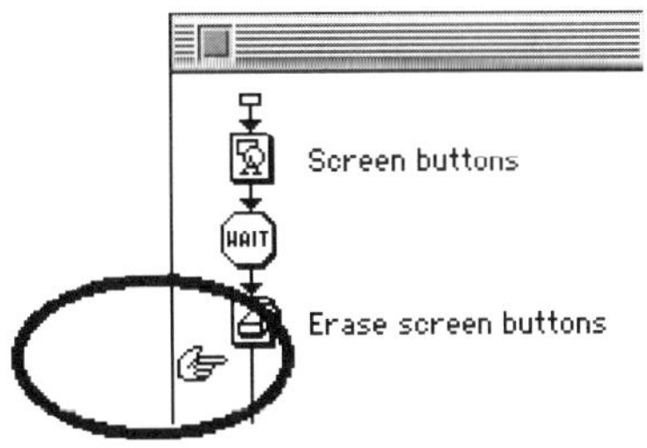

Often, you will want to copy an icon's name without copying the entire icon. Copying and pasting an icon's name is often faster than typing the name and helps prevent potentially important typos. To copy an icon's name, first use the selection tool to highlight the icon whose name you want to copy.

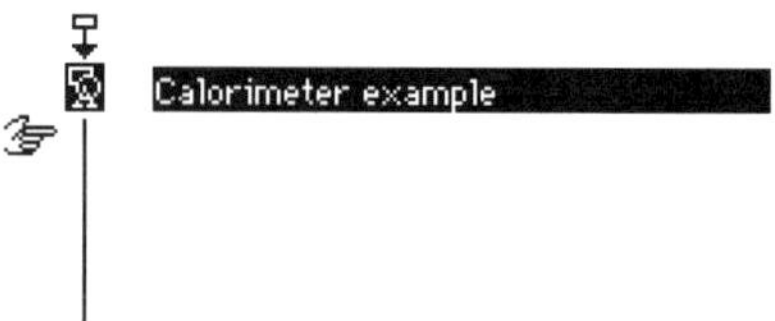

Now use the mouse to click on the icon's name. The selection tool will change to an I-beam when it enters the icon's name field. Click on the icon's name with the mouse and highlight the text you want to copy.

To copy the text, select Copy from the Edit pulldown menu. To paste the text, place the cursor where you want the text to appear and select Paste from the Edit menu.

How Can Authorware Create Icons for Me?

The title to this section may sound like a joke, but it is not. Authorware can create Display icons for the designer. The trick to this approach is to use Authorware's capability to import what are known are Rich Text Format (RTF) files. RTF files keep the text formatting applied in a word processor.

To create an RTF file, create your display in a word processing file and save the file in *RTF* format. (Check the manual that accompanies your word processor for more information on this topic.)

Next, go to your Authorware lesson file and open a Display icon into which you want to place the text. Select Import from the File menu.

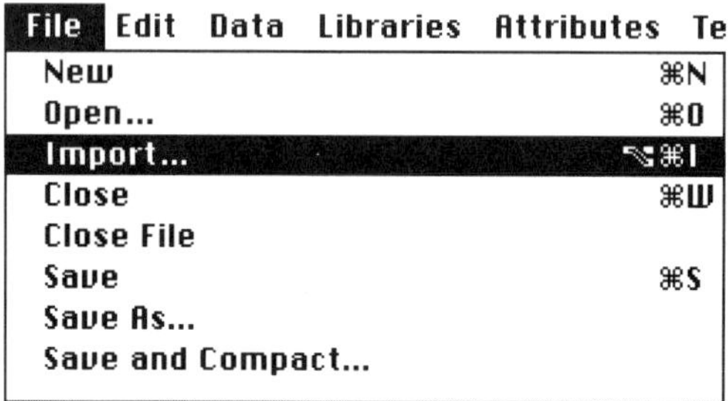

Authorware will prompt you to locate the file you want to import. After identifying the file you want to import, the following dialog box will appear.

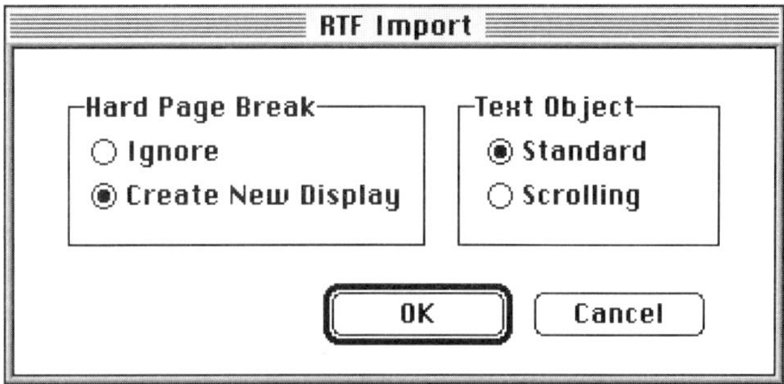

Pressing OK tells Authorware to open the selected file, fill the screen with the first page of text from the word processing file, and to create additional Display icons containing subsequent pages from the file. The following illustration shows an original Display icon titled *Introduction* and two additional Displays. The icons titled *a : 2* and *a : 3* were created automatically whenever Authorware encountered a page break in the imported RTF file. The titles of the new icons are taken from the text in each Display.

Note: It is important to place "Hard Page Breaks" into your word processing file rather than accepting the usual pagination created by the word processing application.

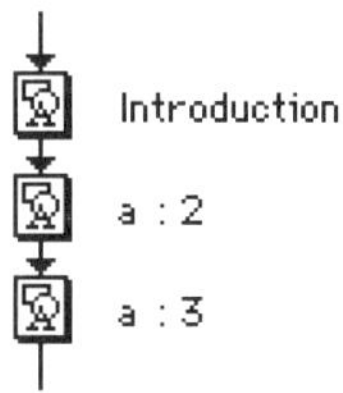

How Do I Organize Icons?

As you have already seen, creating lessons in Authorware involves navigating between Design and Presentation windows. As you add icons to the Course Flow Line to create presentations, you will soon run out of space to add more icons. When the Course Flow Line is full, it is necessary to use Map icons to group icons.

Map Icons

You will need to group icons because there is a limit to the number of icons that can be placed on a flow line. This limit is determined by the size of your computer's monitor. The following techniques can be used to place icons into Maps.

- Drag and Drop. You can add icons to an existing Map simply by dragging and dropping icons into the Map. First, open the Map icon. Drag an icon onto the Course Flow Line in the open Map icon.

- Highlight two or more adjacent icons on the Course Flow Line and then select Group from the Edit pulldown menu.

The highlighted icons will be placed into a new Map icon on the Course Flow Line. Try to group icons logically to help you to edit and troubleshoot your lesson.

Several levels of design windows can be created by grouping icons into Maps. The level of the design window in which you are working is displayed in the upper right corner of the Design Window. There is no limit to the number of levels you can have. Just remember that the deeper the level, the more time it will take you to access it.

In the following figure, the first flow line (Level 1) has three Map icons. Opening the first Map icon displays its contents-the flow line designated as Level 2. In turn, opening the Map icon in Level 2 gives you its contents-the Level 3 flow line.

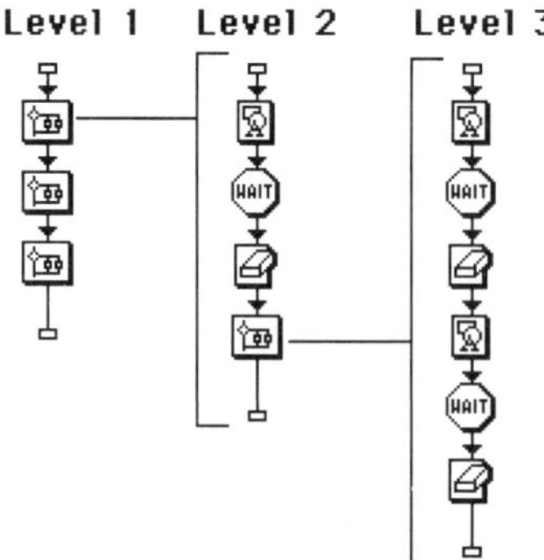

How Do I Align Objects Located on Different Display Icons?

Because presentations often consist of several Display icons, it is often necessary to align objects in separate displays to ensure that they don't overlap and are well spaced. For example, objects in Displays are often carefully placed to maintain a sense of balance and spaciousness among the objects. Aligning objects requires you to select and move objects to desired positions. There are two main ways to align objects: by jumping from icon to icon or by aligning objects while running a file.

To Align Objects by Jumping from Icon to Icon

- Access the Course Flow Line that contains the Display icons you want to align.
- Double-click on the first Display icon in the series of icons.
- After the icon opens, return to the Course Flow Line by
  - Executing the Jump to Icon command

    or

  - Clicking on the Close box of the toolbox
- While holding down the Shift key, double-click on the second Display icon in the icon series. The selected icon will open, and the contents of both the first and second Display icons will be displayed.
- Continue this process of Shift-opening icons until the contents of all icons in the series you want to align are displayed.
- To select a specific icon, double-click on an object of that icon. Margin handles will be displayed along with the Toolbox for the selected icon.
- Move the contents of the selected icon to the desired location.

You can also edit while running a lesson. In fact, this is often the most efficient way to make small changes and align objects.

To Align Objects While Running the Lesson

- Be sure that you can stop your lesson at the end of the series of icons that you want to align. Do this by
  - Inserting a Wait icon at the end of the icon series

    or

  - Inserting a Stop flag at the end of the icon series

    or

  - Being ready to execute the Pause command
- Run the lesson.
- When the lesson stops at the end of the icon series, the contents of all icons in the series you want to align will be displayed.
- To select a specific icon, double-click on an object in that icon. (Margin handles will be displayed along with the Toolbox for the selected icon.)
- Move the contents of the selected icon to the desired location.

Note: Object alignment discussed here concerns objects in different icons. Aligning two or more objects in a single icon is performed using the Align Objects command and is discussed in Chapter 5.

How Do I Hide Displays?

Sometimes it is important to ensure that information in one display is always dominant over information in another display. However, this can be difficult to guarantee. When Authorware draws text or graphic objects, the newly presented information is dominant over the old.

One solution to ensure that information is presented as intended involves layer effects. Layering establishes a dominance hierarchy that controls how displays appear: Displays that appear higher in the hierarchy are dominant over others.

To set a Layer level, either highlight (with the selection tool) or open a Display icon. Select Effects from the Attributes window and enter a number into the Layer field. Higher-layer numbers result in dominance over displays with lower-layer number

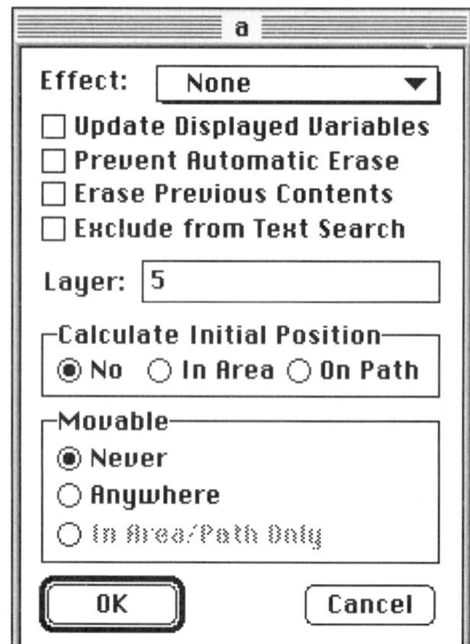

Use layering effects cautiously. They can provide "quick fixes" to irritating design problems. However, Display icons with changed layer numbers can also prove difficult to hide and are sometimes used when designers don't understand how other icons operate. Layering effects can come back to haunt you.

STUDY EXERCISES

1. How can you control where Authorware places the Continue button in the Presentation Window?

2. Use Wait icon options to create presentations in which the uses move to the next screen:
   - by clicking the mouse.
   - by pressing a key on the keyboard.
   - by waiting 10 seconds before moving on automatically.

3. Create a blackboard to display a class lecture. On the blackboard, build a presentation that gradually unfolds several steps that together complete an activity.

4. Use at least three Display icons to build an electronic resume:
   - Display parts of the resume sequentially (i.e., one line at a time) by placing words in different Display icons.
   - Use Transitions (fade in, dissolve, push, strips, etc.) to make the presentation visually interesting.
   - Create special effects by drawing objects in one pattern and changing the fill to make objects appear to shimmer.

5. Use Display, Wait, and Erase icons to build an outline for a speech, a plan for a lesson, or a description of a sequential process. For example, a mathematician might outline the steps for solving quadratic equations using the quadratic formula. Use Start and Stop flags to test subsets of the presentation.

Multimedia

CHAPTER OVERVIEW

One of Authorware's greatest strengths is its ability to incorporate multimedia into files. Multimedia lessons, those that use animated objects, sound files, and video, as well as text and still graphics, are not only possible, but are relatively easy to create with Authorware.

CHAPTER OBJECTIVES

By the end of this chapter, you will be able to
- Animate objects between two points.
- Animate objects on a path or along a curve.
- Incorporate sound files into lessons.
- Incorporate QuickTime digital video files into lessons.
- Combine images from videodisc or videotape with Authorware files.

KEY TERMS

Animation
Sound
Digital Movie
Video interface

SUPPORT MATERIALS

On the CD-ROM disc, run **BEGIN.PKG** if you are a Macintosh user or **BEGIN.APP** if you are using a PC. When the file opens, click once on the title page to begin. Select **Chapter 4** and run the video to learn how to animate an object along a straight line or on a path.

   The folder on the CD-ROM titled MACDEMOS or PC_DEMOS contains several demonstration files that you can run and examine. The folder contains two versions of each file: a packaged file that you can run and an unpackaged file containing the icons used to create the file. Run the file and examine the icons to see how to incorporate sound files and animation into your lessons.

Macintosh users:
Run the file CHP04.pkg to view its contents.
Open the data file CHP04.A3M to examine how the file was created.

PC users:
Run the file CHP04.APP to view its contents.
Open the data file CHP04.A3W to examine how the file was created.

Note: You must have a copy of Authorware on your computer to open the data files.

STUDY TOPICS

Incorporating Sound Files

Sounds can be used for several types of tasks. Most commonly, sound is used to amuse or motivate. Sound files are often used as an alternative to text to transmit information or to reward students for correct answers.

Sounds are also used to add a degree of realism to a lesson. Images on computer monitors are, of course, simply electronic pulses. Consequently, a danger exists that learners may not value learning from a computer or invest sufficient effort to learn lesson content deeply. Sounds help users to believe that the environment in which they are interacting is, indeed, real. For example, adding a sound to a button often helps to persuade the user that the object being clicked is really a button and not simply an electronic image.

Where Do Sound Files Come From?

Sound files are available from many sources. Many companies distribute sound files that can be used in lessons. Others are available for free from bulletin boards and the Internet. However, if the exact sound for your needs is missing, you may have to create one yourself.

Sound files are not created with Authorware. Instead, sound files are created with an application such as SoundEdit Pro that converts voice or sounds stored on a tape recorder, CD, or other media from analog signals into digital formats. Once created, the sound can be loaded into and saved as part of an Authorware file. This chapter assumes that you either know how to create your own sound files or that you have access to a library of digital sounds.

Sound files, like graphics, can be created in many formats. However, Authorware will only recognize certain types of files. The most common formats are probably AIF, SoundEdit, and WAV files. The range of file formats tends to change, so check your manuals to determine which file formats will work.

How Do I Play a Sound File?

Playing a sound file involves using a Sound icon. To play a file, drag a Sound icon onto the Course Flow Line.

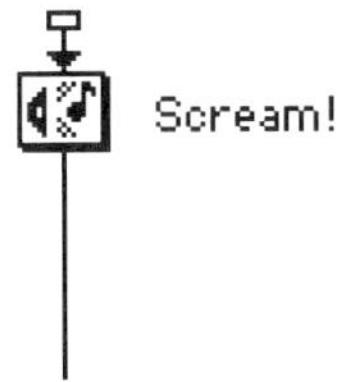

The Sound icon should be placed at the point on the Course flow Line where the sound is to be played. Open the Sound icon by double-clicking on its icon. Opening the Sound icon produces the following dialog box:

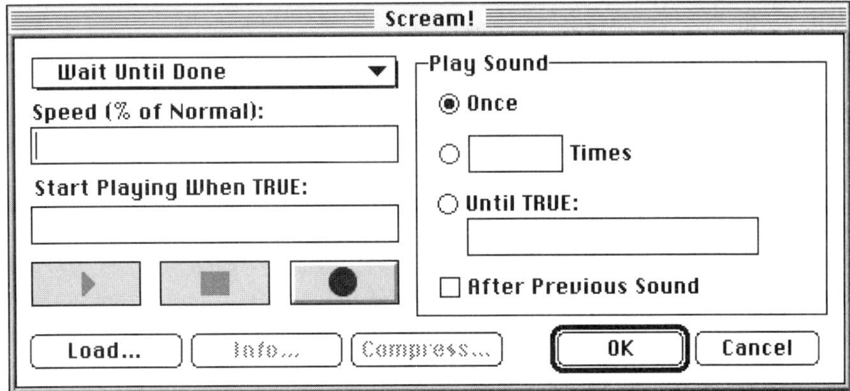

Several decisions (some may not require action by the designer) must be made every time a Sound icon is used. These include the following:

- Locating the sound file that is to be used.

Choosing a sound file to play is quite easy. Simply select the Load button with your mouse and identify the location of the sound file on a disk. Once the file has been found, Authorware loads the file into the computer to become a permanent part of the lesson file. In other words, once located, an additional sound file does not need to be loaded with the finished product.

- The speed at which the files will be played.

Playing a sound file at more than 100% increases the pitch of the sound. Many cartoon characters voices are created by increasing the actor's voice pitch. In contrast, playing sounds under 100% slows the sound and deepens tone. Sometimes, files are stored at high speed to save disk space and must be slowed for playback in Authorware.

- How many times the sound file will be played.

Most sounds are played only once. However, creative use of this option can save time and storage space. For example, a cuckoo clock striking midnight might involve playing a sound file 12 times in rapid succession.

- Whether a sound is to be played before or while other events occur.

This decision is important. Sometimes it is necessary to play a sound before another event occurs. For example, a designer may want students to listen to corrective feedback completely before proceeding with the lesson. In such cases, select the *Wait Until Done* option. However, at other times, simultaneous events are important. For example, a sound file may be used to introduce a concept that unfolds visually in front of users. In such cases, select the *Concurrent* option.

In general, don't overuse sound. If used sparingly, sound files can help to focus learners' attentions and motivate them to continue to work. However, when overused, or used carelessly, sounds tend to lose their impact.

How Do I Play a Digital Movie?

The process involved in playing a movie is similar to that used to play a sound file. However, unlike sound files, Digital Movies are not usually loaded into the lesson file. Instead, they are stored on a disk alongside the Authorware file. The most common way to play a movie involves placing a Digital Movie icon on the Course Flow Line at the point in the lesson where the movie is to begin, and setting several options that control how the movie will be displayed.

First, place a Digital Movie icon on the Course Flow Line. Double-click on the Digital Movie icon to reveal its dialog box. Authorware will now ask you to identify the movie that you want to play.

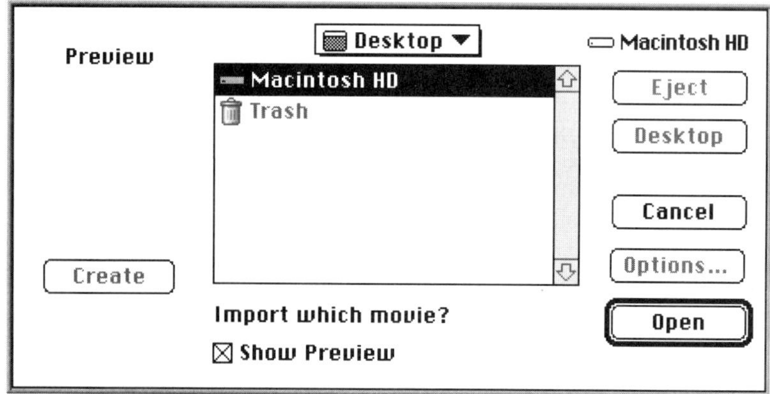

After locating the movie, a dialog box, similar to the following, will appear.

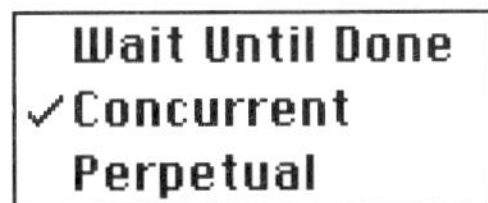

As you can see, several options can be controlled.   Often, files do not need to be adjusted. However, if you wish, you may change which frames are displayed, the presentation rate, and the number of times the movie shows.

Also, as was possible with the Sound icons, you may control the Timing. That is, you may decide whether Authorware stops and displays the entire video before proceeding (Wait Until Done), continues with the lesson while the movie is playing (Concurrent), or is available as a Perpetual option.

```
Wait Until Done
✓ Concurrent
  Perpetual
```

The relevance of Perpetual options will not become apparent until that topic is addressed in Chapter 8.

You can also control where the movie will be shown. To do so, drag the Digital Movie window to a new location while the video is showing. You can also use Transition effects to present or erase movie files.

How Do I Create an Animation?

You can create animations that would usually take many hours to develop, in just a few minutes using the Motion icon. Designing animation with a traditional programming language is often a complex and tedious process. It involves creating subroutines that systematically, and repeatedly, draw, erase, and move objects on the computer monitor to create the illusion of motion. Creating animation with Authorware is much simpler. Simply identify the object to be animated and trace the path along which the object will move.

It should be noted that Authorware's animation capabilities are limited. When faced with the need for sophisticated animation, Authorware designers often use tools such as Director. Animations created with other programs often can be imported into Authorware and displayed via the Digital Movie icon.

The first step in creating an animation is to place an object, on its own, into a Display icon. This object is the one that will be animated. Next, place a Motion icon below the Display icon on the Course Flow Line.

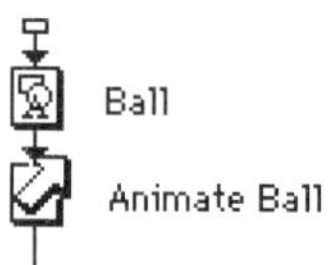

Opening the Motion icon reveals the following dialog box.

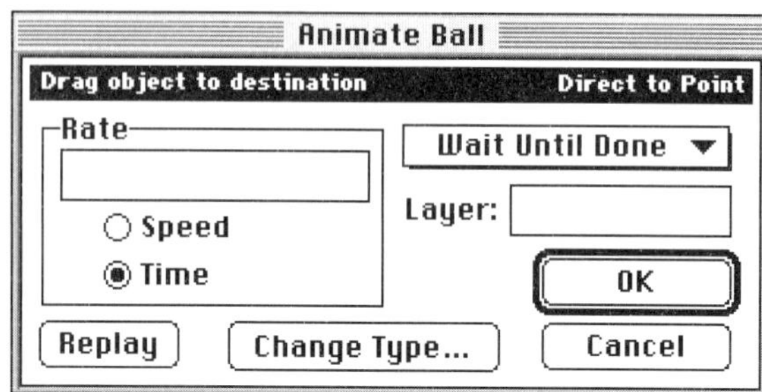

The top right-hand corner of the dialog box indicates the animation type, which in this case is Direct to Point. Authorware offers five classes of animation, although only two will be addressed in this text. The other three animation types allow greater flexibility, but require the developer to use Variables to control the animation. Selecting the box titled *Change Type* reveals all five classes.

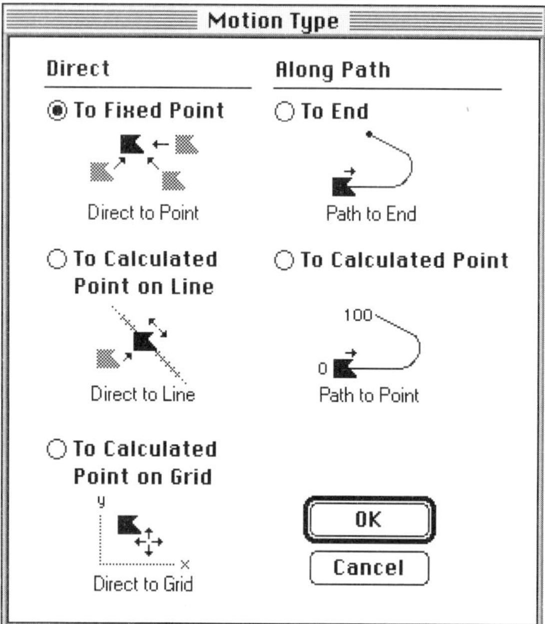

Those we will examine are Direct: To Fixed Point and Along Path: To End. Direct to Fixed Point is the simplest class of animation. It moves objects from one screen location to another in a straight line. Along Path To End is more sophisticated. It allows you to specify a path along which an object will be animated. This path is essentially unlimited in length or the number of turns.

Note: Authorware animates Display icons. That is, when an object is animated, all objects that exist in the same Display icon will also be animated. If you want to animate a single object then the object must exist in its own Display icon.

Guiding Activities: Motion Icons

The following activities provide step-by-step guidance to create animations.

Task 1

Goal: Animate a ball moving across the computer screen in a straight line.

- Create an object in a Display icon. *Note:* Filled, solid objects are easier to animate than empty or shaded objects.
- Place a Motion icon on the Course Flow Line below the Display icon.
- Open the Motion icon by double-clicking on the icon on the Course Flow Line.
- The default animation class is *Direct: To Fixed Point.*
- Complete the instruction to "Drag object to destination" by dragging the object to be animated to its destination.

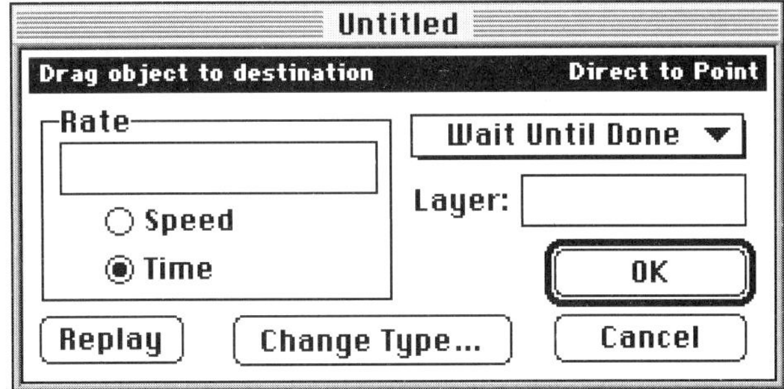

- Adjust the Time/Speed selection to meet your needs. You may select either Time or Speed for the animation timing. If you select Time, the animation will be completed in the number of seconds specified. If you select Speed, the animation moves at the rate of 1 inch per number of seconds specified. If you want objects to move at identical speeds, select Speed as the option and set a common rate for both animations.
- Select Wait Until Done or Concurrent for Timing.

Note: Selecting Wait Until Done pauses the lesson until the animation has been completed. Selecting Concurrent causes the next icon on the Course Flow Line to be executed immediately. If you want two or more Display icons to be animated simultaneously, you must select the Concurrent option.

- Click Replay to test the animation you have just created.
- Click OK when you are satisfied with the animation.
- Run the file to test the animation.

Task 2

Goal: Animate two or more objects moving across the screen.

- Place two solid objects in two Display icons (one object in each icon). Remember to label each Display with different names.
- Place a Motion icon on the Course Flow Line for each object to be animated.
- Run from the flag to set each Animation.
- Follow the instructions that appear for each object to be animated.
- Set the Timing to Concurrent for the first Motion icon.
- Run the file to test the animation.

Task 3

Goal: Animate an object moving around the perimeter of the monitor.

- Place a solid object in a Display icon before a Motion icon.
- Run the lesson. At the Motion icon, select *Along Path: To End* as the animation type.
- Notice the instruction in the top left corner of the dialog box. Authorware needs to know which object (i..e., which Display icon) will be animated. Identify the object by clicking on it once with the mouse.

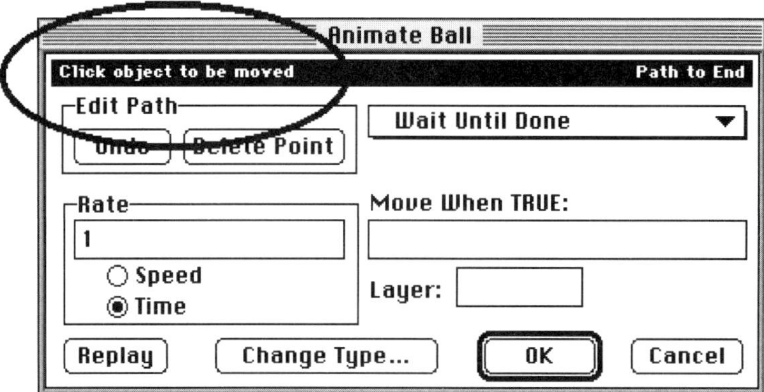

- Clicking on an object drops a triangular anchor onto the screen in the center of the object. (Sometimes the anchor may be hidden behind the object to be moved.)

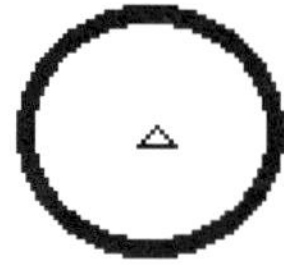

- Notice how the message in the animation dialog box changes to *Drag object to create path.*

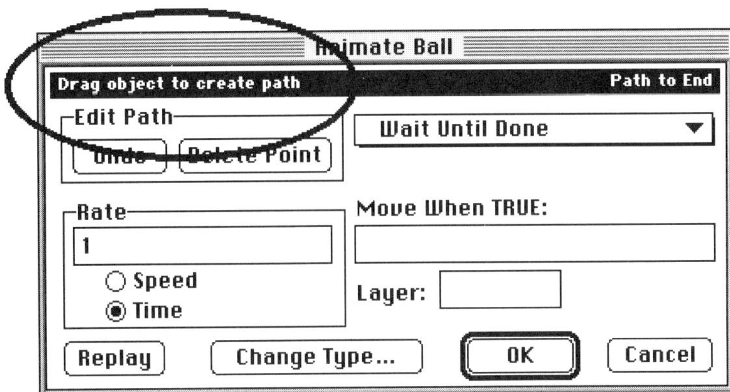

- To create the path along which the object will be animated, click on the object with the mouse, and, with the mouse button still depressed, drag the object to a new screen location. When the object is in the desired location, deselect the mouse. Deselecting the mouse button places a new anchor on the screen. Each time you drop the object (by releasing the mouse button), you will create another anchor. The anchors define the path along which the object will be animated. Repeat this process of selecting—dragging—deselecting until the desired path has been created.

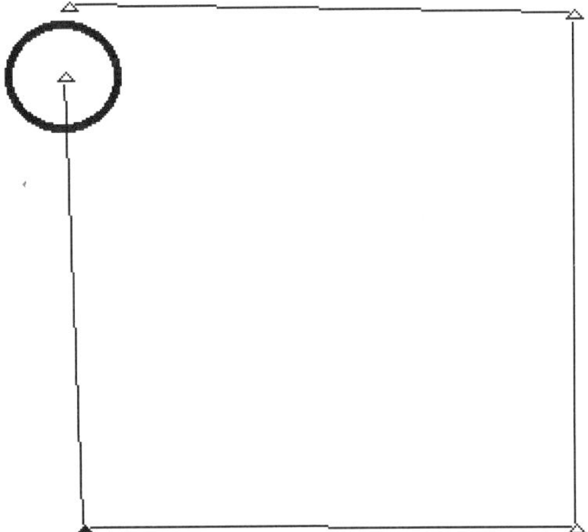

- Press the Replay button to test the animation.

Note: You may need to move the animation dialog box to place anchors. Also, be careful that you don't accidentally move the anchor (the small triangle located at the center of the object to be moved) instead of the object.

Task 4

Goal: Animate an object "orbiting" the screen (i.e., create a curved path rather than a linear one).

- Place a solid object in a Display icon before a Motion icon.
- Run the lesson. At the Motion icon, select *Along Path: To End* as the animation type.
- With the mouse, click once on the object to be animated as in the previous example. Once again, clicking on an object drops a triangular anchor onto the screen in the center of the

object. Create at least five animation anchors.

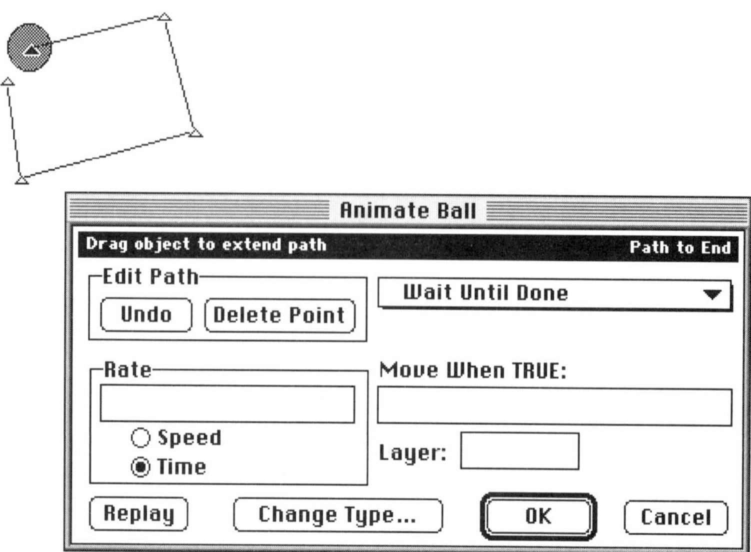

- Move the anchors with the mouse for more accurate placement. Shift-click and drag an anchor to move it.

- You must now change the straight-line animation to curved animation. To do this, double-click on each of the triangular anchors. Notice that the triangles change to circles to indicate curved animation. Be careful with curved animation. Some paths are very unusual!

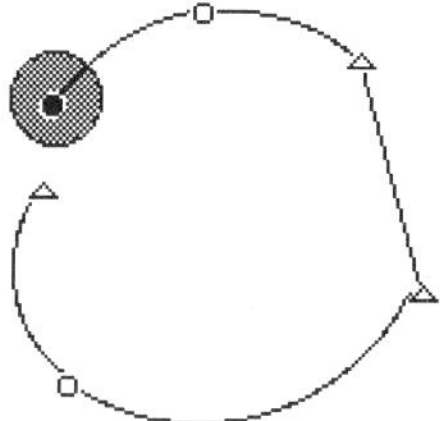

- Click OK in the animation box when you are done. Run the animation to test it.

STUDY EXERCISES

1. What is the difference between the *Wait Until Done* and *Concurrent* options in the Motion dialog box?

2. Place one or more Sound icons onto the Flow Line to deliver music or speech. If you have access to a microphone, you may be able to create your own sound files to create a narrated presentation.

3. Use a Digital Movie icon to play a movie in a file. Include several icons that explain the content of the movie for the user. *Note:* You need a Digital Movie file such as a QuickTime movie to complete this exercise.

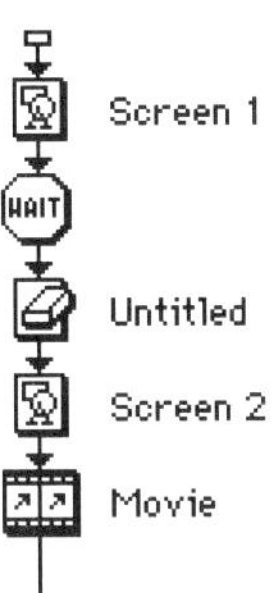

4. Animate an object around the perimeter of a rectangle.

5. Create three planets orbiting simultaneously around a static sun. The icon sequence for this exercise is as follows:

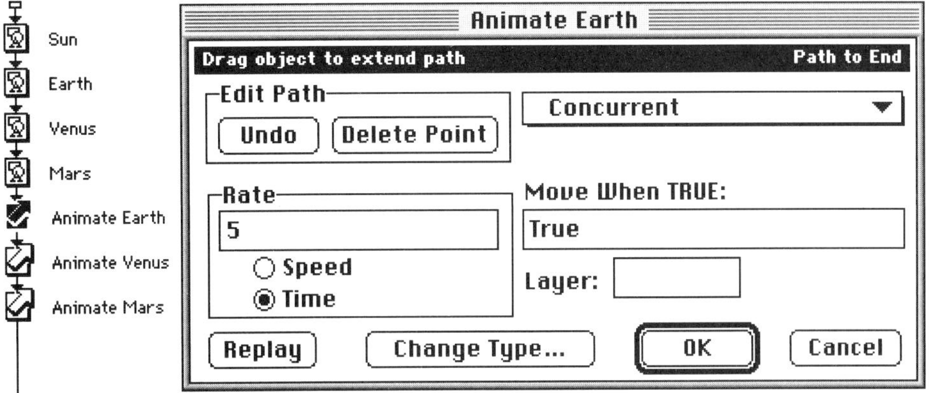

Notice that the field titled Move When TRUE: contains the value True. Setting this value to True assures the animation will never stop. That is, the Earth icon will continue to orbit the Sun for as long as the file is running.

6. You may need to read Chapters 6 to 8 before attempting the following exercise.

Use the Interaction icon to ask a question and Sound icons to deliver feedback. The illustration following shows how Sound icons can be used for feedback.

Note: You will need to have two sound files available to complete this question.

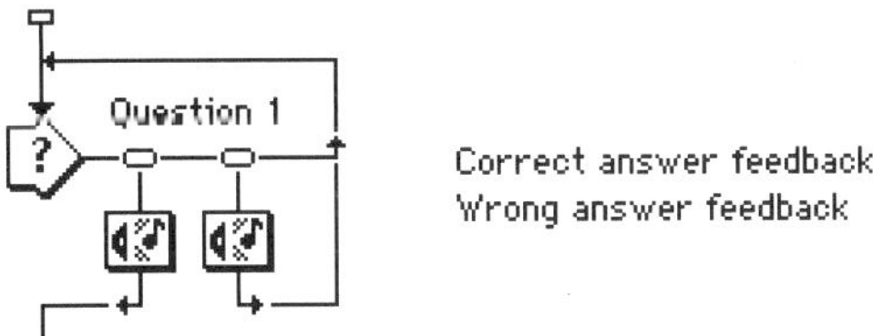

5

Odds and Ends

CHAPTER OVERVIEW

Learning to use Authorware to develop instruction can be a daunting task at first. The volume of information that must be learned to complete even modest tasks may be overwhelming. However, with practice, it becomes much easier and even the most complex structures become clear.

Up to now, the purpose of this text has been on learning the essential features that you need to learn to use Authorware effectively. Along the way, you have probably noticed that several options have been ignored. The reason for ignoring these options is not because they are unimportant. Rather, we have attempted to prevent you from experiencing the type of mental overload that is often experienced when learning new information.

In this chapter, you will examine some of those options we skipped in earlier chapters. We hope that the mental picture you have developed while studying the first four chapters of the book will place you in a much better position to understand these new concepts.

CHAPTER OBJECTIVES

By the end of this chapter, you will be able to
- Use the Tool Bar to execute actions quickly.
- Understand and control the options in the File Setup pulldown menu.
- Use the Grid to place objects accurately on the screen.
- Use the Align Object option to balance objects or align two or more objects in horizontal or vertical planes.
- Define and apply styles to text.
- Use the Trace window to debug lessons.

KEY TERMS

Tool Bar
File Setup
Show Grid
Snap to Grid
Align Objects
Define Styles
Apply Styles
Trace window

SUPPORT MATERIALS

On the CD-ROM disc, run **BEGIN.PKG** if you are a Macintosh user or **BEGIN.APP** if you are using a PC. When the file opens, click once on the title page to begin. Select **Chapter 5** and run the video to learn how to create and apply a style sheet to text in Display icons.

The folder on the CD-ROM titled MACDEMOS or PC_DEMOS contains several demonstration files that you can run and examine. The folder contains two versions of each file: a packaged file that you can run and an unpackaged file containing the icons used to create the file. Run the file and examine the icons to learn how to control several important options available in the File Setup dialog box.

Macintosh users:
Run the file CHP05.pkg to view its contents.
Open the data file CHP05.A3M to examine how the file was created.

PC users:
Run the file CHP05.APP to view its contents.
Open the data file CHP05.A3W to examine how the file was created.

Note: You must have a copy of Authorware on your computer to open the data files.

STUDY TOPICS

In the following sections, you will examine several Authorware tools that are designed to enhance effectiveness and improve productivity.

Tool Bar

Have you noticed a menu with several icons close to the top of the screen in the Design Window? This menu is the Tool Bar. The Tool Bar allows you to activate several commands with a single mouse click. Many of the tools will be familiar to users who have worked with other word processing, spreadsheet, or similar applications.

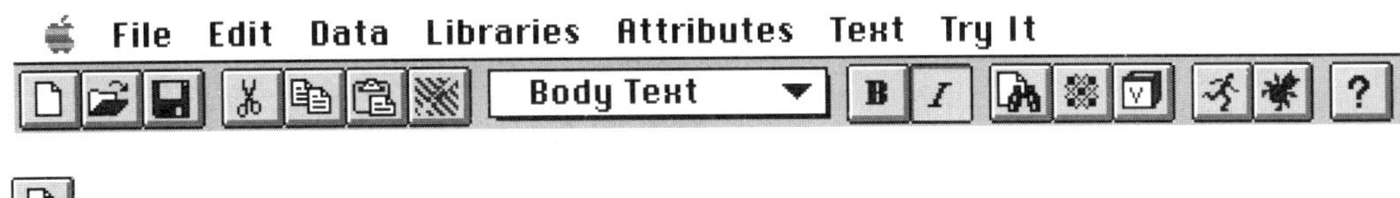

New file: Opens a dialog box to create a new Authorware file.

Opens an existing Authorware file.

Saves a file to disk.

Cuts a selected object or text (cuts the object from the current window into the computer's memory).

Copies a selected object or text (copies the object into the computer's memory, but leaves the original object in place).

Pastes a copy of the current temporary storage buffer.

Reverses the last action (very useful when you accidentally erase an object).

Body Text ▼   Applies a predetermined style to a selected text object.

Adds boldface to the selected text object.

Italicizes the selected text object.

Finds and/or Changes text in Display icons. Use this feature to find/replace words in different Authorware displays. This feature is very useful when name changes are needed.

This icon is titled Show Connections. It shows links created with Navigate icons to other icons in the file. To use this feature, highlight a Navigate icon and select the Show Connections button.

This icon is titled Show Variables. It has the same effect as using the Show Variables option from the Data pulldown menu.

Run/Run from Flag icons: The Run icon has the same effect as using the Run option in the Try It pulldown menu. The Run from Flag icon has the same effect as using the Run from flag option in the Try It pulldown menu. *Notice that the icons change when the Start Flag is placed/ removed from the Course Flow Line.*

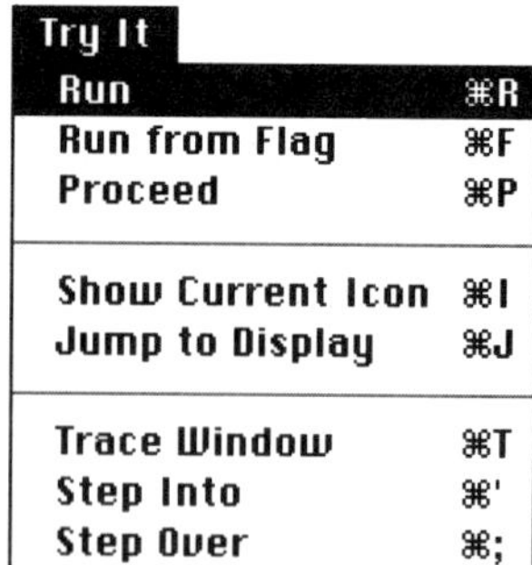

Trace window: One of the most complex and frustrating activities in courseware design involves finding and fixing errors (known as bugs). Selecting the Trace window opens a window that helps the debugging process. The Trace window is a valuable tool to help identify troublesome icons during a lesson run. As the lesson executes, the Trace window maintains a list of the precise order in which icons are executed. This list can be used to follow the lesson's logic and to identify precisely where the actual lesson flow deviates from the intended flow. Items in the Trace window indicate the flowline depth, the icon types, and icon titles.

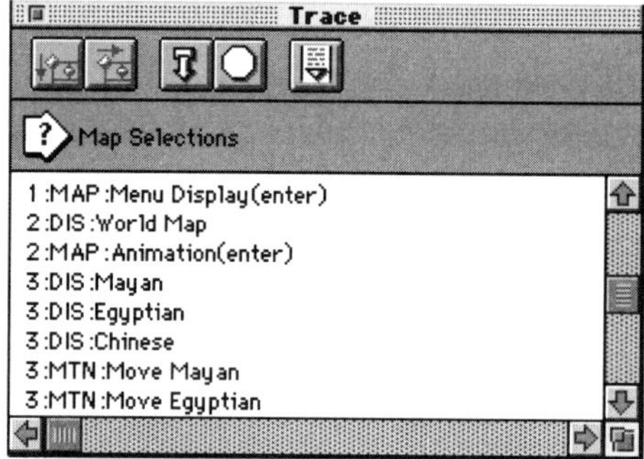

To activate the Trace window, select the Trace button from the Tool Bar or from the Try It pulldown window before running the lesson.

Help: Use this button to access the help system.

File Setup

The File Setup dialog box contains several important options that must be set before completing a lesson.

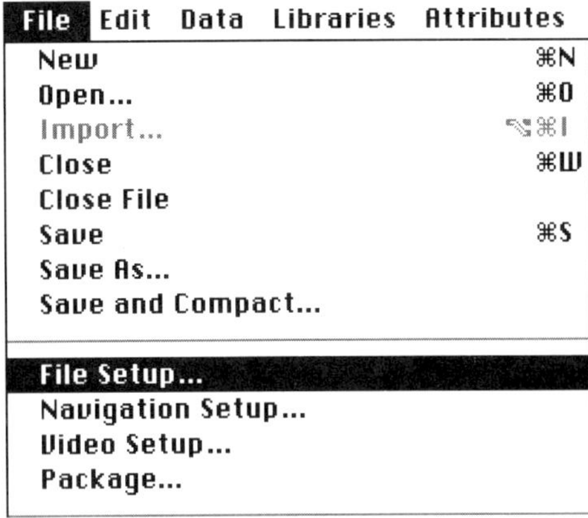

Selecting File Setup brings up the following dialog box. There are many options, some of which are quite specialized. We will describe only the more commonly used options.

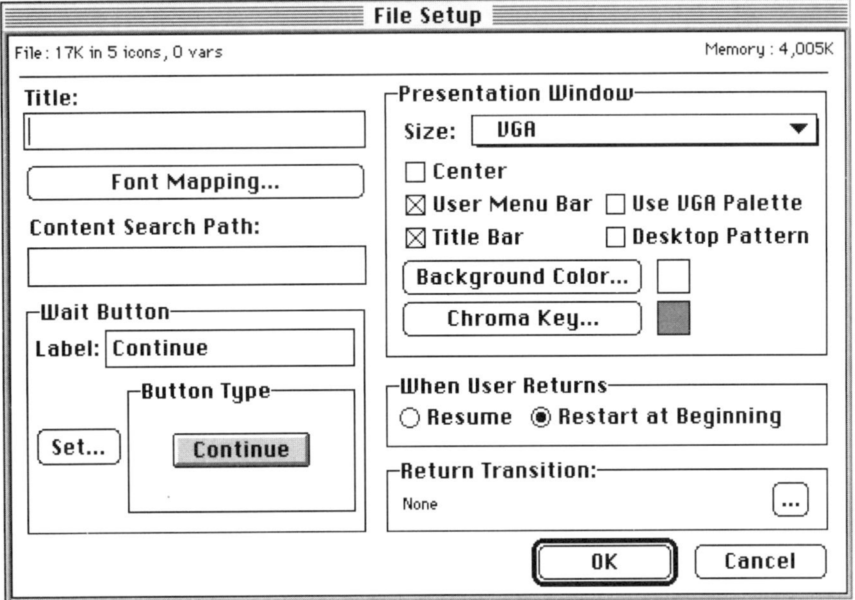

Lesson Title

Later in this text, we will examine Packaging courses. Packaging a course converts your raw lesson file into a finished product. Packaging also prevents the user from accessing the Design Window in which you create the lesson flow.

The Title option allows you to control the name that appears in the Title Bar. The Title Bar contains the text that appears at the top of the Presentation Window of the packaged file. While designing the course, "Presentation Window" appears in the Title Bar. Once the file has been packaged, the user only sees the Presentation Window and the default title given to the Presentation Window is the file name. The default title is the name given to the design file and often has to be changed. For example, you would probably want to change the title of a file on fractions titled *fctns5.a3m* to one that reflects the lesson content more accurately.

The Wait Button

The Wait icon places a button onto the Presentation Window. The default text in the button is *Continue*.

Continue

You can modify the message in the button by changing the contents of the field titled Label. Choosing the Set... option allows you to select from several button styles or to import your own buttons created in a graphics program.

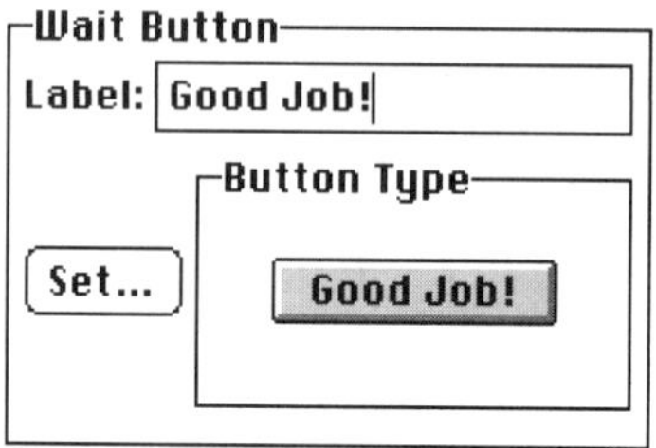

Presentation Window Size

Determining the monitor size that will be used to run the completed lesson is an important task that must be determined early in the needs assessment phase of any design project. The Presentation Window size refers to the size of the monitor that will be used to present the lesson.

Variable
Classic, 9"
Color, 16"
EGA
High-Res RGB, 13"
Monochrome, 12"
Portable
Portrait
PowerBook
RGB, 12"
Two-Page, 21"
✓VGA
Use Full Screen

It is important to carefully examine the equipment that will be used to present the lesson because Authorware does not automatically scale content in Display icons to fit the user's monitor. If you select a large monitor (e.g., a color 16-in. monitor) on which to design a lesson and the lesson file is used on a laptop computer with a small monitor, lesson content may be masked or navigation buttons maybe missing.

Background Color

The default background color for your lesson is white. To change the default color, select the Background Color button and choose from the color palette. The color you choose will appear in the File Setup Window.

Changing the default background color can cause problems, because the color cannot be erased. An alternative approach to creating a color background, and a strategy that permits greater design flexibility, involves using a Display icon that contains a background color. This Display icon is simply left on the Course Flow Line until it is no longer needed and is erased using an Erase icon.

To create a new background color in a Display icon:

- Place a Display icon on the Course Flow Line. Label the icon.
- Double click on the Display icon to open its Presentation Window.
- Select the Rectangle tool from the Authorware toolbox and draw a large rectangle.
- Select Lines... and Color... from the Attributes pulldown menu to display their palettes.
- Select the desired color for the background color.
- Select transparent lines from the Lines palette.
- Use the Selection tool to stretch the rectangle across the entire Presentation Window. To completely cover the window, it may be necessary to move the rectangle and resize it. To do this, select and drag the rectangle to a corner of the Presentation Window. Now, stretch the rectangle before moving so that it covers the entire window.

You may have noticed that when working with a colored background that text entered into a Display appears on a white background rather than on the desired background color. To make the text background the same color as the default background, you must change the background color for the text object.

- Click on the text object with the Selection tool or drag over the text with the Text tool.

- Select Color from the Attributes menu.

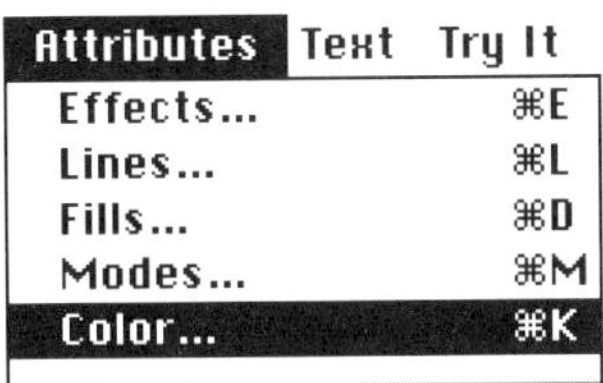

- Click on the Background Color box.

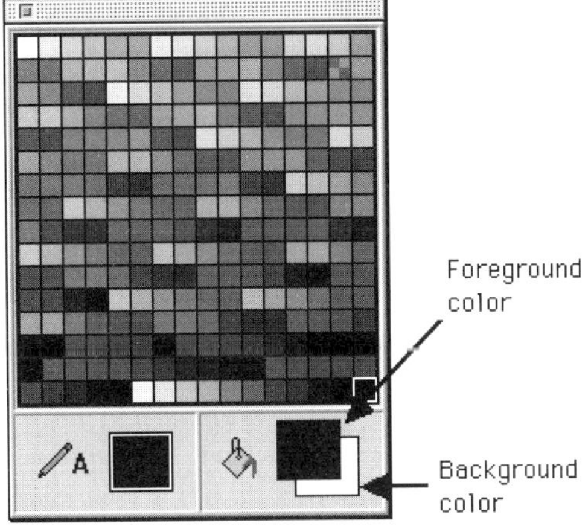

- Select the desired background color.

Setting the "When User Returns" option

As the designer, you control where the lesson begins each time a user quits and restarts a lesson. The default value is to restart the lesson each time from the beginning.

However, it is sometimes beneficial to allow the user to restart a lesson from the point at which it was stopped. In such cases, check the Resume button. However, it is important to realize that this option should be used with caution. Unless an option is included for the user to restart the lesson from the beginning or to navigate easily through the lesson file, the lesson may be unusable after it has been completed once. The usual strategy to circumvent this potential problem is to include the Restart() Function in a Calculation as the final icon on the Course Flow Line. Functions will be examined in detail in Chapter 14.

You can use Transitions to display a special effect each time the user returns to the lesson from the Return effects menu. These Transitions are the same options as those that exist for Erase icons.

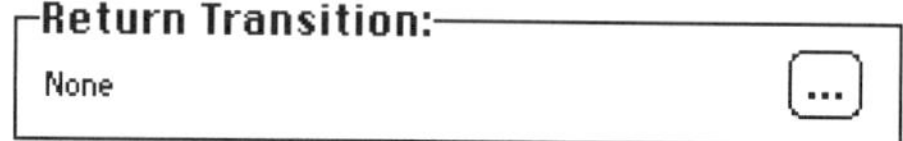

Miscellaneous Options

Show Grid and Snap to Grid

Show Grid creates a series of grid marks on the monitor. These marks can be used by the designer to help align objects on the screen.

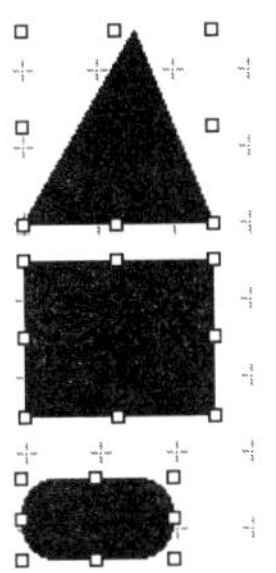

Closely related is the Snap to Grid command. Snap to Grid prevents the designer from placing screen objects more than half a grid distance away from the grid.

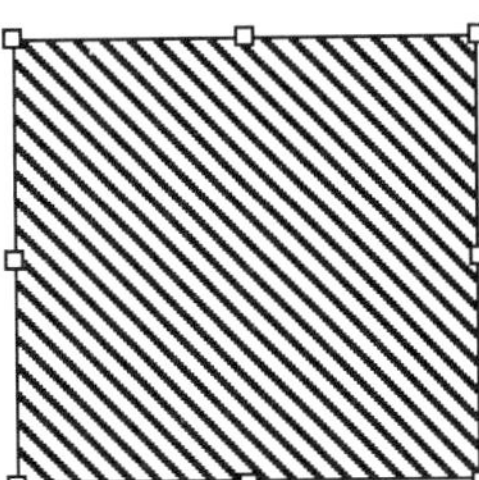

Note: "Show Grid" does not need to be ON to use the Snap to Grid option.

Align Objects

The Align Objects option allows the designer to align two or more objects in the same horizontal or vertical plane. Alternatively, it can be used to space three or more objects horizontally or vertically. Spaced objects generally appear more balanced on the screen and balance is often cited as a factor that makes attractive presentations.

To align or space objects, you must be in the Presentation Window (i.e., open a Display icon). First, select the Align Objects option from the Attributes menu. This brings the Alignment palette to the forefront.

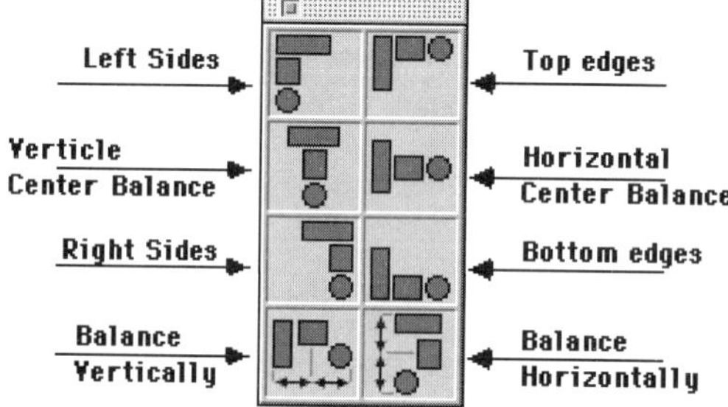

The operation of this palette is clear from its visual appearance. For example, the top left option is used to align objects along their left edges. To align objects, first select two or more objects to be aligned by "Shift-clicking." Next, use the mouse to select the appropriate option from the alignment grid.

Define and Apply Styles

Before applying a text style, the style must be defined. Defining styles is generally performed in one of two ways.

- Copying styled text from other Authorware files and pasting the copied text into the current file. Pasting styled text not only places new text onto the Display icon, it also places a copy of the style sheet into the current lesson. This style sheet now can be applied to any other text objects as described in what follows.

- Selecting Define Styles from the Text pulldown menu and setting options in a dialog box.

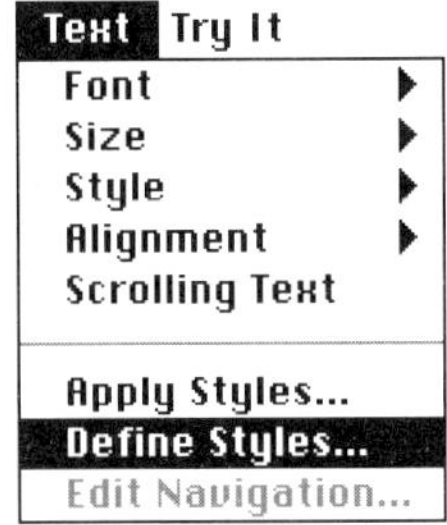

To create a new style:

*   Select the Add button. The default name New Style will appear.
*   Type the desired name for the new style.
*   Select the text formatting options from the dialog box.
*   Select Modify to complete the new style.
*   Select Done to return to the lesson.

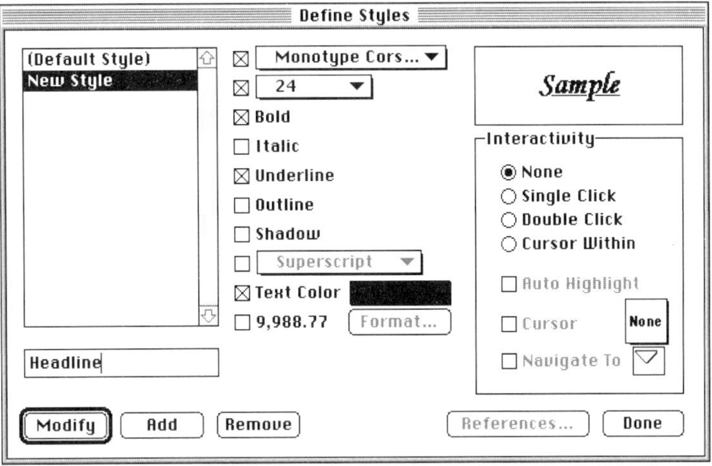

Applying styles

To apply a style, highlight text with the mouse and choosing the appropriate style from the Apply Styles pulldown menu or from the Tool Bar.

In the following example, a style is applied to text in a Display icon by selecting a style from the Tool Bar. First, the text is selected.

Next, a style is selected from the Tool Bar. In this case, a style titled Body Text is selected.

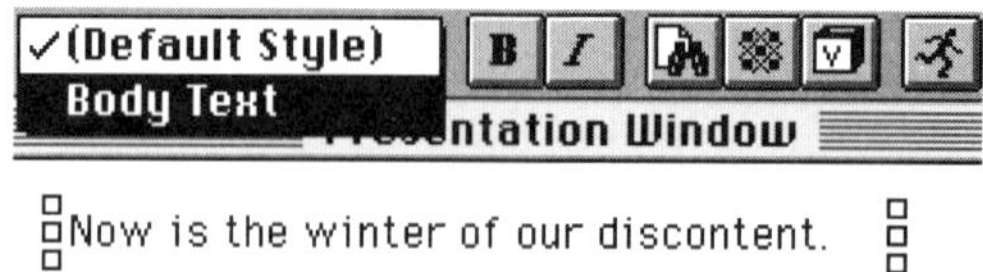

The text reappears in the desired style.

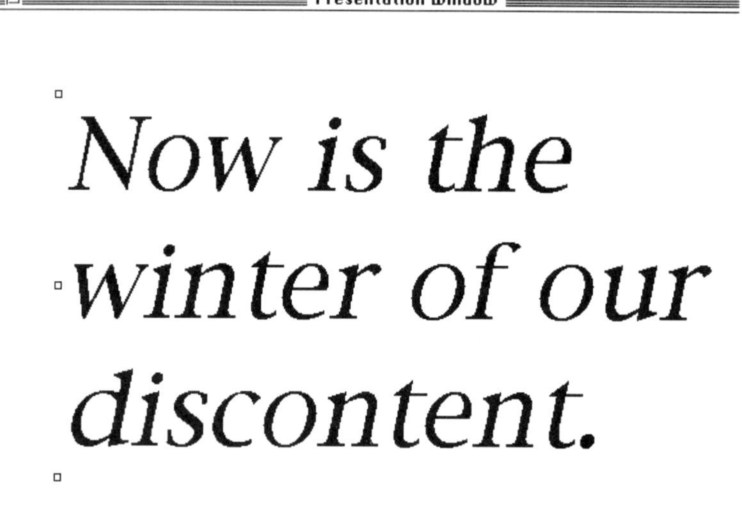

STUDY EXERCISES

1.   Name the keyboard equivalent for each of the following commands.

Example: Command   Keyboard equivalent

                    Run   Command-R

   • Show Variables

   • Pause

   • Jump to Presentation window

   • Show Lines palette

   • Show current icon

- Proceed
- Show Fills palette
- Show Functions
- Show Color palette
- Jump to Design window
- Left-justify text
- Center-justify text

2. The default name given to the button for a Wait icon is "Continue". How can you change the default name to "Next"?

3. Create a lesson with the following default settings:
   - A blue background
   - The Pulldown Menu Bar and Title Bar removed in the Presentation window
   - A Wait button that reads "Press the spacebar to continue"

4. Create three different objects in a Display icon (e.g., a rectangle, an oval, and a hexagon). Align the three objects as follows:
   - Vertically along their left borders
   - Horizontally along their top borders
   - Vertically along their center axes

5. Define and name a Text style with the following attributes:
   - Times font
   - 30-point text
   - Bold text
   - Red text
   - Underlined text

   Create a presentation and apply the style to several words or phrases in the display.

6. Run a file by selecting the Run option from the Tool Bar in the Design Window.

   Place a flag on the Course Flow Line and rerun the file from the Flag by selecting the Run from Flag button in the Tool Bar.

   Rerun the file using the Trace window. Observe the entries in the Trace window while the file is running. When the lesson stops, try to follow the lesson logic by observing each line in the Trace window.

6

The Interaction Icon: Part 1

CHAPTER OVERVIEW

You have learned how to use Authorware to create presentations. Although presenting information is often an important task in the educational process, simply displaying content to users rarely results in deep or lasting learning, and barely scrapes the surface of the types of activities that can be created within Authorware.

Effective instruction engages students with lesson content. In this and the following chapters, you will learn how to create interactive lessons that ask users to type, move objects, select hot spots with the mouse, use pulldown menus, and perform other tasks that require thought. Creative use of these options can result in more active and engaging learning.

The Interaction icon is probably the most complex of all the Authorware icons. In addition to learning how the Interaction icon operates, it is important to learn each of the ten interaction types that accompany Authorware. In this chapter, you will examine the basic structure of an interaction and three interaction types. In the following chapters, you will examine the other types of interactions.

CHAPTER OBJECTIVES

Following this chapter, you will be able to

- Understand the general structure of an Interaction.
- Construct questions that require the following types of responses:

  -Keypress

  -Button

  -Hot Spots

KEY TERMS

Interactions
Interaction Structures
Feedback icons
Response Options
Judging
Looping
Erasing
Keypress responses
Button responses
Hot Spot responses
Hot spots
Wildcard

SUPPORT MATERIALS

On the CD-ROM disc, run **BEGIN.PKG** if you are a Macintosh user or **BEGIN.APP** if you are using a PC. When the file opens, click once on the title page to begin. Select the button titled **Chapter 6**, and watch Parts 1 to 4 to see how an interaction is created and how to use Keypress, Button, and Hot Spot interactions.

The folder on the CD-ROM titled MACDEMOS or PC_DEMOS contains several demonstration files that you can run and examine. The folder contains two versions of each file: a packaged file that you can run and an unpackaged file containing the icons used to create the file. Run the file to examine the icons used to create Keypress, Button, and Hot Spot interactions.

Macintosh users:
Run the file CHP06.pkg to view its contents.
Open the data file CHP06.A3M to examine how the file was created.

PC users:
Run the file CHP06.APP to view its contents.
Open the data file CHP06.A3W to examine how the file was created.

Note: You must have a copy of Authorware on your computer to open the data files.

STUDY TOPICS

The process of creating interactions may seem complex at first, but with practice it soon becomes straightforward. You will learn about the Interaction icon in three phases.
- First, you will follow a series of steps to give you some firsthand experience on which you can build.
- Second, you will learn the general process of creating an Interaction.
- Finally, you will apply the process to three different Response types.

What Is an Interaction?

It may help at first to think of an Interaction icon as Authorware's method for asking questions.
Follow these steps to create a question.

- Place an Interaction icon on the Course Flow Line. Label the Interaction icon "Question 1".

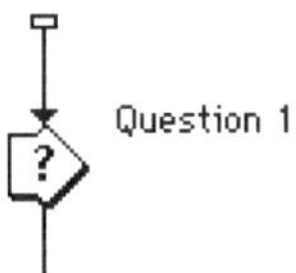

- Double-click on the Interaction icon. A dialog box will appear. Check (i.e., X) the box titled
  Pause Before Exiting. This dialog box controls how information is erased from the screen
  and several options associated with Text Entry Interactions. It will be examined later.

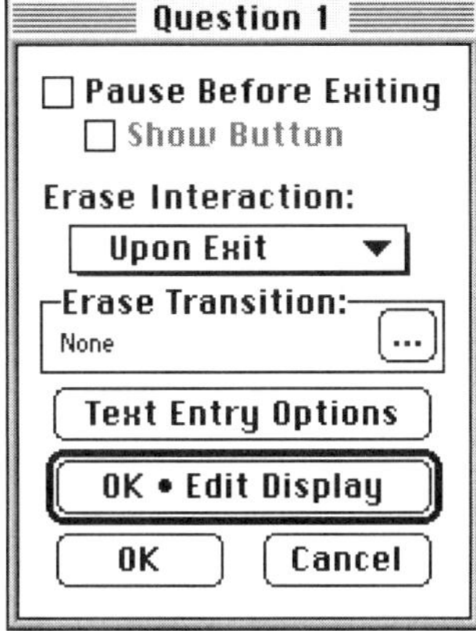

- Click on *OK • Edit Display* to open the Presentation Window associated with the Interaction
  icon. This Presentation Window is typically used to display questions or provide instructions.
  Enter the following text into the window.

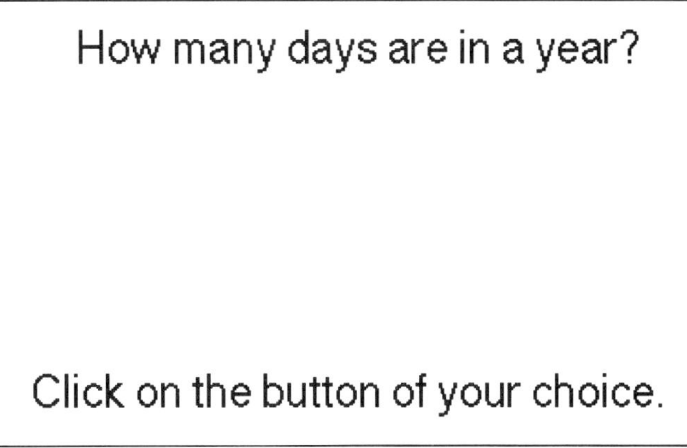

- Jump back to the Design Window and drag a Display icon to the right of the Interaction icon.
  The icon attached to the Interaction icon is known as a Feedback icon.

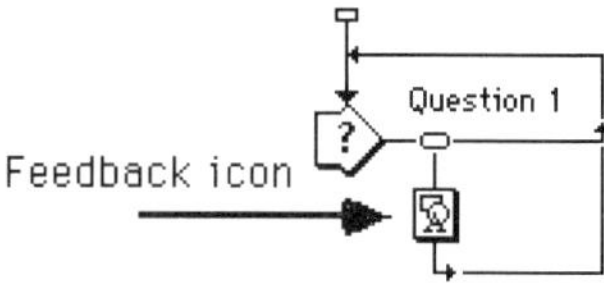

Immediately, a dialog box will appear. The dialog box asks you to identify how the user will respond to the question. Select Button and click OK.

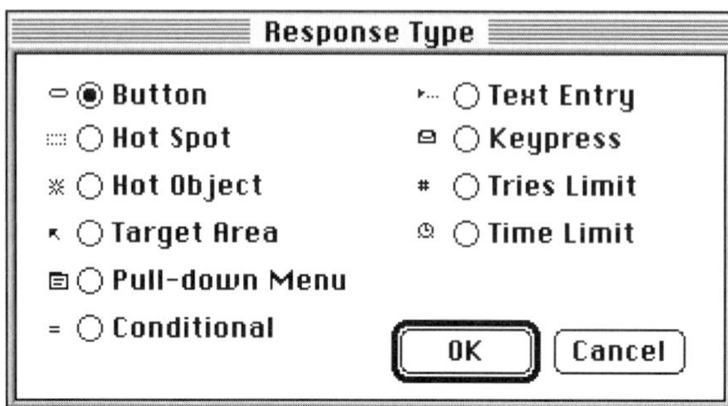

- Notice that immediately above the Feedback icon is a small button. The button is a window to the Response Options for this anticipated response. The Response Options contain many settings that you can modify.

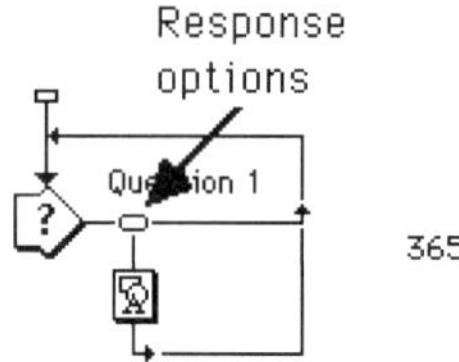

- Double-click on the Response Options button to access the following window. The window contains many features that will be examined later. In the field titled Button Name, replace the word "Untitled" with "365". The button name will appear in the button on the screen. Click OK to continue.

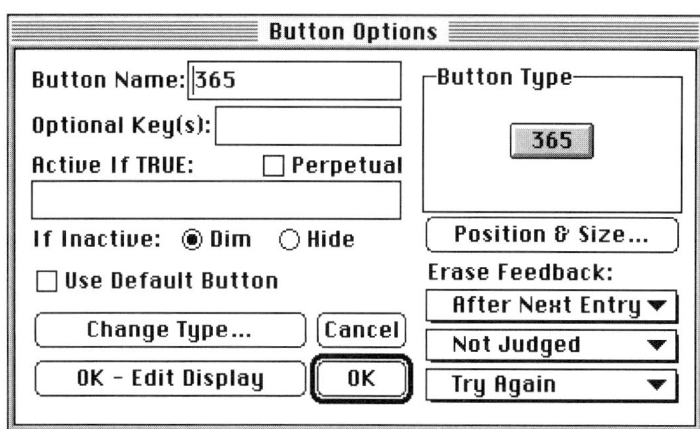

- Now add another Display icon to the right of the icon titled "365" and label this icon "366".

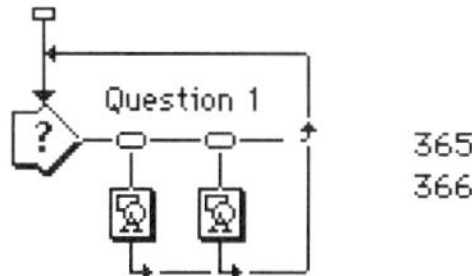

- Open the Display icon titled 365 by double-clicking on its icon. The information entered here will appear if the user selects this button. Type the following text:

That's right.   Well done!

- Open the Display icon titled 366 and enter the following text:

Sorry, but you must be thinking about a leap year.

- Jump back to the Design Window when you are done.
- Double-click on the Response Options icon for 365.

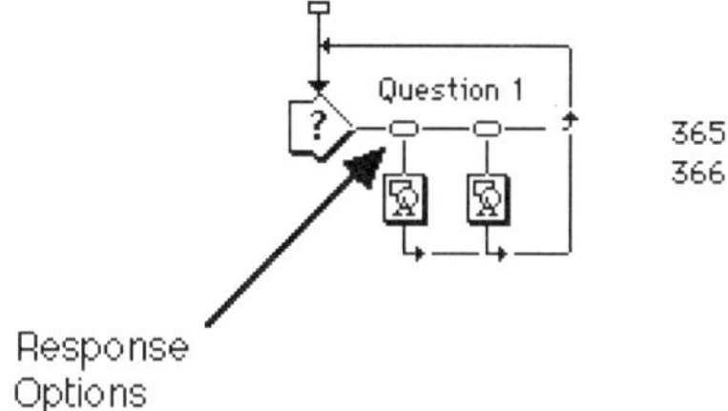

- Change the three pulldown menus at the bottom right of the window. These menus determine when the feedback will be erased from the screen; whether this answer is correct, incorrect, or not judged; and the path that will be followed next.

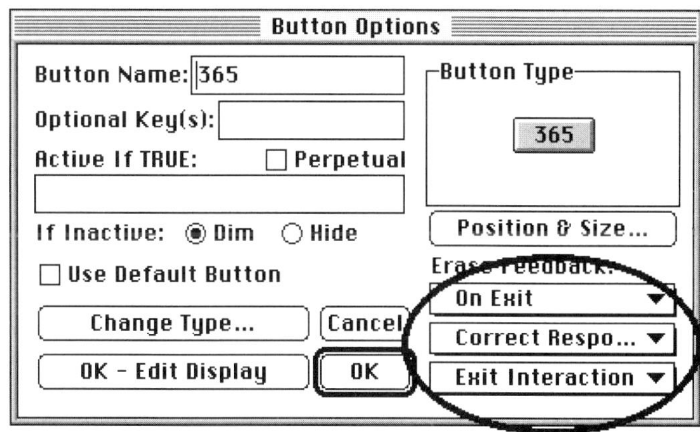

- Select *OK* to close the window and repeat the steps for the Display icon titled "366". Use the following three settings:

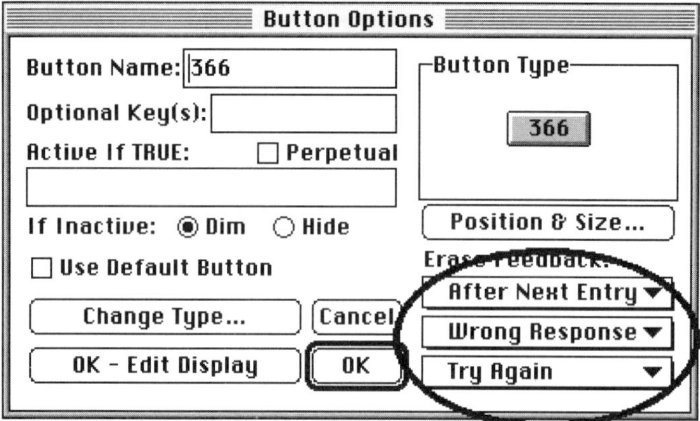

- Select *OK* to return to the Course Flow Line. The icons should now appear as follows:

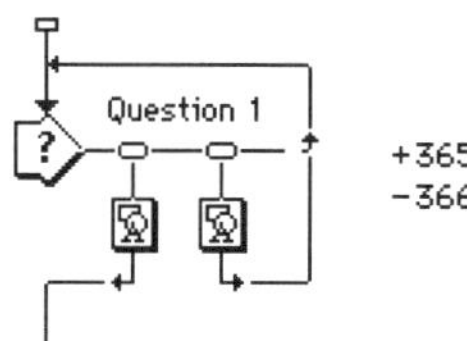

- Save your file and run the lesson. Notice that two buttons appear at the upper left corner of the screen. To place the buttons, Pause the lesson and then move each button by clicking and dragging.

- Run the file again and answer the question by first clicking on the incorrect answer, followed by the correct button. Notice the feedback associated with each response. Also, notice that the question repeats when you click on the incorrect answer, but ends on a correct response.

The General Process

You have created an interaction. How did it work?

Although Authorware permits many different response types, the design process is the same for each. Once you have learned the process of creating an interaction, you can apply it to all response types. The following section explains this process. Subsequent sections examine additional options specific to each interaction type.

Creating interactions involves building Interaction Structures. Interaction Structures include the following:

- An Interaction icon that presents the question and controls when the question is erased from the screen.

- One or more icons that are used to match users' responses against predicted responses. These are called Feedback icons. Once matched, Feedback icons present additional information to the user or initiate other actions.

- Response options for each Feedback icon. Each response type offers different choices, but three options, Judging, Looping, and Erasing, must be set for every Feedback icon.

An Interaction Structure

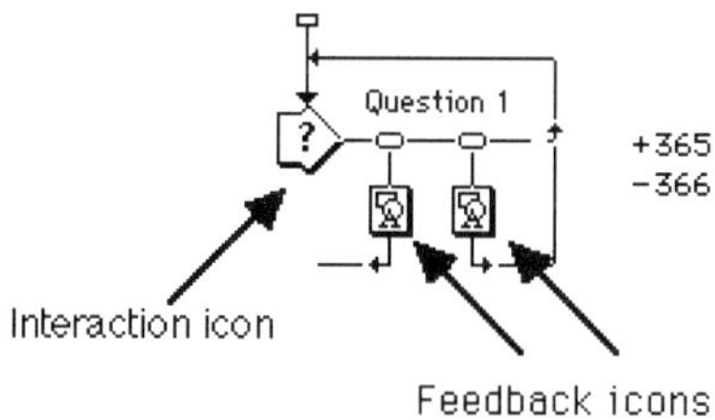

The Interaction Icon

The Interaction icon usually contains the question and controls how it is erased. To enter information into an Interaction icon:

- Place an Interaction icon on the Course Flow Line and label the icon.
- Double-click on the Interaction icon.

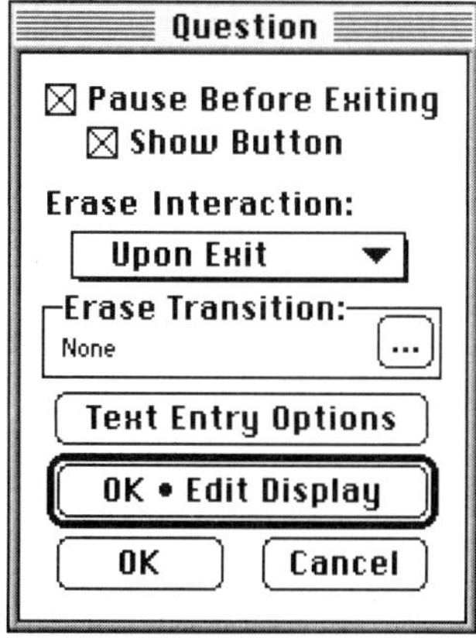

Notice the Erase Interaction pulldown menu. The menu offers three options that control when the question is erased. The default setting (Upon Exit) ensures that the question remains on the screen until the interaction is completed.

After Next Entry removes the question from the screen as soon as the user responds. This option is frequently used for pulldown menu interactions. The final option, Don't Erase, ensures that the question remains on the screen until it is removed with an Erase icon.

Notice the box titled "Pause Before Exiting". Checking this option helps to prevent feedback from being erased from the screen before the user has had a chance to react. In effect, this option places a Wait icon onto the Course Flow Line when the question is finished.

- Clicking on *OK•Edit Display* opens a Display in the Interaction icon. This is where the designer enters the text and graphics that form the question and instructions on how to interact. You will usually include at least one text or graphic object in an Interaction icon. However, in some cases, you may have entered the question stem and instruction on preceding icons. In these cases, you can leave the Interaction icon empty.

Feedback Icons

Feedback icons provide distinct responses to different user input. They allow the designer to customize feedback. Response Options must be set for each Feedback icon. These options vary for different response types, but give the designer considerable flexibility.

- Before using a Feedback icon, you must decide how the user will interact. In other words, will the user type a response, move an object, select from a pulldown menu, or use another interaction type?

- Next, decide what type of feedback you will use. Initially, it is easiest to use Display icons for feedback. However, with experience, you will recognize that your options are almost unlimited. For example, a Sound icon could be used to play a sound file or a Motion icon could be used to animate an object. More complex feedback can be put into Map icons.

- To add a Feedback icon, drag an icon from the Icon Palette and drop it to the right of the Interaction icon.

- One Feedback icon is added for each anticipated response. Anticipated responses are the different ways that you believe the user will respond to the interaction. When the first Feedback icon is added, a dialog box will prompt you for a Response Type. Subsequent Response Types follow the first choice, but can be modified.

- To enter text into a Feedback icon, double-click on each Display icon and enter the relevant information.

Setting Response Options

You will learn about the options for each response type in this and the following two chapters. However, three options are common to all Feedback icons: Judging, Looping, and Erasing. Judging refers to whether an answer is correct or incorrect. Looping controls whether the user will repeat a question or continue with the lesson. Erasing controls when feedback is erased from the screen. Although the options for each response type differ, they all include the same menus for judging answers, looping, and erasing feedback.

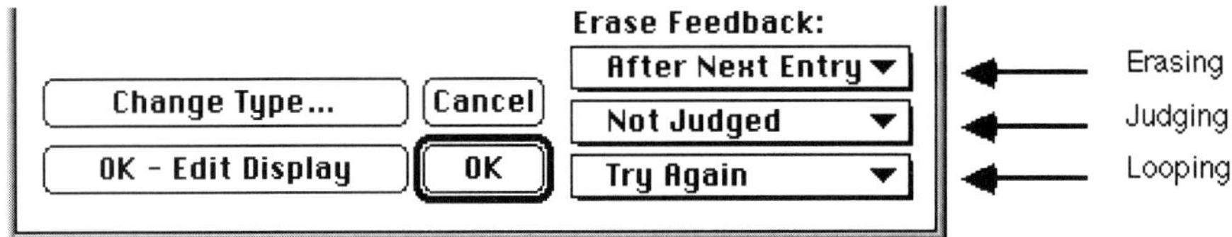

To Set Judging

Three judging options facilitate tracking of correct and incorrect responses:

Setting judging is important because this updates the System Variable used for tracking the number of correct and incorrect responses. When you set answer judging, Authorware keeps track of the number of correct and incorrect answers made during the lesson. This information is often used by designers to help decision making later in the lesson. For example, sometimes users are only allowed to exit a lesson when they have answered a given number of questions correctly. Selecting *Not Judged* turns off the judging System Variables. (System Variables will be examined in Chapter 13.)

To Set Looping

Three looping options control whether the user repeats a question or lesson segment. A fourth option (Return) is available only for Perpetual responses, which will be introduced later (see Chapter 8). In general, set looping to Exit for a correct response and Try Again for an incorrect response.

- *Try Again*: Authorware repeats the current Interaction icon. Try Again is often used with wrong answers and is particularly useful when you want the user to repeat a question.

- *Exit Interaction*: Authorware exits the interaction and returns to the next icon on the Course Flow Line. Exit Interaction is typically used with correct answers.

- *Continue*: Authorware checks whether the learner's response matches more than one anticipated response. Continue is used when more than one response or condition could be true.

Looping options for each feedback icon are indicated by arrows attached to the Feedback icons.

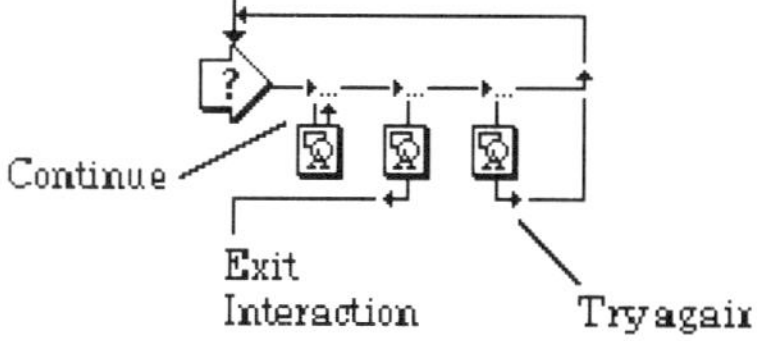

Note: To change the looping, you do not need to access the Response Options for each anticipated response. By holding down the Command key while clicking on the arrowhead of the looping symbol (immediately above or below the feedback icon), you can change the looping type (the arrow will change direction). Continue clicking until the looping is set to the desired option.

To Set Erasing

You can control when feedback is erased from the screen. As with erasing of the question, understanding how feedback is erased from the the screen is very important. Four options exist for erasing feedback.

- *Before Next Entry*: Erases feedback for the current answer before the learner enters another response. Be careful with this option. The lesson needs some way to pause to ensure that the user has time to read the feedback.

- *After Next Entry*: Feedback for the current answer stays displayed until the learner enters another response. This option is most commonly used with wrong answers and " Try Again" looping.
- *Upon Exit*: Feedback is erased when the Interaction icon is exited. This option is usually used with correct answers and "Exit Interaction" looping.
- *Don't Erase*: Feedback remains displayed. If you select *Don't Erase* you will need to use an Erase icon to remove feedback.

The following illustration shows the components of an Interaction Structure for a Text Entry response.

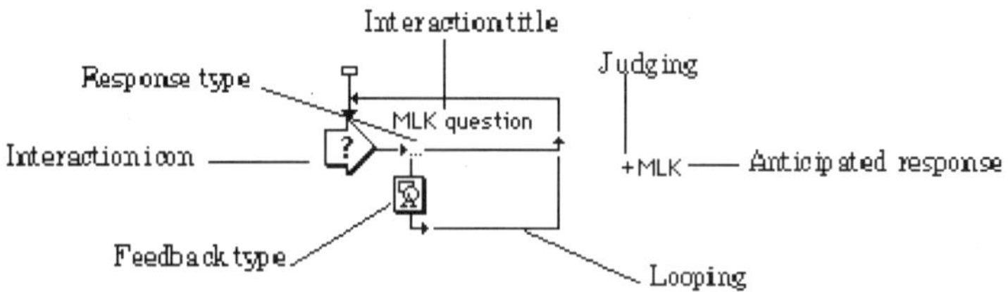

Response types

The Interaction icon supports 10 response types. Although the process of creating an interaction is essentially the same for each, their Response Options are very different. In the remainder of this chapter, we will examine three commonly used response types: Keypress, Button, and Hot Spot.

Keypress Responses   

Keypress Responses are the simplest to create and use. To use a Keypress Response, the user presses a key on the keyboard. Authorware responds if the designer has anticipated that response. Keypress Responses are often associated with multiple-choice questions, but may be used for a wide range of interactions. For example, the designer could use Keypress Responses to control navigation.

The Following Exercise Demonstrates How to Create Keypress Interactions

- Place an Interaction icon on the flow line. Title the interaction "Keypress interaction".
- Open the Interaction icon. Mark the *Pause Before Exiting* option. Click *OK•Edit Display* and use the Text tool to place an interaction in the Presentation Window. For example, you might enter the following multiple-choice question.

Which city is the capital of Pennsylvania?

a. Philadelphia

b. Harrisburg

c. Pittsburgh

Type a, b, or c to make your response.

- Jump back to the flow line and attach four Display icons into the Interaction Structure for feedback.

- At the prompt, select Keypress for the response types and enter appropriate icon names. For a Keypress Response, the icon names specify the keys that the user will select. For this multiple-choice question, the icon names will be "a", "b", "c", and "?", for Philadelphia, Harrisburg, Pittsburgh, and a wildcard, respectively.   The key for the wildcard (which catches any other entries) is "?".

- Open each Feedback icon and type appropriate feedback for each anticipated response. For the wildcard, include a comment that the user pressed the wrong key.

- Open the Response Options to modify judging, looping, and erasing.

  For the correct answer (b):

  Set erasing to On Exit

  Set judging to Correct Response

  Set looping to Exit Interaction

  For the wrong answers (a and c):

  Set erasing to After Next Entry

  Set judging to Wrong Response

  Set looping to Try Again

  For the wildcard (?):

  Set erasing to After Next Entry

  Set judging to Not Judged

  Set looping to Try Again

- The icons should now appear as follows:

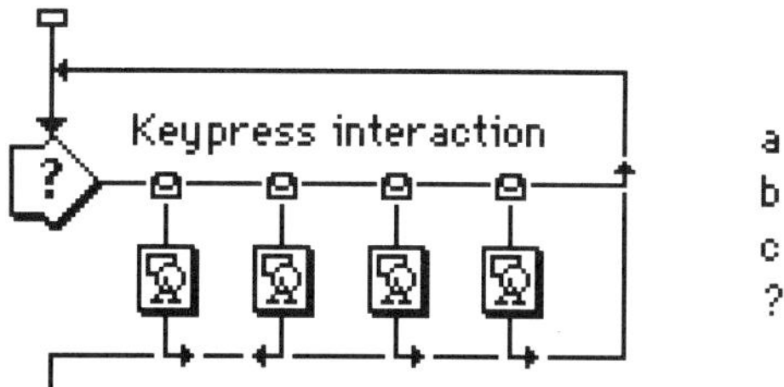

- Run the file to test the interaction.

Things You Should Know About Keypress Options

- Keypress Responses are case-specific. Therefore, if you want to allow the learner to enter either an uppercase or a lowercase letter, you must include them both in the list of anticipated responses, separating them with a vertical bar.
  - *Example:* A | a

- To use special function keys as anticipated responses, type their names; do not just press their keys.
  - *Example:* CmdQ requires the user to press Command-Q.

Button Responses 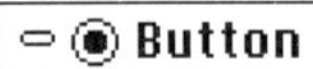

A Button Response was used earlier in the chapter to introduce the Interaction icon, and is probably already familiar to you. The following activity gives you a chance to see how the question used for the Keypress Response is designed for a Button Response. Button Responses create buttons on the screen that can be used to answer questions, make selections, or navigate. Button Responses are very easy to use because they provide users with visual clues about how to enter responses.

The Following Exercise Demonstrates How to Create Button Interactions

- Place an Interaction icon on the flow line. Title the interaction "Button interaction".
- Open the Interaction icon. Mark the *Pause Before Exiting* option. Click *OK•Edit Display* and use the Text tool to place an interaction in the Presentation Window. You might type the following question:

Which city is the capital of Pennsylvania?

Click on a button to make your response.

- Jump back to the flow line and place a Display icon into the Interaction Structure for feedback.
- At the prompt, select Button for the response type.
- Type Philadelphia for the title of the Feedback icon.
- Add two more Display icons to the right of the first Feedback icon. Title the icons "Harrisburg" and "Pittsburgh". The icon names will appear on the screen in the buttons.
- Open each Feedback icon and type appropriate feedback for each anticipated response.
- Open the Response Options to modify judging, looping, and erasing. For the correct answer (Harrisburg):

  Set erasing to On Exit

  Set judging to Correct Response

  Set looping to Exit Interaction

  For the other answers:

  Set erasing to After Next Entry

  Set judging to Wrong Response

  Set looping to Try Again
- The icons should now appear as follows:

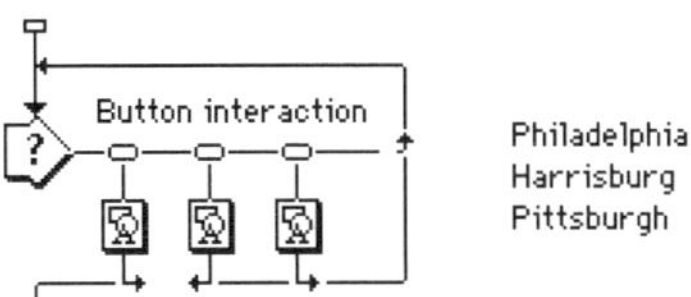

- Authorware places buttons at the top left corner of the screen. You will need to move them to their appropriate locations. To access the buttons, either reopen the Interaction icon and edit the display or run the lesson and Pause at the interaction. Select and drag with the mouse to move a button.

- Select Run to test the interaction.

Things You Should Know About Button Options

- Selecting the Default Button option enables the learner to press Return to select the button. Only one Feedback icon can have a Default button.

- To move or resize a button, first Pause the lesson and then select and drag the button to its desired location. You can also modify a button's size and location by selecting the *Position and Size* option. This window allows you to specify button placement precisely by specifying distances in pixels. You can also use Variables in these fields to determine button placement.

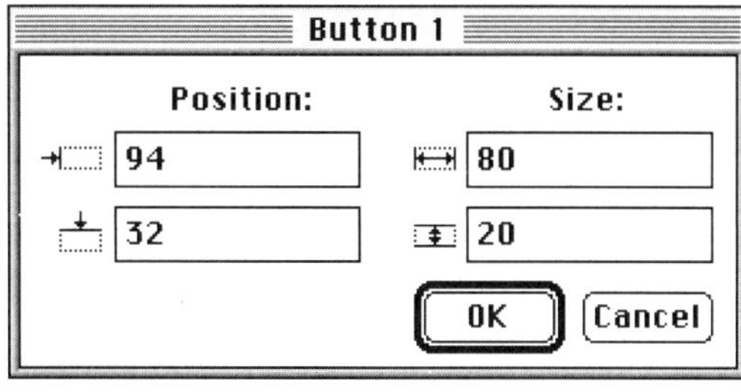

Hot Spot Responses 

When a Hot Spot is created, rectangular areas of the screen become sensitive to the location of the mouse. When the user clicks in the rectangle (or sometimes when the mouse enters into the area), the lesson provides feedback

The Following Exercise Demonstrates How to Create Hot Spot Interactions

- Place an Interaction icon on the flow line. Title the interaction "Hot Spot interaction."

- Open the Interaction icon. Mark the *Pause Before Exiting* option. Click *OK•Edit Display* and use the Text tool to type the following question:

Which city is the capital of Pennsylvania?

Philadelphia
Harrisburg
Pittsburgh

Click on the correct answer with your mouse.

- Jump to the flow line.
- Place a Display icon into the Interaction Structure for feedback.
- At the prompt, select Hot Spot for the response type.
- Type Philadelphia for the title of the Feedback icon.

- Add two more Display icons to the right of the first Feedback icon. Title the icons "Harrisburg" and "Pittsburgh". The icon names will label the Hot Spots, making them easy to identify.

- Open each Feedback icon and type appropriate feedback for each anticipated response.

- Open the Response Options to modify judging, looping, and erasing. For the correct answer (Harrisburg):

  Set erasing to On Exit

  Set judging to Correct Response

  Set looping to Exit Interaction

  For the other answers:

  Set erasing to After Next Entry

  Set judging to Wrong Response

  Set looping to Try Again

- The icons should now appear as follows:

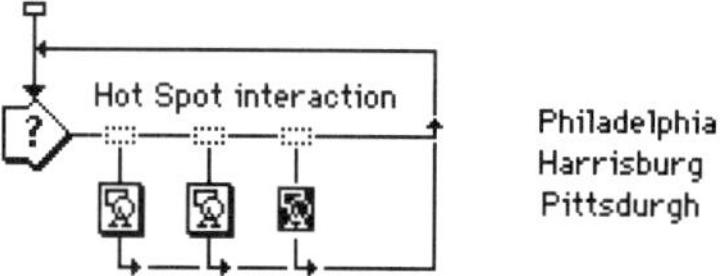

- You will need to move the Hot Spots to their appropriate locations. In this case, each Hot Spot should cover the name of a city. To access the Hot Spots, either reopen the Interaction icon and edit the display or run the lesson and Pause at the interaction.

- Use the mouse to move and resize the Hot Spot. Make sure that each Hot Spot completely covers the appropriate area of the screen, but don't allow hot spots to overlap (unless you are creating a wildcard).

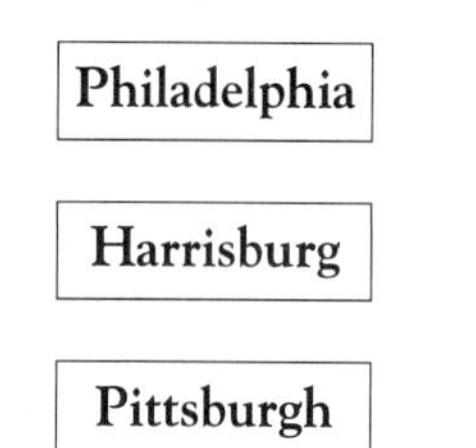

- Select Run to test the interaction.

Things to Know About Hot Spot Options

- For each Hot Spot feedback icon, Authorware sets aside an area, called a hot spot. Double-clicking on a hot spot opens the Response Options for that icon.

- Each hot spot is represented by a dotted rectangle. Hot spots are not visible to the learner.
- You can overlap hot spots to trap for clicks that are out of range (like wildcards). To do this, create a Hot Spot icon for out-of-area clicks; make the hot spot for this icon cover the entire screen. Any mouse click that misses the other feedback hot spots will be caught by the large one. You must place this icon to the right of any other hot spots in the interaction structure.

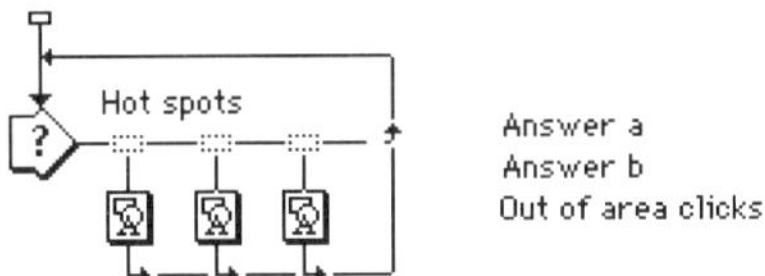

- Optional keys can be used as an alternate way to select a hot spot. Specify special optional keys by typing the key name in full.

  Examples:

  Return

  Tab

  Left Arrow

  Backspace

  Esc

- Don't use the Active if True and Perpetual options yet. They are more complex and will be dealt with later. The Active if True option causes the hot spot to be active only when a Variable is true. This option is especially useful for hiding options. Perpetual hot spots can be active during some lesson sections (e.g., when the Variable is true) and inactive during other lesson sections (e.g., when the Variable is false).

- In addition to setting the Response Options, you must place the Hot Spot for each anticipated response. Like buttons, Authorware places Hot Spots at the top left corner of the screen. There are two ways to place or resize the Hot Spots:

  1. Open the Response Options. A Hot Spot will appear in the Presentation Window. Modifying the Hot Spot involves clicking and dragging on the handles that appear in the Presentation Window. Moving or resizing the hot spot modifies the location and dimensions of the Hot Spot.

  2. Run the lesson and Pause at the interaction to highlight the Hot Spots. Resize the area where you want the learner to click. Resize and move the Hot Spots as necessary for each anticipated response.

STUDY EXERCISES

1. Examine the Response Options for Keypress, Button, and Hot Spot responses to find answers to the following:

   Name which response types offers the following features:

   - Custom cursors
   - Mark the area after matching a response
   - Permit use of the "Perpetual" option
   - Allow the designer to control button placement

- Match a response by placing the cursor within a "hot" area
- Require the designer to move "touch-sensitive" areas

2. Experiment with the following Hot Spot options to discover how each operates.

   - Optional Keys
   - Custom Cursor
   - Auto Highlight
   - Match with: Single- or Double-click, or Cursor in Area

3. Use a Keypress interaction to create a multiple-choice or true/false test. Include approximately five questions in the test. Do not allow users more than one chance to answer each question. Include a wildcard for "out-of-bounds" responses, but do not count this as an answer (i.e., allow the user another chance to answer the question).

4. Create another multiple choice test, this time using Hot Spot response. Allow users to repeat questions they answer incorrectly. Use the Mark After Match option to indicate past answers. Create a help button that pops up when the user places a mouse in a specific screen area.

5. Use Button responses to create a navigation system that leads to two or more sets of multiple-choice questions. Use the tests you created in Exercises 2 and 3 for the test content. Include a Quit button that allows the user to escape from the tests and to continue with the lesson. Experiment with the Button Types option in the Response Options to find buttons that you like.

6. Create an entertainment center with a sliding door. Include a button on the front. When the button is pressed, the door should open to reveal a TV and a radio inside. Click on the TV to play a movie. Click on the radio to play a sound file.

7

The Interaction Icon: Part 2

CHAPTER OVERVIEW

In the last chapter, you learned the basic structure of an interaction and three response types. In this chapter, you will learn how to use four more response types: Hot Objects, Text Entry, Target Area, and Pull-down Menus. Hot Objects allow you to specify an entire object as "hot" without needing to define a rectangular target area around the object. Text Entry responses require the user to type text into the computer. Target Area responses create interactions in which users must move objects to specific screen locations.   These can be particularly useful when learning steps to complete procedural tasks.   Lastly, Pull-down Menus allow you to create navigation structures that control lesson flow via Pull-down Menus.

CHAPTER OBJECTIVES

Following this chapter, you will be able to create interactions using the following response types:

- Hot Objects
- Text
- Target Areas
- Pull-down Menus

KEY TERMS

Hot Object responses
Text Entry responses
Target Area responses
Pull-down Menus
Feedback icons
Response Options

Judging
Looping
Erasing
Wildcard

SUPPORT MATERIALS

On the CD-ROM disc, run **BEGIN.PKG** if you are a Macintosh user or **BEGIN.APP** if you are using a PC. When the file opens, click once on the title page to begin. Select the button titled **Chapter 7**, and watch the videos for Parts 1 and 2 to see how Hot Object and Text Entry interactions are created.

The folder on the CD-ROM titled MACDEMOS or PC_DEMOS contains several demonstration files that you can run and examine. The folder contains two versions of each file: a packaged file that you can run, and an unpackaged file containing the icons used to create the file. Run the file to examine the icons used to create Hot Objects, Text Response, Target Area, and Pull-down Menu interactions.

Macintosh users:
Run the file CHP07.pkg to view its contents.
Open the data file CHP07.A3M to examine how the file was created.

PC users:
Run the file CHP07.APP to view its contents.
Open the data file CHP07.A3W to examine how the file was created.

Note: You must have a copy of Authorware on your computer to open the data files.

STUDY TOPICS

The following sections examine Hot Object, Text Entry, Target Area, and Pull-down Menu responses.

Hot Object Responses 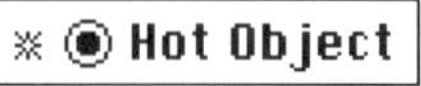

Have you noticed that Hot Spot interactions are imprecise and will accept any response within the defined rectangular area? This may cause problems; for example, when hot spots overlap, the user might click on one object, but receive feedback associated with another. In the following illustration, a user who clicks on the circle could receive feedback intended for the star.

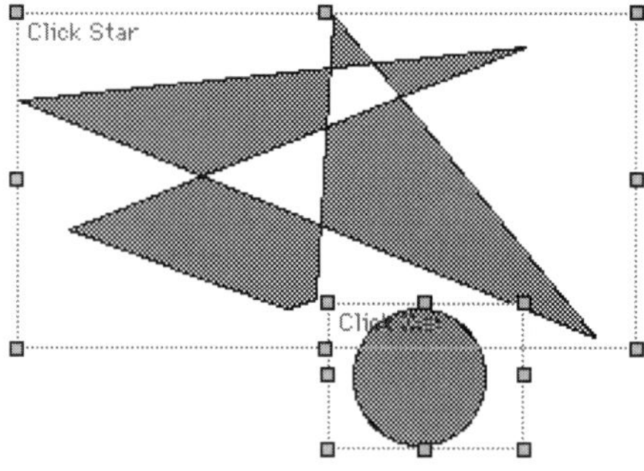

One solution to this problem involves using Hot Object interactions. Hot Objects are like Hot Spots: They require the user to interact with the computer by clicking on an area on the monitor. However, Hot Objects use entire objects instead of rectangles to define the target areas. Although the physical actions involved in using Hot Object and Hot Spot interactions are essentially identical, different processes are employed in creating the interactions.

The Following Exercise Demonstrates How to Create Hot Object Interactions

The goal of this exercise is to create a Hot Object interaction in which the user must use the mouse to click on one of two objects (a triangle or a square). Different feedback is given for correct and incorrect responses.

- Place two Display icons on the flow line. Title the icons Triangle and Square. Open each Display and use the graphics tools to create a triangle and a square in their respective icons. Fill each object with a solid fill to make it easier to click on the objects.
- Place an Interaction icon on the flow line. Title the interaction "Hot Object question."
- Open the Interaction icon. Mark the *Pause before Exiting* option. Click *OK • Edit Display* and type the following:

Click on the Triangle with the mouse

- Jump to the flow line.
- Select a Display icon for feedback and place it into the Interaction Structure.
- At the prompt, select Hot Object for the response type.
- Type "Click the Triangle" for the title of the Feedback icon.
- Open the Feedback icon by double-clicking.
- Enter appropriate feedback for a correct response and jump back to the flow line
- Open the Response Options:

  Set erasing to On Exit

  Set judging to Correct Response

  Set looping to Exit Interaction

  Click OK to return to the flow line
- Add a second Display icon to the right of the first Feedback icon.
- Type "Click the Square" for the title of the Feedback icon.
- Enter appropriate feedback for a wrong response and jump back to the flow line. Appropriate feedback could be

No, that's a square. Click on the Triangle.

- Open the Response Options:

  Set erasing to After Next Entry

  Set judging to Wrong Response

  Set looping to Try Again

  Click OK to return to the flow line

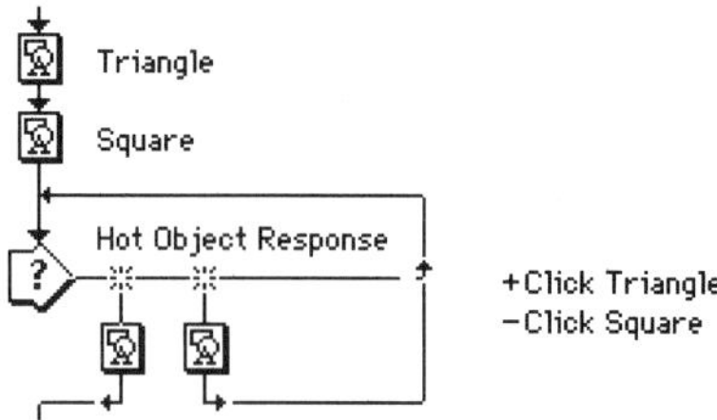

- Run the file. The lesson will stop at the Response Options for you to identify the appropriate object. The title of the object to be selected will appear in the window labeled *Title.*

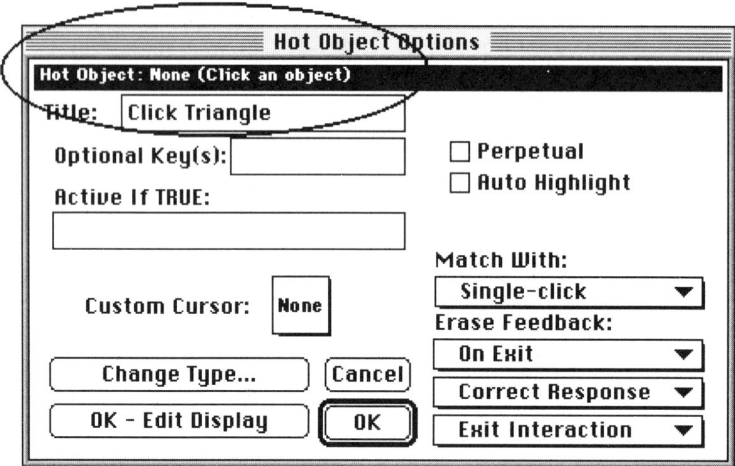

Click on the appropriate object with the mouse. The name of the selected object will appear in the Response Options window:

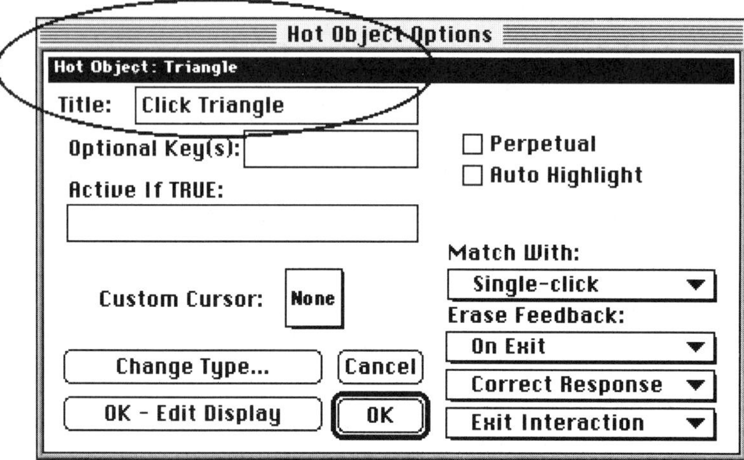

- Click OK to proceed. Repeat the exercise for the second object.
- Run the file again and test the lesson by entering both the correct and incorrect responses.

Things to Know about Hot Object Options

- Match With: Allows you to select an object with a single-or double-click, or just by placing the cursor over the hot object.

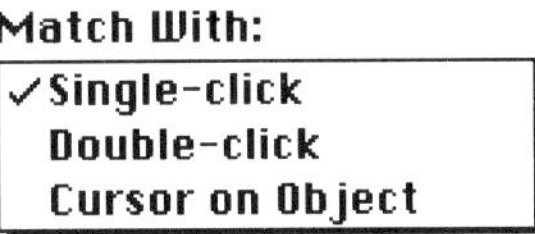

Text Entry Responses   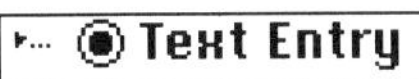

In the last chapter, you learned how to construct a Keypress Response that responds to the pressing of a single key on the keyboard. Use Text Entry responses whenever you want the user to type more than one character into the computer. The text that the user types can be judged for accuracy.

The Following Exercise Demonstrates How to Create Text Entry Interactions

The goal of this exercise is to create a question in which the user types a response and receives feedback. Different feedback is given for correct and incorrect responses.

- Place an Interaction icon on the flow line. Title the interaction "MLK question".
- Open the Interaction icon. Mark the *Pause Before Exiting* option. Click *Text Entry Options*. The Presentation Window will open, showing the text entry marker and the text entry box along with its move and resize handles. The entry marker shows where text will appear on the screen when the user starts typing and sets the size of the text entry box.

Click and drag on the handles to move or resize the text entry marker and box.

- When the entry marker is appropriately placed, type the following text into the Presentation Window:

Whose birthday do we celebrate on January 15?

Type your answer and press Return.

- Jump to the flow line.
- Select a Display icon for feedback and place it into the Interaction Structure.
- At the prompt, select Text Entry for the response type.
- Type MLK as the anticipated response.
- Open the Feedback icon by double-clicking.
- Enter appropriate feedback for a correct response and jump back to the flow line.
- Open the Response Options:

  Set erasing to On Exit

  Set judging to Correct Response

  Set looping to Exit Interaction

  Click OK to return to the flow line
- Add a second Display icon to the right of the first Feedback icon.

- Select the wildcard (*) as the anticipated response.
- Enter appropriate feedback for a wrong response and jump back to the flow line.
- Open the Response Options:

  Set erasing to After Next Entry

  Set judging to Wrong Response

  Set looping to Try Again

  Click OK to return to the flow line

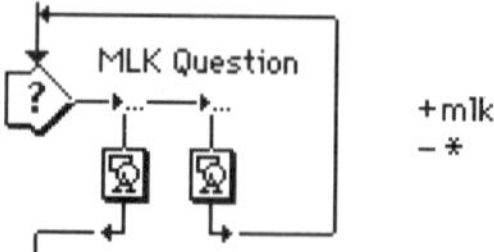

- Run and test the lesson by entering both correct and incorrect answers.

Things You Should Know About Text Entry Options

- A feedback icon can be set to respond to any of several alternate student responses. Different correct responses are separated by a vertical bar (|).
  - *Example:*   city | town | village | township | suburb
- Separate a comment from an anticipated response with two dashes.
  - *Example:*   St. Paul--capital of Minnesota
- Make a text response active only on a specific try by preceding the response with a pound sign (#) and the attempt number.
  - *Example:*   #1Blue | #2Red

    Blue is judged correct on the first try; red, on the second try.
- Text Entry responses need not be limited to brief answers. Text responses can be up to 400 hundred characters long.
- Special characters used in answer judging:

  (Shift, Backslash key) means "or"
  Example: 8|eight
  means either response will be accepted

       *   wild card character accepts anything

  Example: Minneapolis|Min*
  means Min followed by any other characters will be accepted as the correct response

       ?   accepts any single character

  Example: receive|rec??ve
  means the characters rec plus any two characters plus the characters ve will be accepted as the correct response
- Some Text Entry Options are quite sophisticated, but rarely used. Check the Authorware manuals to examine Incremental Matching, Word Order, Extra Words, and other options.

Target Area Responses

Target Area responses allow you to create questions that involve moving objects from one screen location to another. For example, you may want the user to connect words with their definitions. By linking a list of randomly ordered words to their meanings, it is possible to check a student's comprehension.

The Following Exercise Demonstrates How to Create Target Area Interactions

The goal of this exercise is to create a Target Area interaction in which the user must move a ball from one part of the screen to another. Feedback is included for correct and incorrect responses. The *Snap to Center* option is used for a correct response and *Put Back* is used for an incorrect response.

- Place an object such as a circle into a Display icon. Title the Display icon with an appropriate name.

Note: Filled objects are easier to move than unfilled objects.

- Place an Interaction icon on the flow line. Title the interaction "Target Area question."

- Open the Interaction icon. Mark the *Pause before Exiting* option. Click *OK • Edit Display* and enter the following directions and graphics.

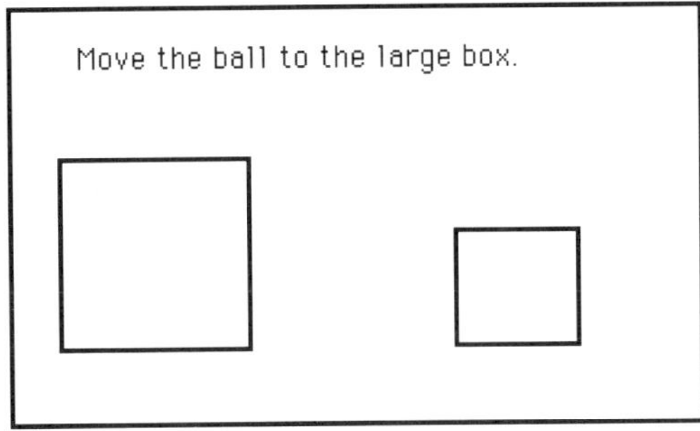

- Jump back to the flow line. Include two Display icons for feedback, one for each anticipated response, and select Target Area as the response type.

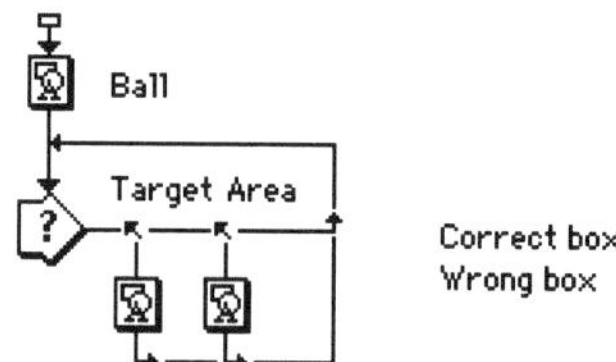

- Title the Feedback icons and enter appropriate feedback into each Display icon.

- Run the lesson. The lesson will pause for you to define the target areas. For each Target Area: Move and resize the target area to cover the appropriate box.

  Drag the object that is to be moved (i.e., the ball) to the center of the target area. For the second object, you may need to rerun the lesson to move the ball if it is hidden behind the first target.

- For the correct response, set the Response Options as follows:

  Set erasing to On Exit

  Set judging to Correct Response

  Set looping to Exit Interaction

  Set destination to Snap to Center

  Click *OK* to return to the flow line

- For the wrong response, set the Response Options as follows:

  Set erasing to After Next Entry

  Set judging to Wrong Response

  Set looping to Try Again

  Set destination to Put Back

  Click OK to return to the flow line

The icons should appear as follows when you are done:

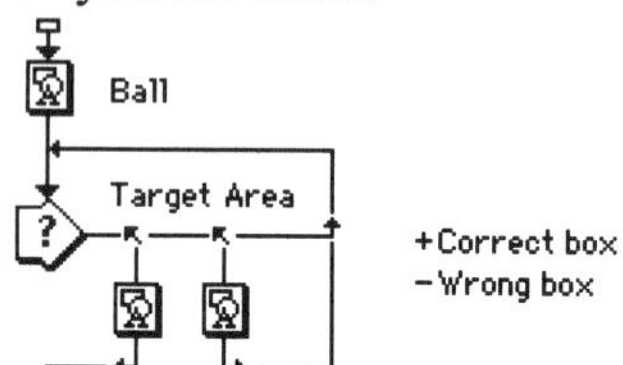

- Run the lesson and test each option.

Things to Know About Target Area Options

- Place each object to be moved in a separate Display icon that precedes the Interaction icon on the flow line.

- Separate Feedback icons are required for each object to be moved.

- The instruction at the top of the Target Area Options directs the designer to move an object to a target. When the link between the two has been made, the object's name appears in the window. To link an object and its target location you can either move the target area to the object and then select the object to be moved with the mouse, or select the object to be moved with the mouse and then move and resize the target area. The methods work equally well, but circumstances sometimes require you to use one method or the other.

Before:

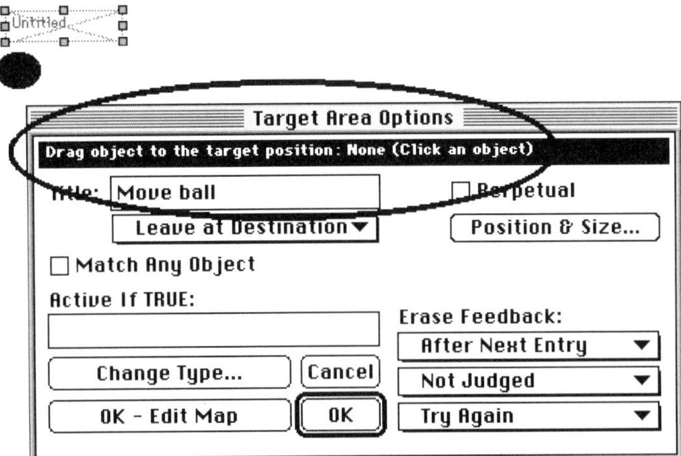

After:

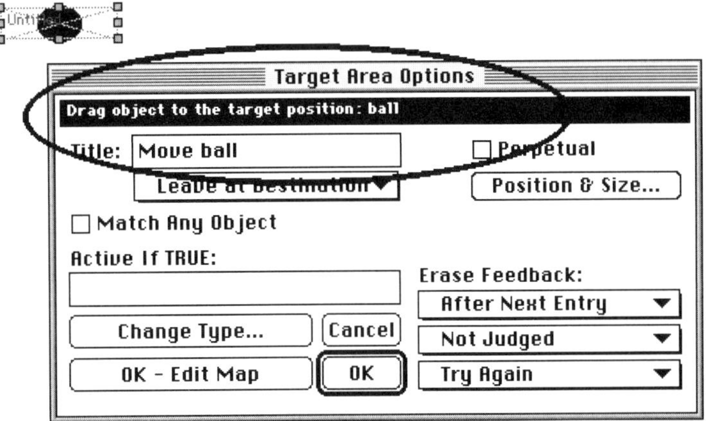

- When you double-click on the Target Area Response Options, both the Response Options and the current Presentation Window are displayed. This window contains the objects that the user can move.

- You must select one of the following three options for each anticipated response:

Leave at Destination: The object is left where the user moves it.

Snap to Center: The object will snap to the center of the destination rectangle if the user moves the object within the target area. This is the normal selection for a correct answer.

Put Back: The object immediately returns to its original position after the user moves the object. This option is especially useful for incorrect responses.

Pull-down Menus   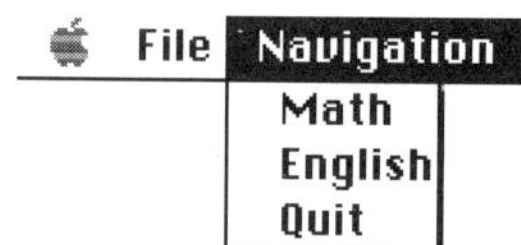

Pull-down Menus are generally used for lesson navigation.   In the following example, a Pull-down Menu is used to move between two lesson sections, Math and English, or to Quit the lesson.

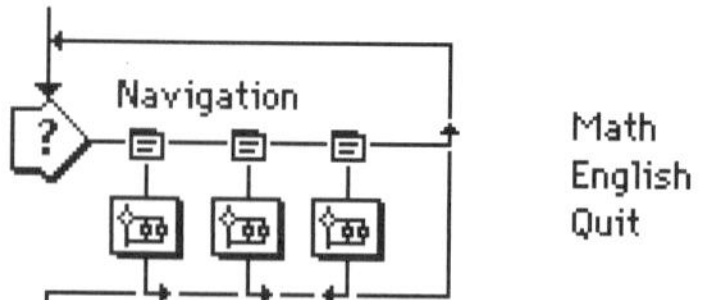

As illustrated, feedback for a Pull-down Menu is usually placed into a Map icon. The Map icon contains the content relevant to the path selected by the user.

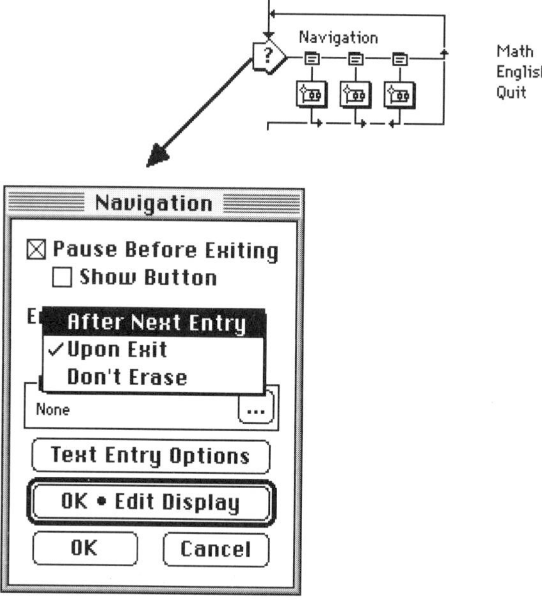

The Following Exercise Demonstrates How to Create Pull-down Menu Interactions

- Place an Interaction icon on the flow line. Title the interaction "Navigation". The title of the Interaction icon appears in the menu bar during the lesson.

- Open the Interaction icon and set the Erase Interaction option to *After Next Entry*. This is important. Without changing the Erase Interaction option, any information that is placed into the Interaction display will clutter the screen.

- Click *OK • Edit display*. For a Pull-down Menu response, the interaction often includes instructions to select from the Pull-down Menu. Type the following text into the Presentation Window.

SELECT AN OPTION FROM THE PULL-DOWN MENU.

- Attach two or more Feedback icons (use Map icons) to the Interaction Structure. At the prompt, select Pull-down Menu as the response type. Name each feedback icon with the text you want to appear under the Pull-down Menu (Math, English, and Quit).

- Place the appropriate content into each Map icon. For this practice exercise, a single Display icon followed by a Wait icon and an Erase icon is appropriate.

- Open the Response Options for Math and English:

  Set erasing to After Next Entry

  Set looping to Try Again

  It is unusual (but not necessarily inappropriate) for a response to be judged correct or wrong from a Pull-down Menu response.

  Click OK to return to the flow line

- Open the Response Options for Quit:

  Set erasing to On Exit

  Set looping to Exit Interaction

  Click OK to return to the flow line

- Run the Interaction and test each option.

Things You Should Know About Pull-down Menu Options

- Options in the Pull-down Menu appear in the order in which the Feedback icons are positioned in the flow line.

- You can control the text style of the menu option by placing a style code at the beginning or end of the Feedback icons. The style code consists of the symbol for "less than" (<) and a letter:

  <B   **Bold**

  <I   *Italic*

  <U   <u>Underline</u>

  <O   **Outline**

  <S   Shadow

- The icon name (-   causes a dotted line to be put into the Pull-down Menu. The icon name (causes a blank line to be put into the Pull-down Menu.

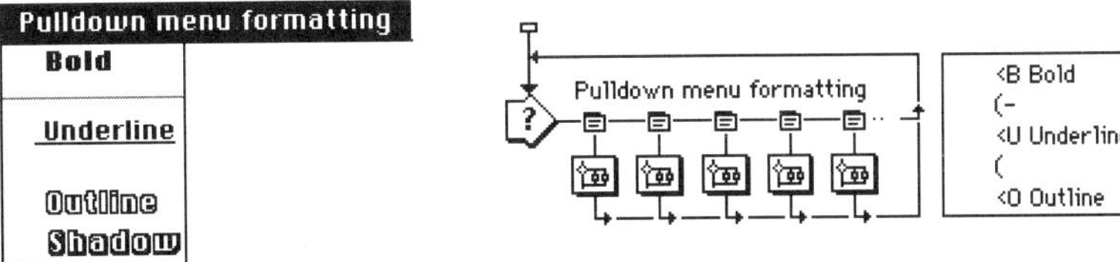

STUDY EXERCISES

1. A designer created an interaction with the following settings for a correct response:
   - looping was set to *Exit Interaction*
   - erasing was set to *On Exit*

   When the question was answered correctly, feedback was erased from the screen before the user had an opportunity to read it.

   How could the designer have prevented feedback from being erased too quickly?

2. How do you display and move the Entry Marker for Text Entry interactions?

3. Total Physical Response is a foreign-language learning technique that encourages users to learn a language by following commands. Create a brief lesson in which users must move objects to various places in a room.

   To do this, you will first need to create a room with some objects in it. Remember that each object must be placed into a separate Display icon.

   Use several Target Area interactions to instruct the users to move objects from one location to another. For example, you could tell users to " Move the book from the table to the chair".

   Move to the next question if a correct answer is given. Move the object back to its original position and repeat the question for an incorrect response. Use appropriate feedback for correct and incorrect responses.

4. Create a navigation structure that uses Pull-down Menus to create a navigation structure that allows the user to switch lesson segments.

5. Create a Text Entry interaction that quizzes the user for the name of the President of the United States. Use appropriate feedback and looping for correct and incorrect responses.

6. Create a Target Area interaction in which the user must assemble three objects in a specific order. Use the Put Back option to return objects that are moved out of order.

The Interaction Icon: Part 3

CHAPTER OVERVIEW

This chapter presents the final three response types and introduces one of Authorware's most powerful and flexible programming techniques: Perpetual Interactions. The three response types we will examine are Time Limit, Tries Limit, and Conditional. Time Limit responses provide a tool to prevent users from struggling unnecessarily long on a question. Tries Limit responses are similar in operation to Time Limits, however, rather than reacting to the time taken, they monitor the number of attempts a user has made. Conditional responses provide even greater flexibility. They allow the designer to create an interaction that matches a specified condition. Together, these three response types provide designers with valuable tools to help identify students in need of help or to respond to special instructional conditions.

Perpetual Interactions provide design flexibility. Once a student has completed an Interaction icon, that icon is essentially "dead." That is, the icon cannot be easily reused. Very often, however, the designer would like the student to access an interaction at any time during a lesson. For example, the designer may wish the user to have permanent access to a series of help buttons or a glossary. Perpetual interactions provide this capability by keeping interaction structures "'alive" during lessons.

Perpetual Interactions also increase programming efficiency. They often contain information that is to be accessed frequently (i.e., they operate like subroutines in traditional programming languages), and reduce the need to duplicate programming structures.

CHAPTER OBJECTIVES

Following this chapter, you will be able to create interactions using the following response types:
*   Conditional
*   Time Limit
*   Tries Limit
*   Perpetual Interactions that allow the learner (or the designer) to access important information throughout a lesson

KEY TERMS

Conditional responses
Time Limit Responses
Tries Limit Responses
Perpetual Interactions
Return Looping
Auto-match option

SUPPORT MATERIALS

On the CD-ROM disc, run **BEGIN.PKG** if you are a Macintosh user or **BEGIN.APP** if you are using a PC. When the file opens, click once on the title page to begin. Select the button titled **Chapter 8** to see how Conditional interactions are created.

The folder on the CD-ROM titled MACDEMOS or PC_DEMOS contains several demonstration files that you can run and examine. The folder contains two versions of each file: a packaged file that you can run and an unpackaged file containing the icons used to create the file. Run the file to examine the icons used to create Time Limits, Tries Limits, Conditional, and Perpetual Interactions.

Macintosh users:
Run the file CHP08.pkg to view its contents.
Open the data file CHP08.A3M to examine how the file was created.

PC users:
Run the file CHP08.APP to view its contents.
Open the data file CHP08.A3W to examine how the file was created.

Note: You must have a copy of Authorware on your computer to open the data files.

STUDY TOPICS

Tries Limit, Time Limit, and Conditional responses enable the designer to provide feedback when the following exist:

- The user has attempted a question a given number of times
- A given amount of time has elapsed
- A condition defined by the designer has been matched. This sounds vague, but in practice provides considerable design flexibility.

Tries Limit Responses   `# ⊙ Tries Limit`

When Would I Use Tries Limit?

Tries Limit Interactions allow the designer to give hints and help to prevent the user from entering an endless question loop. An endless loop occurs when the user cannot give a response that the computer expects, and the machine simply repeats the question. Imagine the following scenario: You are asked to name the capital city of Liechtenstein. You vainly attempt to answer the question by typing the names of European cities that come to mind. Each time you enter a response the computer delivers the same reply: Wrong. Try again.

>Hamburg
  Wrong try again.

>Belgrade
  Wrong try again.

>Berlin
  Wrong try again.

and so the lesson continues until you turn off the machine in frustration.

Tries Limit Interactions help prevent such frustrating experiences by providing feedback after a given number of attempts. For example, you could provide clues that gradually steer the user toward the correct response.

How Do I Set Tries Limit?

The following question provides more information to prompt the learner or to provide additional instructional opportunities. A branch is triggered based solely on the number of attempts the user has made.

- In an existing Interaction Structure, insert a Display icon at the end of your set of feedback icons.
- Change the response type to Tries Limit. (The Tries Limit Options will be displayed.)

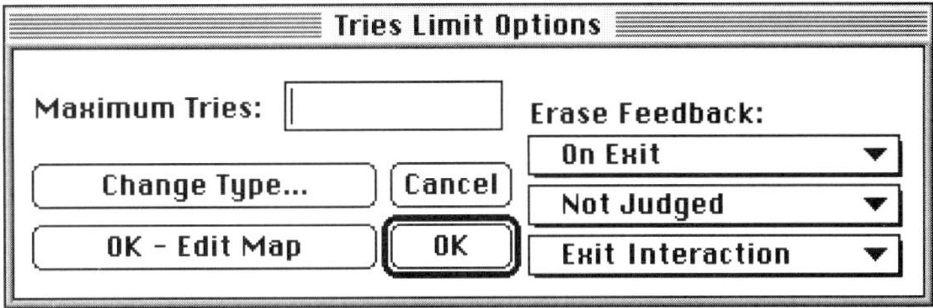

- Enter the maximum number of tries. This is the number of responses the users can enter before the event is triggered.

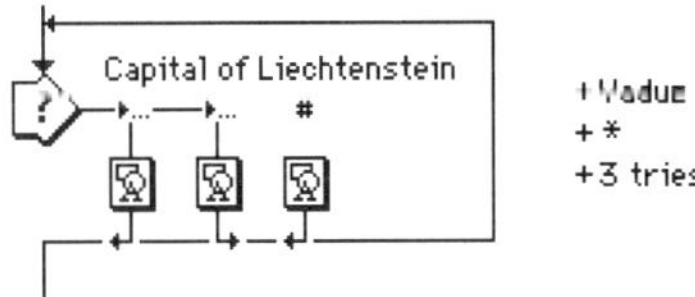

- Set the judging option to Not Judged so the System Variables for correct and incorrect answers are not updated.

- Set Looping to Exit Interaction if you want the user to exit the question after a given number of tries. Set Looping to Try Again if you want to display a hint, but do not want the user to exit the question

- Click on *OK • Edit display* to enter feedback for the Tries Limit.

Things to Know About Tries Limit Options

Be careful where you place Tries Limit responses. Placing a Tries Limit response at the beginning of the flow line causes the Tries Limit to bypass any other options. However, by placing it at the end of a series of anticipated responses, Authorware can match other responses and still present the feedback associated with the Tries Limit.

Time Limit Responses   ⏱ ⦿ Time Limit

When Would I Use a Time Limit?

Use a Time Limit whenever you want to branch a lesson based on the amount of time a user has spent on an interaction. Time Limits operate like Tries Limits. Whereas Tries Limits allow you to branch after some number of tries, Time Limits allow the designer to intervene after a set time period. Time limits are often used to create time challenges to stimulate motivation. They are also used to give hints when the learner is taking a long time to respond.

To Set Time Limits

- In an existing Interaction Structure, add a Display icon to your Feedback icons. Insert a Time Limit icon either at the beginning or end of the Feedback icons.

- Change the Response Type to Time Limit. (The Time Limit Options will be displayed.)

- Enter the Time Limit, in seconds.

- Decide whether you want a clock, which indicates time remaining, to be displayed. If so, click on the Show Time Remaining option.

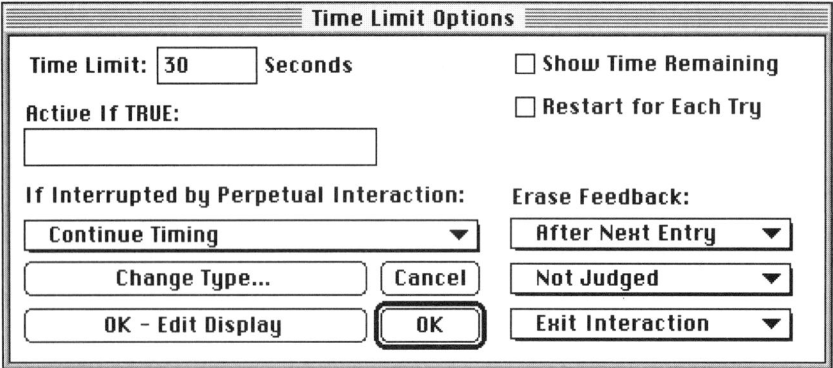

- In the Interaction icon shown a Feedback icon appears after 30 seconds.

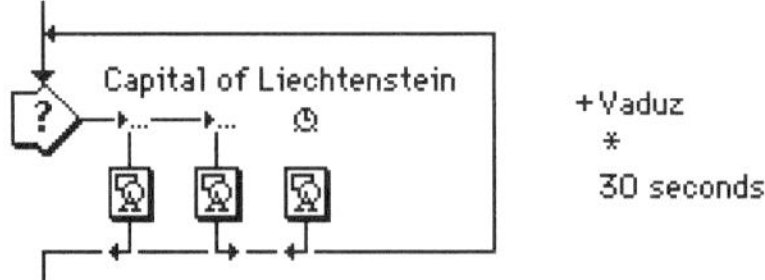

Things to Know About Tries Limit Options

- Show *Time Remaining* places a clock on the screen to indicate the proportion of time gone versus time left.

- Perpetual Interactions (which will be addressed later in this chapter) can ruin timed responses. The option *If Interrupted by Perpetual Interaction*: provides options that allow you to control whether timing is reset, ignored, or repeated when a Perpetual Interaction is activated by the user.

If Interrupted by Perpetual Interaction:

```
✓ Continue Timing
  Pause, Resume On Return
  Pause, Restart On Return
  Pause, Restart If Running
```

Conditional Responses   `= ⦿ Conditional`

When Would I Use a Conditional Response

Watch out! This section may be confusing!! Unless you understand how Functions and Variables work in Authorware, Conditional Responses will not make much sense. Functions and Variables will be introduced in Chapters 12 and 13.

In general, Conditional Responses are activated when Authorware notices that some condition has been met. For example, Authorware might notice that a user has just answered five successive test items correctly. Alternatively, Authorware might notice that the time is 10:00 a.m. or that the user has just clicked his or her mouse. The most important point to understand is that Authorware executes the feedback icon associated with the Conditional response when some condition is matched.

The Following Exercise Demonstrates How to Create a Conditional Interaction

In the following interaction, Marvo the magician will attempt to read your fortune! The computer checks the day of the week on the system clock and uses this information to make a prediction. The day of the week is stored in the System Variable titled *DayName*. One prediction is made if *DayName* contains Monday, Tuesday, or Wednesday. Another prediction is made for Thursday and Friday, and a third prediction if *DayName* contains Saturday or Sunday.

To create the Interaction:

- Place an Interaction icon on the flow line. Title the interaction "Marvo's prediction".

- Open the Interaction icon. Mark the *Pause Before Exiting* option. Click *OK • Edit Display* and use the Text tool to type the following:

My name is Marvo the
magician. Let me
predict your future

- Jump to the flow line.
- Place a Display icon on the flow line for feedback.
- Select Conditional for the response type.
- Open the Conditional Response Options icon and type:

    DayName="Monday"|DayName="Tuesday"|DayName="Wednesday"

- Add two more Display icons to the right of the first Feedback icon. Open the Response Options and type the following conditional statements into their respective icons:

    DayName="Thursday"|DayName="Friday"

    and

    DayName="Saturday"|DayName="Sunday"

- Add a Map icon to the end of the Interaction Structure. Set the response type for the Map icon to Button. Title the Button response *Continue for my Prediction.*
- For each anticipated response:

    Set looping to Exit Interaction

    Set erasing to On exit

The icons should appear as follows.

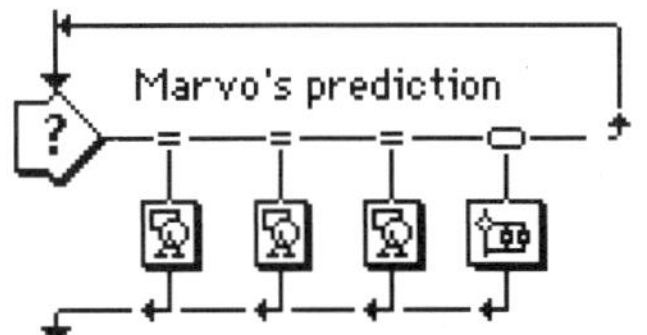

DayName="Monday "|DayName="Tuesday "|DayName="Wednesday
DayName="Thursday "|DayName="Friday "
DayName="Saturday "|DayName="Sunday "
Continue for my prediction

- Enter feedback for each anticipated Conditional response. The illustrations that follow are for
    (a) Monday, Tuesday, or Wednesday
    (b) Thursday or Friday
    (c) Saturday or Sunday

(a)

> # My senses tell me that three to five work days will fall before the weekend.

(b)

> # The weekend will soon arrive. I predict rest and relaxation within the next two days.

(c)

> # Today appears to be a Saturday or a Sunday. I predict relaxation today.

- Run the file and observe the results.

Things to Know About Conditional Options

The Auto-match option is a powerful feature.

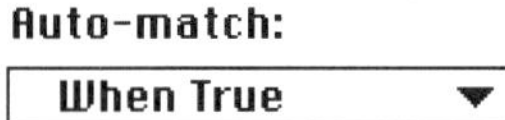

The default value is Off. When Auto-match is Off, Authorware waits for the user to enter information into the computer at an Interaction icon before checking to see whether a condition has been met.

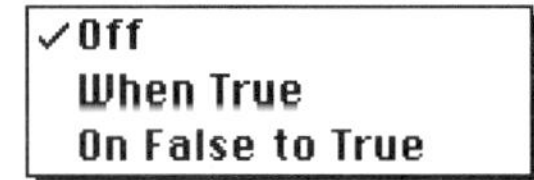

However, instead of waiting for the user to make a response before checking for a match, Authorware automatically matches a response when a condition exists if *When True* is selected. This is a powerful tool because it allows the lesson to take a particular path even though the user has not made a response.

Perpetual Interactions

Perpetual Interactions are one of the most flexible and important design techniques available in Authorware. Once a student has completed an Interaction icon, that icon is essentially "dead." That is, the icon cannot be easily reused. Very often, however, the designer would like the user to access an interaction throughout a lesson. Perpetual Interactions provide this capability by keeping Interaction structures "alive" during lessons. Perpetual interactions contain information that is to be used repeatedly.

Perpetual Interactions considerably increase programming efficiency. Because they contain information that is accessed often (i.e., they function like subroutines), they remove pressure on the designer to duplicate icons on the Course Flow Line.

When Would I Use a Perpetual Response?

- Use Perpetual Interactions whenever you need permanent access to some section of a lesson.

    Example:

    Imagine that you want to create a Help option. If you employ the "normal" linear lesson structure, the Help option will not be available to the student after it has been used once. How could you make the option permanently available, or turn the option Off/On as needed?

The Following Exercise Demonstrates How to Create a Perpetual Interaction

- Place an Interaction icon on the flow line. Title the interaction "Perpetual help button".

    Note: Perpetual Interactions are often placed at the start of a lesson, before lesson sections that might use the Interaction. This is important because Authorware must store Perpetual Interactions in memory before they can be used.

- Select a Map icon for feedback and place it into the Interaction Structure.

- At the prompt, select Button for the response type.

- Type *Help* for the title of the Feedback icon.   Open the Map icon and place a Display, a Wait, and an Erase icon onto the flow line.

- Open the Feedback icon and enter some appropriate content for a Help screen.

- Open the Response Options. Select the Perpetual check box.

☒ Perpetual

- Controlling Erasing. You must control erasing not only of the information in the Interaction icon, but also in the screen from which you came. You may want to erase the screen from which you came or leave the information showing when you use a Perpetual Interaction. The screen will be erased if the Looping for the Perpetual Response is set to Exit Interaction. However, if Looping is set to Return then no erasing will take place. In the latter case, it may be necessary to use "masking"to temporarily hide a screen. Masking is achieved by covering a display with a (borderless) box filled with paint (usually the background color).

    It is often easiest to control erasing of information in the Perpetual Interaction by using Erase icons rather than the Erase Feedback response options. This is why you used a Map as the feedback icon. By using Display icons followed by Wait and Erase icons, you can ensure that information is erased when the user exits the Perpetual Interaction.

- Do not judge the interaction.

- Choose Return for Looping. "Return" Looping sends the user back to the icon that calls the perpetual response.

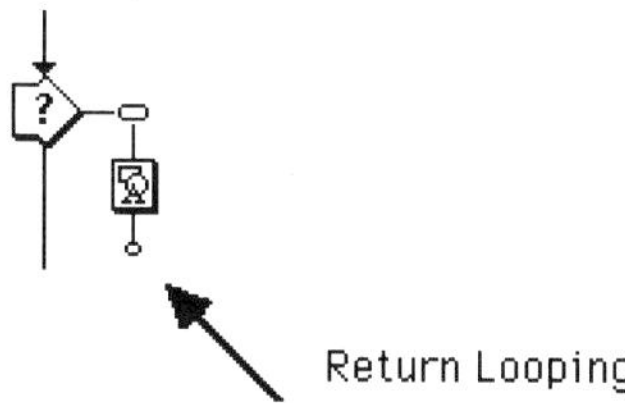

- Add a Display icon to the flow line and enter some text. Run the lesson to test the Perpetual Interaction. Notice that the Help button is available. Selecting *Help* places the content of the Perpetual Interaction onto the screen together with a Wait button. Resize and place the Wait button on top of the Help button so only one button shows at a time.

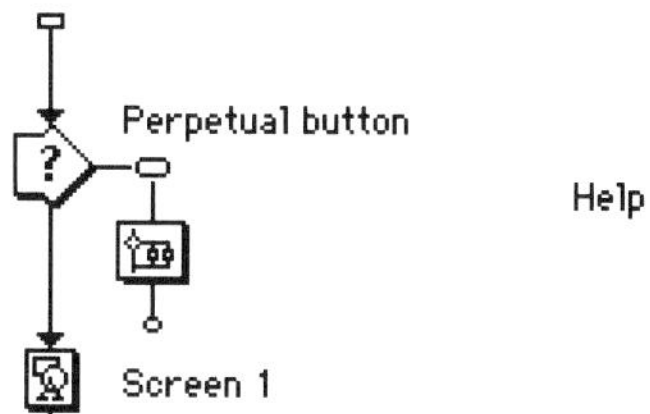

- To use a perpetual response, first create the Perpetual Interaction, then "Call" the interaction whenever it is needed. The method used to call a Perpetual Interaction varies according to the response type. For a Button response, simply clicking the button on the screen activates the interaction.

Things to Know About Perpetual Interactions

- To remember which response types support Perpetual Interactions, notice that with the exception of Conditional responses, the response types require the use of the mouse to interact. Also, the response types that support Perpetual Interactions are the six options in the left of the response type window:

⊖ ◯ **Button**

⠿ ◯ **Hot Spot**

✳ ◯ **Hot Object**

⬉ ◯ **Target Area**

▤ ◯ **Pull-down Menu**

＝ ◯ **Conditional**

STUDY EXERCISES

1. Create an interaction in which the user is given a prompt after two incorrect answers and is given the correct answer after three incorrect answers. Set Looping to Try Again after two incorrect answers and Exit after three incorrect answers.

2. Create an interaction in which the user is given a prompt after 20 seconds (if the correct answer has not been given), and the correct answer after 60 seconds. Set looping to *Try Again* after 20 seconds and *Exit* after 60 seconds.

3. A Pull-down Menu cannot be reused after it has been passed on the Course Flow Line. This can be a problem if you want the options in a Pull-down Menu to be available throughout a lesson. One solution to this problem involves using the Perpetual option in the Pull-down Menu.

    Use this approach to create a perpetual Help button that the user can access at any time during the lesson.

The following questions involve the use of Variables. You may want to complete chapter 13 before attempting these exercises.

4. Create a Keypress interaction in which you ask the user to identify the names of the last three presidents of the United States from a list of six presidents. Use a Conditional response and the System Variable TotalCorrect to match the third correct response. Provide appropriate feedback after each correct/incorrect response.

5. Did you notice in the previous exercise that the user could select the same correct answer three times? How could you make a response inactive once it has been selected?

6. Create an electronic notepad for the user to write notes/comments during the lesson. Use a Perpetual Interaction with a Button response to activate the notepad, which should be available throughout the lesson.

9

Libraries and Models  

CHAPTER OVERVIEW

In this chapter, you will examine two development tools that multimedia designers use to benefit design productivity and lesson execution: Libraries and Models. Libraries accelerate design by providing easy access to commonly used icons. Models play a similar role. However, rather than providing access to individual icons, Models provide access to sets of icons that perform tasks.

CHAPTER OBJECTIVES

By the end of this chapter, you will be able to
- Create Libraries to store and reuse icons.
- Create Models to to store and reuse lesson logic.

KEY TERMS

Libraries
Library links
Broken links
Models

SUPPORT MATERIALS

On the CD-ROM disc, run **BEGIN.PKG** if you are a Macintosh user or **BEGIN.APP** if you are using a PC. When the file opens, click once on the title page to begin. Select the button titled **Chapter 9**, and watch the video to see how Libraries and Models are created.

STUDY TOPICS

What Is a Library?

Libraries store icons that are used repeatedly in a lesson, or even in several lessons. Libraries improve productivity and reduce file size. By reusing icons, Libraries allow you to reproduce lesson content or ideas that you developed elsewhere. Reproducing icons is faster than creating original icons.

Imagine a lesson that uses sound files to deliver spoken feedback. In the following example, a sound file "tells" the user whether an answer is correct or wrong.

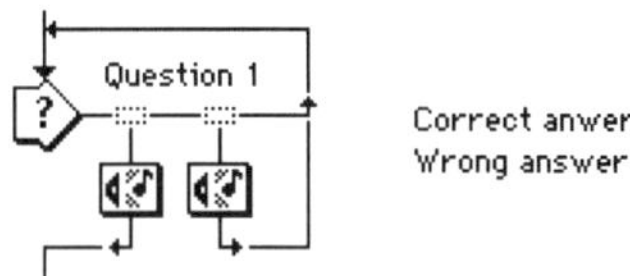

Repeatedly using Sound icons to deliver feedback causes two problems. First, it is labor-intensive. Each time you use a Sound icon, you must identify a sound file. Second, using the same sound file repeatedly increases file size. A small sound file recorded at a low sampling rate often increases lesson size by 50K. Using 2 sound files 10 times in a lesson could increase the file size by at least 1000K. In other words, the lesson could be 1 MB larger to include simple spoken feedback!

A solution to both problems involves using a Library. By placing the original Sound icon into a Library, the designer can select copies of the Sound icon by dragging the icon from the Library onto the Course Flow Line. Better still, each copy is not a real copy! Instead, Libraries use aliases to point from the copy on the Course Flow Line to the original icon stored in the Library. The following illustration shows the Sound icon after it has been reproduced from the Library. Notice the Sound icons' labels are italicized, indicating that the icons come from a Library file.

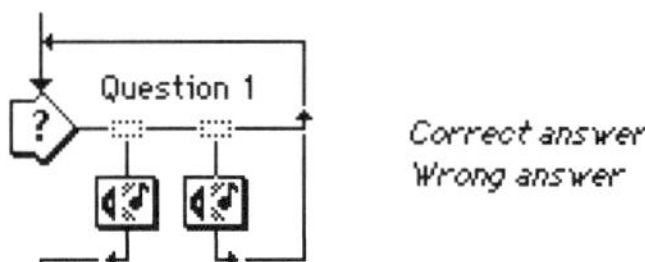

How Do I Create a Library?

To create a new Library, select New Library from the Library pulldown menu.

It is important to remember that the Library is a separate file and that the information in the file must be saved. Libraries must be saved to avoid losing the links to the lesson files. To save a Library, select Save from the File pulldown menu.

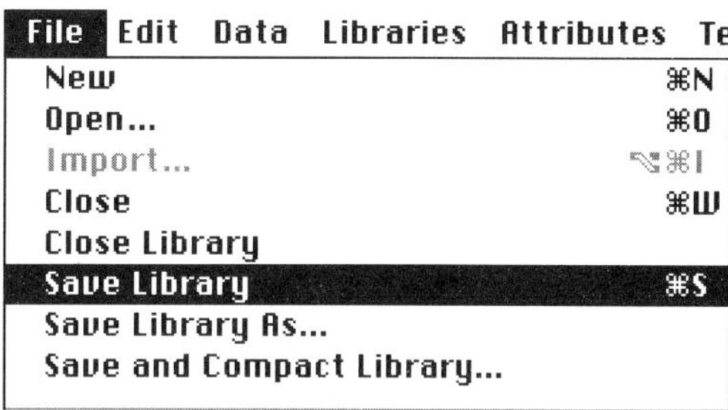

Once opened and saved, the Library window will appear as in the following illustration (this Library was given the name *library*).

At first, the Library is empty. To add items to the Library, drag an icon from the icon palette or from the Course Flow Line and drop the icon in the main Library window. When you add an icon from the Course Flow Line to the Library window, a copy of the Library icon automatically replaces the old icon. To place copies of Library icons into lessons, simply drag the icons from the Library window rather than from the icon palette.

  The following Library file shows four icons, although others are available by scrolling down with the scroll bar. In addition to each Library icon being named, each icon is labeled to remind the designer of the icon's contents at a later date.

Notice that the title of the Sound File on the following Course Flow Line appears in italics to indicate that it is an alias.

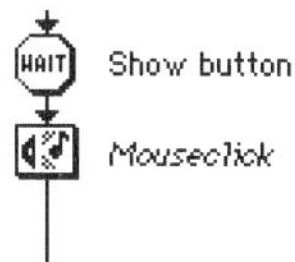

You can edit the contents of a Library icon and instruct Authorware to apply the changes to all, or just a subset of icons. First open and edit an icon in the Library. Next, highlight the icon and select Show Library Links from the Libraries pulldown menu.

At the dialog box, select the icons you want to update using standard shift-clicking techniques to choose multiple items from the list. Click Update when you are ready to apply the edits to the selected icons.

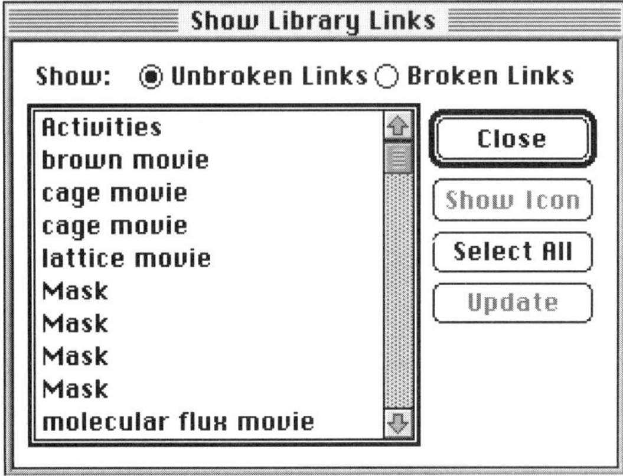

Not all icons can be added to a Library. Notice that some icons will produce the following error message if you attempt to drag them to a Library.

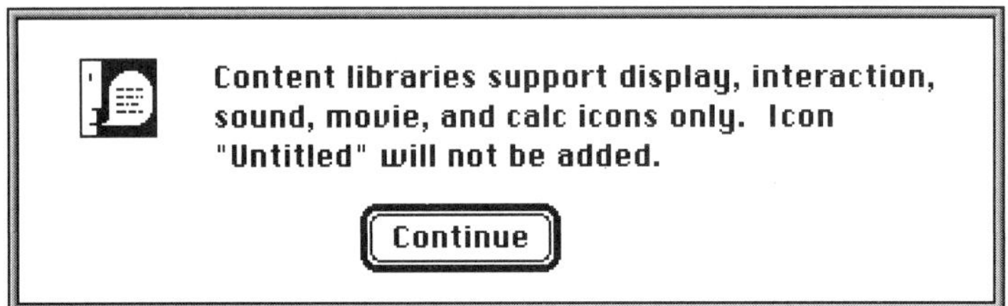

When a lesson file is finally Packaged (see Chapter 15), it is very important to include any Library files with the finished product. However, Authorware is smart enough to include only those Library files that are critical to smooth lesson performance. Consequently, Authorware designers can develop extensive Library files containing icons that may be used frequently in several different files without being concerned that the entire Library content must accompany every lesson.

What Is a Model?

A Model is a set of icons that you can save and reuse. Designers often design parts of lessons that take many hours to develop. Once created, designers frequently want to use the same logic in other lessons. To do so (without using Models) requires copying and pasting icons from the original into the new lesson file. This process can be quite time-consuming. However, by saving lesson logic into a Model, designers have immediate access to the desired icons without having to leave the lesson.

Many computer programmers will be familiar with the concept of a Model, although they often use a different language. Programmers often develop subroutine libraries containing frequently used sections of programming code. A Model is Authorware's version of a subroutine library. Once a Model has been saved, it becomes a permanent part of the Authorware application (although it can be removed) and can be easily pasted into another lesson.

At first, it is easy to confuse Libraries with Authorware Models. The difference between a Library and a Model is that a Library contains many different icons, but without any accompanying lesson logic, whereas a Model contains icons that have been carefully arranged in a predetermined logical sequence.

Models are important productivity tools. Many lessons contain identical lesson sequences. For example, the introductory screens for a series of lessons may include identical elements. Rather than recreating the icon sequence in every lesson, or copying and pasting icons from one file to another, Models allow icons to be immediately available.

Some models contain important logic but little or no lesson content. Saving the icon structure as a model allows the template to be reused simply by pasting the model onto the Course Flow Line. The lesson content would then be supplied by the designer.

How Do I Create a Model?

The Create Model option cannot be used until one or more icons have been highlighted.

To highlight icons, click-on one or more icons while pressing the Shift key. Alternatively, drag several icons across with the mouse.

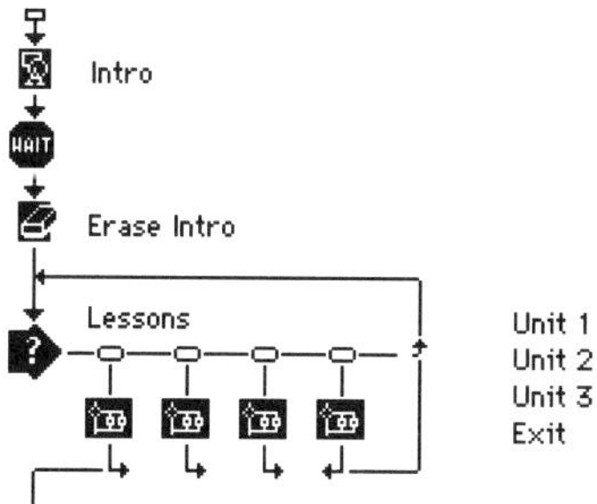

Once icons are highlighted, select Create Model from the Libraries pulldown menu.

A dialog box titled Model Description must be completed and you will be asked to save the Model to a disk.

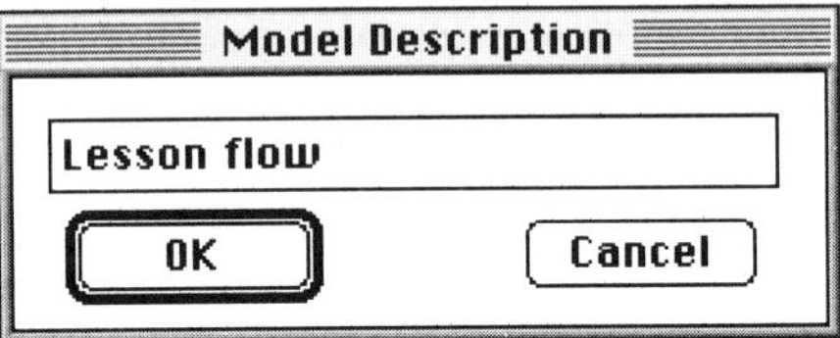

The description given to the Model appears as a name in the Paste Model pulldown menu.

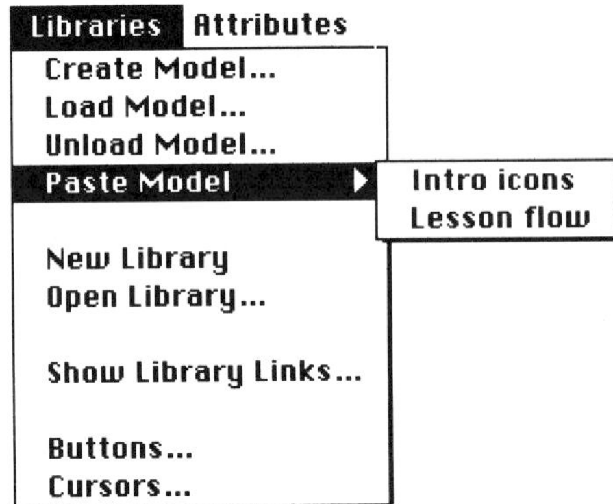

To reuse the Model, simply select the appropriate item from the list. The icons that form the Model will be immediately pasted onto the Course Flow Line.

In addition to creating your own Models, Models created by other designers can be imported into Authorware. Imagine, for example, that you found a sophisticated adaptive testing module that drills students on important lesson content and uses increasing ratio review to retest students on items they answer incorrectly. Such a template could be useful in many different designs, but difficult and expensive to create. Fortunately, such a Model could be distributed on disk and loaded into Authorware using the Load Model option.

STUDY EXERCISES

As an Authorware designer, you should attempt to create a Library containing frequently used icons and models. A library will greatly stimulate your productivity by speeding the development process. The following exercises are designed to stimulate such development.

1. Create a Library containing information that you believe you will use regularly. For example, you might include the following:

    • A Display icon containing a company or institutional logo.

    • A Display icon containing a frequently used background design.

    • Display icons that contain a variety of buttons, navigation arrows, and other frequently used graphics. You may want to create these graphics in a drawing or painting program.

    • A Sound icon containing the sound used to make a button "click."

    • A Calculation icon containing several lines of instructions necessary to complete a complex task. For example, this could involve collecting and writing lesson data to a file that is stored in a lesson folder.

2. Create a Keypress multiple-choice question with one correct answer and three distracters (incorrect answers). In place of real content, create a template indicating where the user should place the questions, answers, and feedback for right and wrong answers. Save the interaction as a Model.

3. Create a Model containing a Framework icon (see the following chapters on the Framework and Navigation icons) that performs customized navigation.

The Decision Icon 

CHAPTER OVERVIEW

In this chapter, you will learn about the Decision icon. The Decision icon is used to control the lesson flow. Attached to the Decision icon are paths that contain different contents. Designers use the Decision icon whenever they wish to select one or more paths from the set of paths.

In programming terms, the Decision icon replaces the If Then/Do-Next function. The Decision icon remembers the number of times paths have been selected and determines which subsequent paths to select.

Chapter Objectives

By the end of this chapter, you will be able to

- Use the Decision icon to control lesson sequencing.

KEY TERMS

Decision icon
Path
Random to any path
Random without repetition

SUPPORT MATERIALS

On the CD-ROM disc, run **BEGIN.PKG** if you are a Macintosh user or **BEGIN.APP** if you are using a PC. When the file opens, click once on the title page to begin. Select the button titled **Chapter 10**, and watch the video to see how Decision icons are used to create branching paths.

The folder on the CD-ROM titled MACDEMOS or PC_DEMOS contains several demonstration files that you can run and examine. The folder contains two versions of each file: a packaged file that you can run and an unpackaged file containing the icons used to create the file. Run the file and examine how each of the four different branching options is created.

Macintosh users:
Run the file CHP10.pkg to view its contents.
Open the data file CHP10.A3M to examine how the file was created.

PC users:
Run the file CHP10.APP to view its contents.
Open the data file CHP10.A3W to examine how the file was created.

Note: You must have a copy of Authorware on your computer to open the data files.

STUDY TOPICS

When Do I Use a Decision Icon?

Decision icons are used whenever the designer wants to control or alter the lesson flow. Consider, for example, a case in which the designer wishes to select a series of test questions from an item pool. The Decision icon allows the designer to select a given number of questions and to do so sequentially, randomly, or according to some specified criteria.

The Decision icon is also an invaluable development tool. Creative uses of Decision icons can result in the solution of many awkward programming problems.

How Does the Decision Icon Work?

A Decision structure comprises two parts: a Decision icon and one or more icons attached to the Decision icon, which are called Paths. The Decision icon manages the logic of the Decision structure and controls Branching and Repeating. Branching refers to the Path that is selected. Repeating refers to the number of times the Decision structure is used.

A Path is an icon attached to the Decision structure. A Path may be any icon except an Interaction, another Decision icon, or a Framework icon. However, because a Map icon can be used as a Path, in effect, any icon can be used as a Path by embedding icons within Maps. In the following illustration, the Decision structure includes a Decision icon and three Map icons as Paths. Each icon attached to the Decision structure represents a new path. Each path is numbered. The leftmost icon is the first Path in the Decision structure, the next icon is the second path and so on.

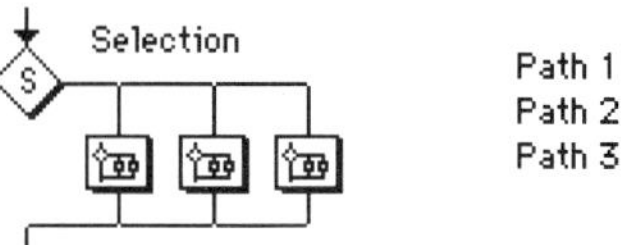

Opening Decision Icons

Two principal decisions must be made concerning the Decision icon:
- The order in which the Paths will be accessed—known as Branch options
- The number of times the Decision icon will be employed—known as Repeat options

Double-click on the Decision icon to access the Branch and Repeat options. The Branch options are shown in the left side and the Repeat options on the right of the display box in the following figure.

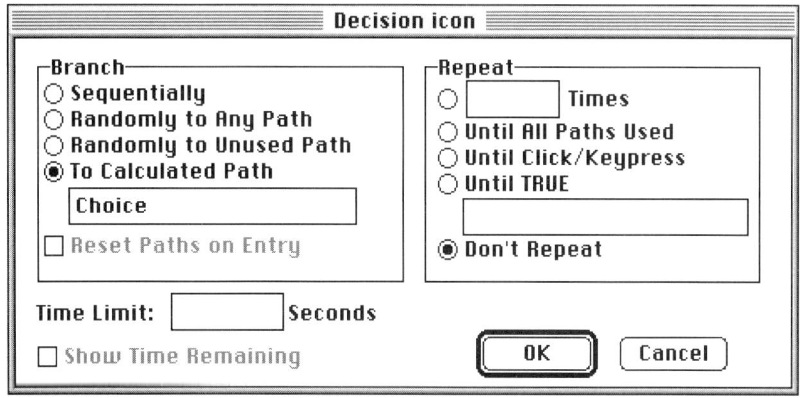

The order in which the paths are chosen is determined by using Branch options:

- *Sequentially* selects the paths, beginning with the leftmost path (path 1) and continuing in order from left to right with the other icons attached to the Decision icon (e.g., path 1, path 2, path 3).

- *Randomly to Any Path* selects a path at random from the paths attached to the Decision icon. Furthermore, the selected path is replaced into the pool and may be reselected (e.g., path 2, path 4, path 2, path 1).

- *Randomly to Unused Path* selects a path at random from the paths attached to the Decision icon. Once it is selected, the path will not be chosen again unless the entire Decision structure is reused (e.g., path 3, path 4, path 1, path 2) .

- *To Calculated Path* uses a Variable to select a path. Calculated Path selects the path number equal to the value stored in a variable. Suppose, for example, that a user Variable titled Choice were placed into the Calculated Path slot.

If Choice=3, then the third path attached to a Decision icon would be chosen. It is important to realize that the Calculated Path option cannot be properly implemented until the concept of Variables is understood.

Repeat controls the number of times a user must follow a path. Returning to the earlier example in which each path of a Decision icon represents a test item, if the designer wants to end the test after the student answers five questions, the designer would repeat the Decision icon five times.

However, if the designer wants the students to continue until answering five questions correctly without errors, the designer might enter the following statement into the Until TRUE box:

FirstTryCorrect=5.

In this case, the designer would be using a Variable to control how many times the Decision icon repeats.

Examples

1. The uppercase S in the Decision icon following indicates that Authorware will select paths sequentially, that is, path 1, path 2, path 3, and so on. However, we can discover how many paths will be selected only by opening the Decision icon.

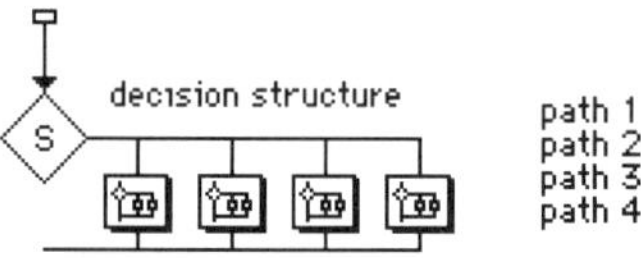

2. Authorware will select a path at random. No item will be selected twice. Authorware will repeat the Decision icon until all the paths have been selected

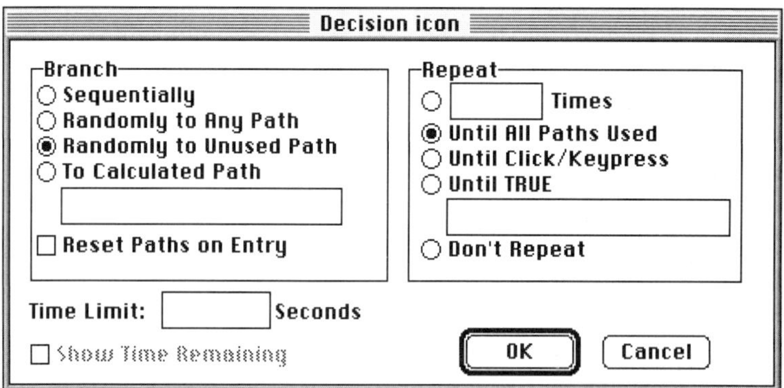

3. In the following case, the path chosen is dependent on a user-defined variable titled "Lesson".

How Can I Use a Decision Icon as a Programming Tool?

It must be emphasized that the following example will make sense only to those who have at least a working knowledge of Variables. Others may want to skip this section until after completing Chapter 13.

One common development problem occurs when the designer wants to vary the lesson sequence for different users. For example, a designer might want to follow a given path only if the user has already completed some part of the lesson. In such cases, the path can be attached to a Decision icon and controlled with a Variable.

The following illustration describes such a case. Here, one path is attached to a Decision icon. On the surface, it may appear that the path (titled *Glossary help*) might be available to all users. However, inspection of the Decision icon reveals that the path is controlled by the User Variable titled Event. In this case, *Glossary help* will only be available if the current value of the Variable = 1. If the Variable = 0, then path 0 will be selected. However, the paths in the Decision icon are numbered, with the leftmost path starting at 1. In other words, no path will be selected.

To provide access to the information stored in path 1, the designer must include the calculation

Event = 1

at some point in the lesson, prior to the Decision icon. This could be done, for example, at the end of an icon sequence presented earlier in the lesson.

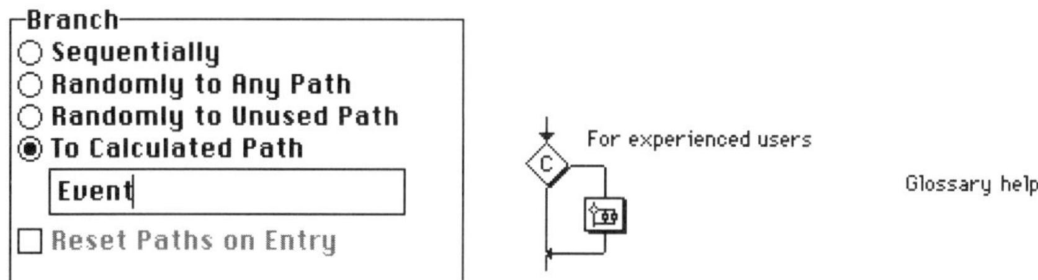

STUDY EXERCISES

1. Construct a five-item quiz that ends when the student has completed four items. Present items in a random order, but present each item only once.

2. (a) Use the Decision icon to simulate the rolling of a single die and display the result in a Display icon.

    (b) Use the Decision icon to simulate the rolling of two dice and display the results in a Display icon.

3. *The following exercise requires the use of a Variable and should not be attempted until after completing the chapter on Variables.* Create three branches for a tutorial and store each branch as a Decision icon path. Place an Interaction icon immediately before the Decision icon to ask the user to type a 1, 2, or 3 to indicate the branch they wish to select (e.g., Type a

"1" to choose math, "2" to choose Science, and so on.). Use a Calculated path in the Decision icon to select Path 1 if the student types a 1, branch 2 if the student types a 2, and branch 3 if the student types a 3.

4. Create a file that randomly selects playing cards from a deck of cards. Each time the user presses a button, a randomly selected card should appear on the screen. The user should be able to select cards until every card has been chosen.

   There are several ways to create such a file. You might use Decision icons to

   (a)   Determine a card number between 1 and 13.

   (b)   Select one of four suits.

   You must also keep track of cards that have already been selected (i.e., make sure that cards are not returned to the deck).

Framework icons 

CHAPTER OVERVIEW

Framework icons enhance navigation. They can be used to move forward and backward though lesson information without using Wait and Erase icons. The Framework icon allows you to design an entirely new set of features that is otherwise difficult or impossible to create. As such, the Framework icon may change the way you think about lesson design.

  This and the following chapter (about Navigate icons) should be studied together because their ideas are so closely connected. The Framework icon uses Navigate icons to create navigation links. Navigate icons connect Pages attached to Framework icons. In practice, Framework and Navigate icons are completely interdependent.

CHAPTER OBJECTIVES

By the end of this chapter, you will be able to
- Use the Framework icon to create navigation structures.
- Edit Framework structures to customize navigation.
- Create hypertext.

KEY TERMS

Framework icon
Entry pane
Exit pane
Navigate icon
Pages
Hypertext
Framework Window
Destinations
Jump to Page
Call and Return

SUPPORT MATERIALS

On the CD-ROM disc, run **BEGIN. PKG** if you are a Macintosh user or **BEGIN.APP** if you are using a PC. When the file opens, click once on the title page to begin. Select the button titled **Chapter 11**, and watch the video to see how Framework Structures are created.

The folder on the CD-ROM titled MACDEMOS or PC_DEMOS contains two versions of each file: a packaged file that you can run and an unpackaged file containing the icons used to create the file. Run the file and use each of the navigation buttons to help you to understand how each button works. Add Display icons to a Framework Structure to create new Pages. Use the mouse to select colored hypertext links to the glossary. To help you to understand how to create hypertext, examine the text style named *Hypertext* and explore the navigation associated with each hyperlink.

Macintosh users:
Run the file CHP11_12.pkg to view its contents.
Run the file CHP11_12.A3M to examine how the file was created.

PC users:
Run the file CHP11_12.APP to view its contents.
Open the data file CHP11_12.A3W to examine how the file was created.

Note: You must have a copy of Authorware on your computer to open the data files.

STUDY TOPICS

Framework Icons

You may have noticed that with the exception of Perpetual Interactions (see Chapter 8), Authorware lessons tend to be very linear. When you create a lesson, Authorware executes icons in a vertical sequence from the top to the bottom of the Course Flow Line. Linear lessons can cause problems, especially when it is important for users to review information. For example, in the following Course Flow Line, you cannot easily access the information on Page 1 after you have moved to Page 2.

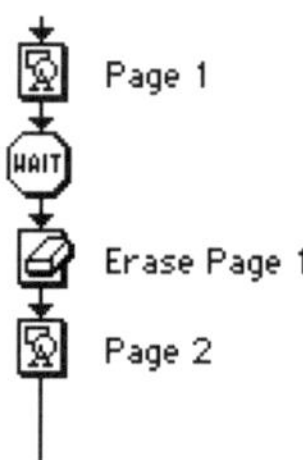

The most important role of a Framework icon is to provide a navigation system that allows the user to easily "page" back and forth between icons to review important information, to move from one lesson unit to another, or to follow a hyperlink.

A Framework icon is made up of two parts: Pages and a Framework Window. A Page is an icon attached to the right of a Framework icon. In the following illustration, Display icons are used for three Pages. The user can move between the Pages by using navigation controls that are built into the Framework Window.

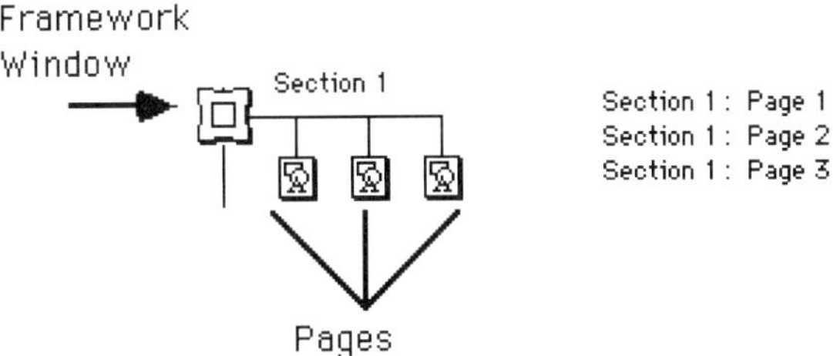

Pages are not limited to presenting information in Display icons. You can attach any of the following icons to a framework: Motion; Erase; Wait; Navigate; Calculation; Map; Movie; Sound; and Video. You can also use the Map icon to store other icons. Map icons often include Display, Wait, and Erase icons to systematically build screens.

The Framework Window contains the navigation controls. These controls determine the order in which Pages are accessed and can be altered to modify navigation. For example, a button in the Framework Window might be used to link to a Page in another framework. To open the Framework Window, place a Framework icon onto the Course Flow Line and double-click on its icon.

The Framework Window includes Entry and Exit panels. These panels contain icons that are executed every time the user enters (Entry panel) or exits (Exit panel) the framework. The default Framework icon (shown in what follows) contains a Display icon titled *Gray Navigation Panel* and eight Perpetual buttons that control navigation.

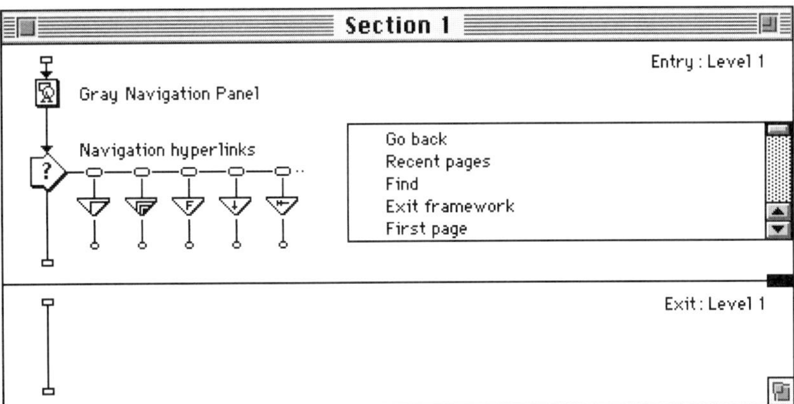

Understanding how navigation is controlled in the Framework Window can be difficult to understand at first. The following examples are designed to help you to learn how navigation works.

Example 1: Using a Framework icon

This example shows the basic operation of a Framework icon. You will create a simple Navigation Structure using a Framework icon and some Display icons as Pages.

- Place a Framework icon on the Course Flow Line. Title the icon Framework 1.

- Add three Display icons as Pages of the Framework Structure (as shown). Label the Display icons Page 1, Page 2, and Page 3.

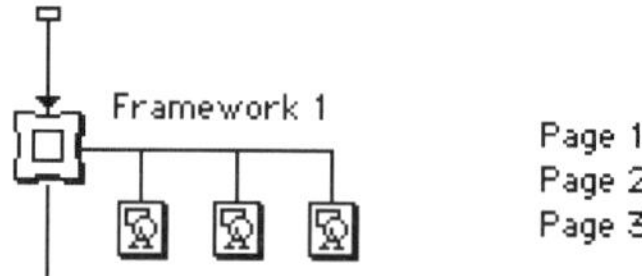

- Open each of the Display icons and type the title of each icon into its Presentation Window.
- Run the file. The following (or a similar) screen will result.

Page 1

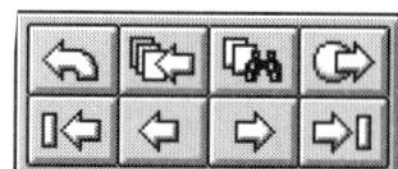

- Experiment with each of the buttons and try to determine how each button works. The exact operation of each option will be addressed later in this chapter.

Tip: Try the following time saver.

You can use a Variable to place different text into Display icons without typing the text into the icons! Paste the Variable titled "ExecutingIconTitle" into a Display icon. Duplicate the icon onto the Course Flow Line. Label each duplicated icon with a unique name.

To use the Variable, first open a Display on the Course Flow Line. Select Show Variables from the Data pulldown menu, select the category titled All, and scroll down to the desired Variable. Click on the Variable's name and press the button titled Paste to place the Variable into the Display.

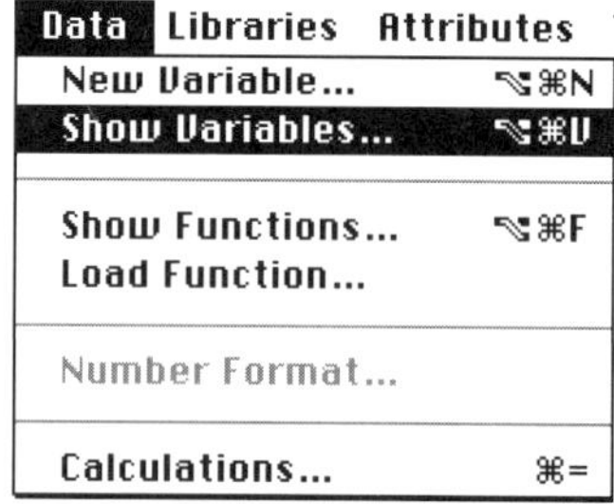

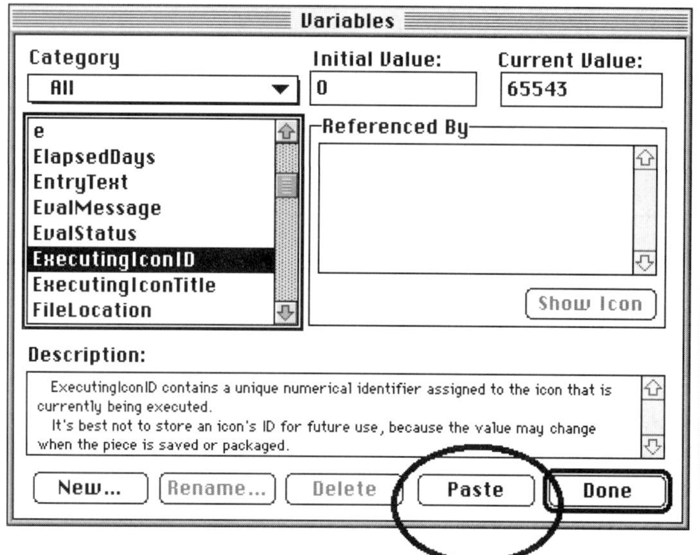

Example 2: Understanding the navigation buttons

This example examines four navigation buttons in the Entry panel. We will "disable" the other four navigation options to prevent you from becoming swamped with new information.

- Place a Framework icon on the Course Flow Line. Title the icon Framework 2.

Next, deactivate some of the default navigation buttons that are built into the Framework icon.

- Double-click on the Framework icon. The following window will appear:

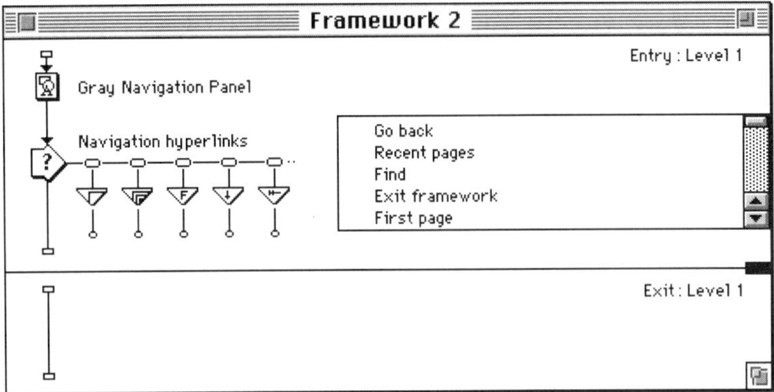

Select and cut the first four Buttons from the Interaction structure titled "Navigation hyperlinks". These four buttons are titled Go back, Recent pages, Find, and Exit framework. When you are done, the following buttons will remain: First page; Previous page; Next page; and, Last page.

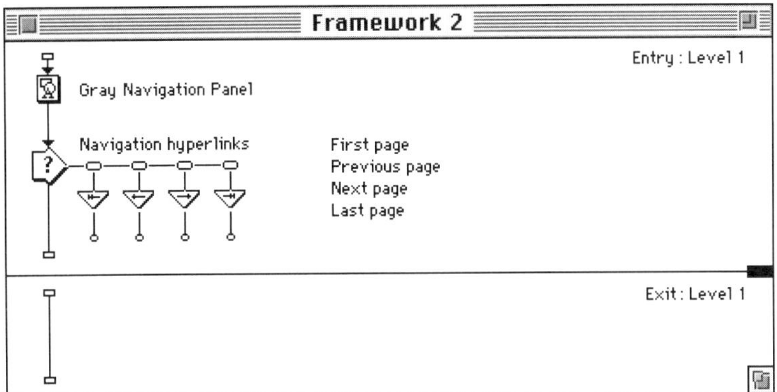

- Next, close the window titled Framework 2 to return to the main Course Flow Line. Attach four Display icons to the Framework Structure.   Each of the icons attached to a Framework icon is a Page. Label the Pages "first", "second", "third", and "fourth".

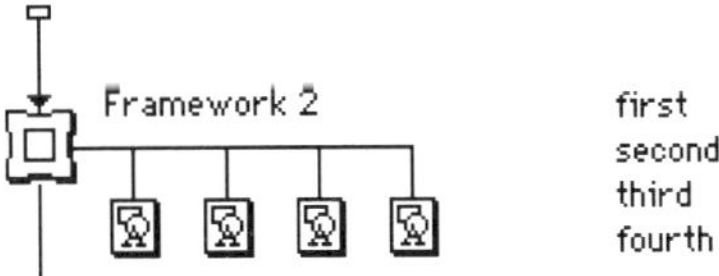

- Open each of the Display icons and type the title of each icon into its Presentation Window (or embed the variable titled "ExecutingIconTitle" as described earlier).

- Run the lesson. Notice that a navigation panel opens at the top-right corner of the Presentation Window and that four of the buttons are missing. These are the buttons we deleted earlier. Removing buttons simplifies the learning task.

- Now experiment with each of the four buttons. You should notice the following:

The two central buttons (Previous page and Next page) allow you to move backward or forward a Page at a time. The other two buttons (First page and Last page) jump to the first or the last Page attached to the Framework icon. Notice that no Wait or Erase icons are needed to control the information flow.

   Try adding additional Pages to the Framework structure and experiment with the buttons. You will find that the navigation controls are automatically applied to all the Pages attached to the Framework structure.

Exercise 3: Understanding the remaining navigation buttons

You will now focus on the other four navigation buttons that make-up the default Framework icon.

- Place a Framework icon on the Course Flow Line. Title the icon Framework 3.
- Place four Display icons to the right of the Framework icon. Label the Display icons first, second, third, and fourth.
- Add a fifth Display icon on the Course Flow Line and title this icon OUT.

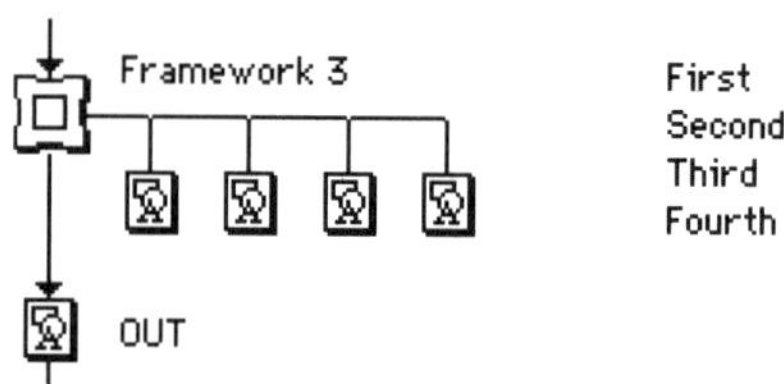

- Open each of the Display icons and type the title of each icon into its Presentation Window (or embed the variable titled "ExecutingIconTitle").
- Run the lesson. Notice that the file is identical to the one created before, with the exception that the navigation controls contain four new options. Before experimenting with these new options, take a few seconds to reuse the Page-Forward, Page-Back, Jump-Forward, and Jump-Back buttons. Do this to create a lesson history that will be revisited in a few moments.
- Select Recent Pages. Recent Pages lists the titles of all the Pages that have been accessed recently. When you select this button, a window similar to the following window will appear. To navigate from here, simply double-click on one of the Page titles in the list.

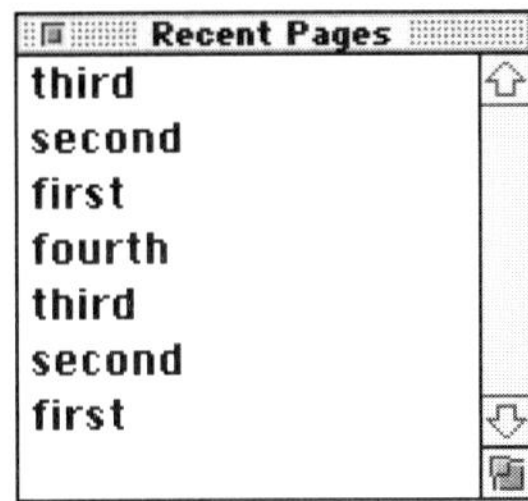

- 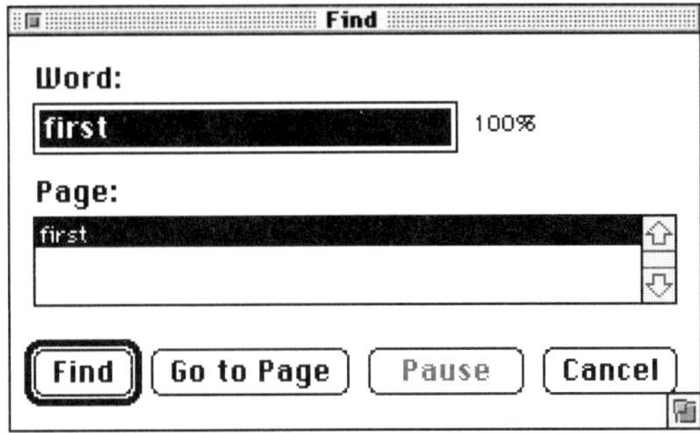 Select Find. Use this option to search for words or terms. The Find button searches for text either in the current or other frameworks and lists the names of all the Pages that include the term.

  To use the Find button, enter the text you want to locate and press the Return key. The names of all the Pages containing the desired text will appear in a window. You can connect to these displays by clicking on the icon names (as you did for the Recent Pages button).

Note: If you use the Variable titled "ExecutingIconTitle" to display icon names in Display icons, the Find button will not be able to locate Pages containing the desired text. Authorware only searches for "real" text, as opposed to text stored in Variables.

- Select the Go Back button. The Go Back button sends the user to the previous page in the current framework. The button is similar but different from the Previous Page button. Whereas Previous Page moves the user though a continuous loop of icons connected to a framework, Go Back retraces the history of Pages that the user has visited. For example, if the user follows the path:

Start
First
Second
First
Second
Fourth

Pressing the Previous Page button three times produces the following result:
Third
Second
First

That is, it revisits the lesson *structure*, whereas pressing the Go Back button three times produces:

Second
First
Second

That is, it revisits the lesson *history*.

- Select the Exit button to move out of the current Framework. In the present example, the lesson moves out of the framework titled Framework 3 and back to the Course Flow Line where the next icon encountered is titled Out.

Creating Hyperlinks

Navigation links are sometimes limited to Pages within a Framework. However, at other times, users want to jump to Pages in other Frameworks. For example, a user may wish to link to a glossary to look up the meaning of a word, or to connect to frameworks containing related ideas. These connections, sometimes called hyperlinks, allow users to follow their personal interests rather than a path that has been prescribed by someone else. Hyperlinks permit users to connect to Pages by clicking on text. Hyperlinks are often cued to the user by using coloring, underlining, or some other form of text highlighting.

Where Do Hyperlinks Come From?

Hyperlinks are created by using Styled Text. Text styling is a common feature in many word processors and desktop publishing programs. It allows a combination of font types and sizes, coloring, and other formatting options to be applied simultaneously from a styles menu. In Authorware, Styled Text can also link text to Framework Pages. If this chapter included Styled Text a link could connect the underlined words <u>styled text</u> to the section in Chapter 5 on Defining Styles.

Creating hyperlinks is a three-step process:
Step 1.   Create a destination Page for a hyperlink and attach it to a Framework icon.
Step 2.   Define a style sheet that formats text and leads to the destination Page.
Step 3.   Apply the style to create a link to the destination Page.

Example

The words *noun*, *verb*, and *adjective* will be highlighted wherever they appear in a lesson, and clicking on the words with the mouse will lead directly to their definitions in a glossary. The glossary will contain definitions of the words. A text style will be created that contains text formatting and a hyperlink. Applying the style will highlight words and create hyperlinks.

Step 1.   Create a destination Page and attach it to a Framework icon.

The destination Page is a Display icon titled Glossary. The Glossary will contain the definitions of the verbs, nouns, and adjectives.

Step 2.   Define a style sheet that formats text and leads to the destination Page.

Hyperlinks are often identified by formatting text to cue the user that a hyperlink exists. Style sheets can be used to format text and to create hyperlinks.

To Create a Hypertext Style Sheet

- Select Define Styles from the Text pulldown menu.

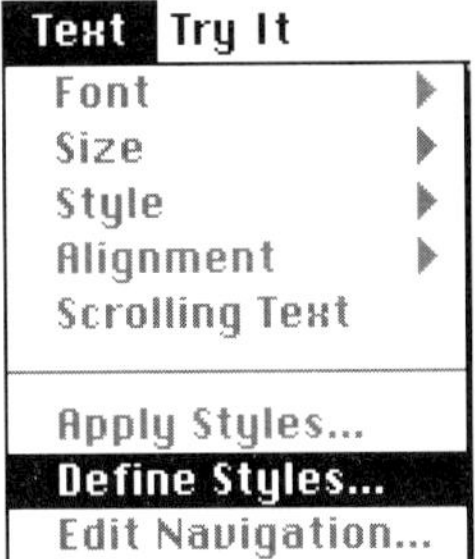

- Click the Add button and type the name of the new style (here, the style name is Hyperlink).
- Click the Modify button when you are done. The title Hyperlink will be added to the list of style sheets.

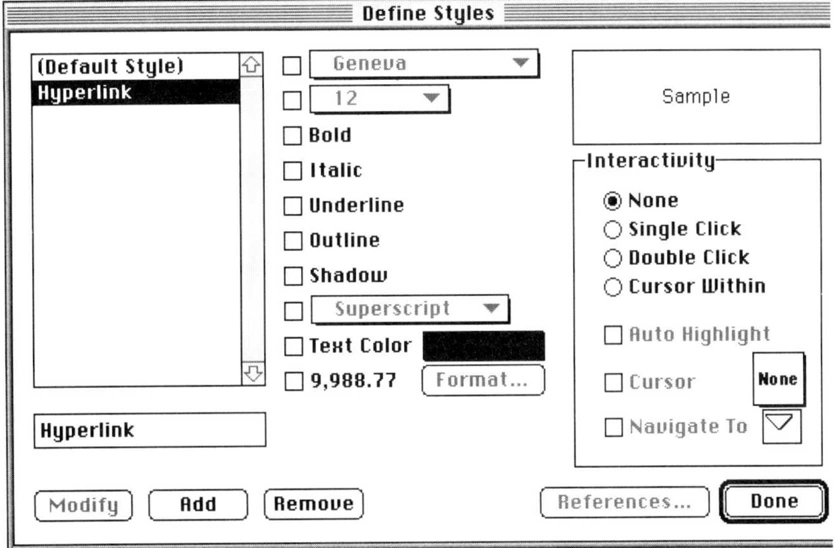

- Select the text-formatting options that you wish to apply to the hypertext. Colored and underlined text are often used to identify links. Text formatting provides users with visual clues that hyperlinks exist. In the following example, the hypertext is highlighted in a dark color, made bold and italicized. Click the Modify button after making changes.

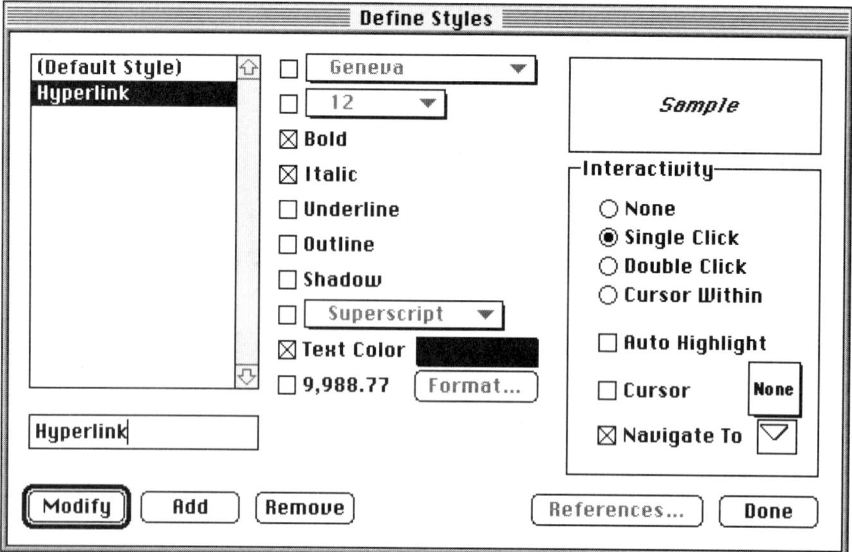

- Now you must create the hyperlink. In other words, you must identify the Page to where the hypertext will go. In the window labeled Interactivity, select "Single Click" and check the "Navigate To" box.

- Single click on the Navigate button ⬇ to show the following window, which displays all the Pages to which you can create a link.

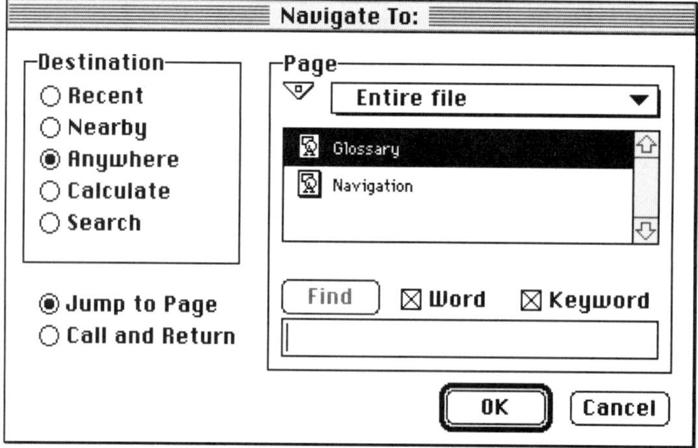

A navigation destination must be a Page attached to a Framework icon. Each Destination offers different navigation options. Selecting *Anywhere* for the destination allows you to select either from the list of all icons in the entire file or more selectively by individual Framework icons. The previous illustration shows that a link can be made to one of two Pages. Selecting the icon titled Glossary will establish a hyperlink to this destination.

The options *Jump to Page* and *Call and Return* determine whether the link is one-way or return. Jump to Page is like a one-way ticket to the specified Page. Call and Return connects to a Page before returning to the icon from which it came. Click OK when you have made a link and determined on a one-way or return ticket.

Step 3. Apply the style to text to create a link to the destination Page.

You can create hyperlinks by applying a style to a word or a set of words. To apply a style, highlight text in a Display icon (using the Text or Selection tools) and apply the appropriate style from the Styles list or from the Apply Styles dialog box. Clicking on a word styled in "Hyperlink" will create a connection to the Glossary.

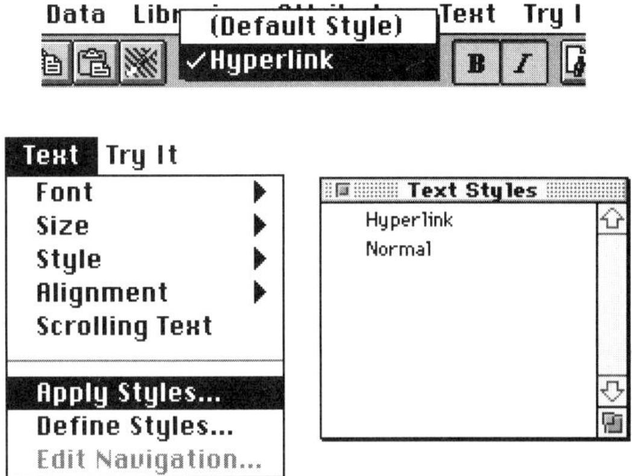

Editing Navigation

The previous example demonstrated a Style Sheet that created a hypertext link to one destination. All styled text landed at the same destination. Sometimes you want to connect to several different Pages. For example, in the previous example, you may want to use different Pages for verbs, adjectives, and nouns.

You can create a Style Sheet that formats text consistently, but prompts the designer to define a destination Page. The primary difference between this approach and the one described previously is that the style sheet will not specify a destination. Instead, after applying a style to text, the designer will choose a destination by selecting Edit Navigation from the Text pulldown menu.

To create different navigation destinations for styled text:

- Open the Display icon from where the hyperlink will be initiated and use the Text tool to highlight the hypertext to be created .
- Select Edit Navigation from the Text pulldown window.

- Select the destination for the hyperlink. In the following example, the designer can choose to link to one of three Pages attached to the Framework icon titled Glossary. Other destinations can be selected by changing the Page organizer.

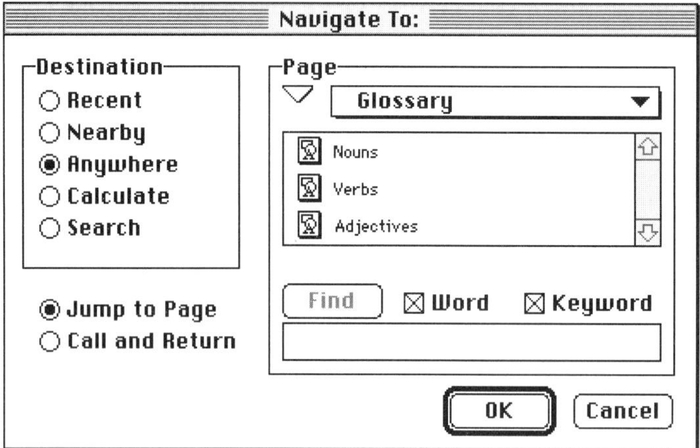

- Once a hyperlink has been created from a Display icon to a Framework Page, the icon containing the hypertext will be marked with a navigation marker (a small triangle), indicating that this icon initiates a link.

Note: Although the Style Sheet will not include the final destination for the hyperlink, the designer must select a level of interactivity in the Define Styles window. It is not sufficient to select text style alone. Instead you must select Single Click in the Interactivity dialog box.

Erasing

You may have noticed that when Pages are attached to Framework icons that erasing occurs automatically. That is, when the user selects a navigation button to move to another Page, information on the last Page is removed. However, sometimes you might want information in a Page to remain on the screen. For example, you might be using a framework to build a presentation in successive Display icons.

A feature exits to allow you to keep presentations on the screen and to ignore the automatic erase option. The option, titled Prevent Authomatic Erase can be found in the Effects menu under the Attributes menu.

Although selecting Prevent Automatic Erase allows you to build presentations without having to recreate screen content, you should be careful in its use. Using navigation icons to backtrack through a presentation will not remove unwanted information from the screen.

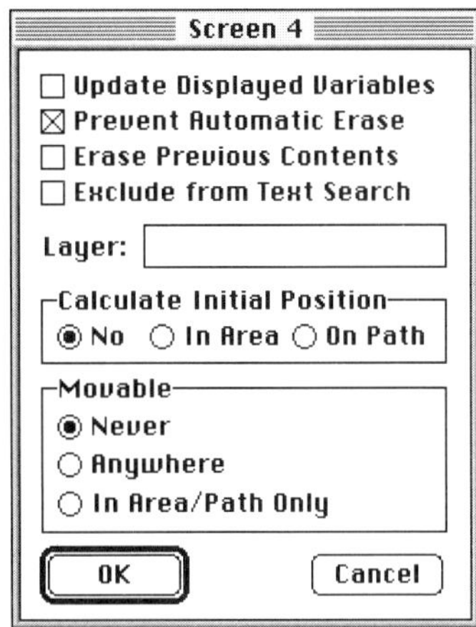

STUDY EXERCISES

1. (a) Use a Framework icon to create a presentation of five different Pages where each Page is a single Display icon. Run the lesson and experiment with each navigation button in the Presentation Window.

    (b) Modify the presentation by including a Map icon as one of the Pages. Into the Map, place a series of Display, Wait, and Erase icons that progressively build a single screen of information.

2. Experiment with the navigation buttons as outlined in what follows.

    (a) Place a Framework icon on the Course Flow Line and modify the navigation buttons to allow only Page-Forward and Page Back navigation. Add three to four Pages to the framework and try to navigate with the buttons.

    (b) Place a Framework icon on the Course Flow Line and modify the navigation buttons to allow only Page-Forward and Recent-Pages navigation. Add three to four Pages to the framework and try to navigate with the buttons.

    (c) Place a Framework icon on the Course Flow Line and modify the navigation buttons to allow only Last-Page, Page-Back, and Recent-Pages navigation. Add three to four Pages to the framework and try to navigate with the buttons.

3. This exercise involves creating hypertext links. Create a Framework containing several Pages that together make a glossary containing definitions of several terms. Place the framework at the end of the Course Flow Line. Create a brief lesson in which the words or terms described in the glossary appear in Display icons in the main lesson.   Create Hyperlinks between each of the terms and the glossary.

4. Create a Framework icon that includes custom navigation buttons.

5. As users go through lessons, they require different levels of support. What starts out being a useful help screen often becomes useless. Framework icons are the perfect tool for creating help screens that change during a lesson according to the users needs.

    Create a brief lesson that includes at least three hyperlinks to different Help screens. The help button should not vary in appearance, but should lead to different destinations for the different types of help. The user should be able to select the Help button to bring up a help window and to use navigation buttons in the help window to access other help screens.

12

Navigate Icons ▼

CHAPTER OVERVIEW

This chapter examines the icon that redirects lesson flow: the Navigate icon. Navigate icons create links to Pages in Framework icons. Most importantly, the Navigate icon creates nonlinear designs. Navigate icons permit forward or backward jumps within a lesson. Instead of using the Course Flow Line to determine lesson sequence, the lesson automatically jumps to the destination identified in the Navigate icon.

CHAPTER OBJECTIVES

After completing this lesson, you will be able to

- Use the Navigate icon to create nonlinear lesson links.
- Customize navigation in Framework icons.

KEY TERMS

Navigate icon
Navigate to
Destinations: Recent; Nearby; Anywhere; Calculate; Search
Jump to page
Call and return
Navigation Structures

SUPPORT MATERIALS

On the CD-ROM disc, run **BEGIN.PKG** if you are a Macintosh user or **BEGIN.APP** if you are using a PC. When the file opens, click once on the title page to begin. Select the button titled **Chapter 12**, and watch the video to see how Navigate icons are used to customize navigation links. The folder on the CD-ROM titled MACDEMOS or PC_DEMOS contains several demonstration files that you can run and examine. The folder contains two versions of each file: a packaged file that you can run and examine. The folder contains two versions of each file: Run the file and open the Entry Panes for each of the Framework icons. Examine modifications to the navigation controls in the Entry Panes.

Macintosh users:
Run the file CHP11_12.pkg to view its contents.
Open the data file CHP11_12.A3M to examine how the file was created.

PC users:
Run the file CHP11_12.APP to view its contents.
Open the data file CHP11_12.A3W to examine how the file was created.

Note: You must have a copy of Authorware on your computer to open the data files.

STUDY TOPICS

Navigate icons can connect any two Pages attached to any Framework icons in a lesson. Navigate icons also can link icons that are not part of a framework to Pages attached to Framework icons. To learn how to navigate, it is important to understand the capabilities of Navigate icons. The purpose of this chapter is to examine these options.

Creating Page-to-Page Navigation

All navigation links connected to Framework icons can be modified. The default Navigation buttons that accompany the Framework icon is actually a Model that is loaded into Authorware each time the program restarts. You can create your own navigation controls, modify the default Framework icon navigation controls, and save other navigation controls as Models that you can reuse.

Double-click on a Framework icon to display the default Navigation buttons in the entry panel.

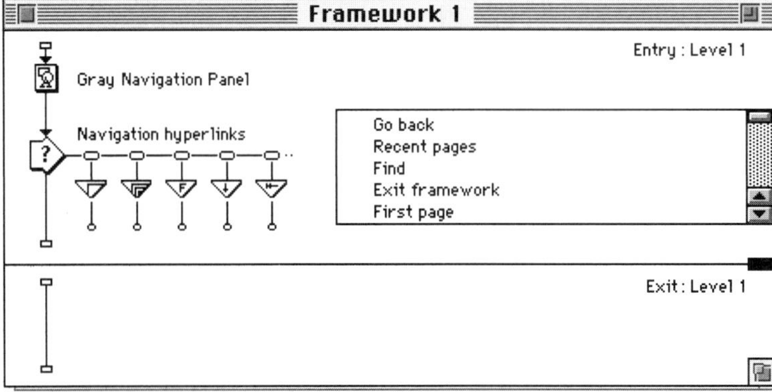

The entry panel establishes the logic that applies to all the Pages attached to the framework. All icons added to the entry panel are executed when the user enters the Framework icon. The default entry panel includes a Gray Navigation Panel that acts as a background for the navigation buttons, and eight navigation buttons. The following figures illustrate the Gray Navigation Panel graphic on which Navigation icons are placed and the default Navigation buttons.

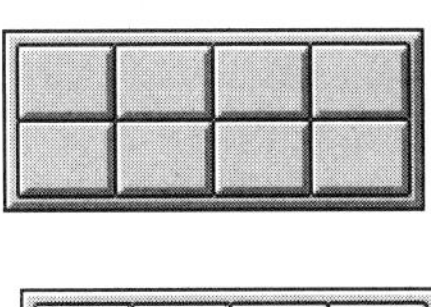

Navigation panel without buttons/icons

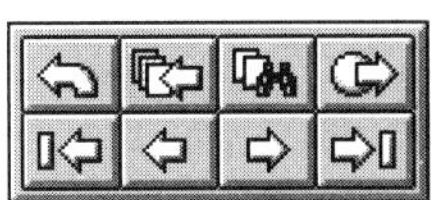

Navigation panel with Navigation buttons

The entry panel contains the navigation. The eight Navigation buttons in the default Framework window are Button responses set to Perpetual. The feedback attached to each button is a Navigate icon that connects to a Page.

The exit panel is used to execute events when the user leaves the Framework icon.   For example, the designer might leave a message indicating that a section of a lesson is done, or an erase icon might be used to ensure information is cleared from the screen.

Using Navigate icons involves identifying Destinations that take the user to a Page. Authorware is very sophisticated in the range of destinations it will allow. To view a Destination, double-click on any Navigate icon.

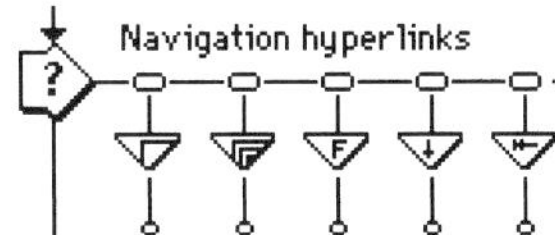

The complete set of Destinations is divided into five classes: Recent; Nearby; Anywhere; Calculate; and Search. The options associated with each destination will be examined in the following sections.

Recent

Recent allows backtracking. In other words, it allows users to repeat Pages attached to Framework icons. The designer can select from two options: Go Back or *List Recent Pages*. Both options are included in the default Framework icon.

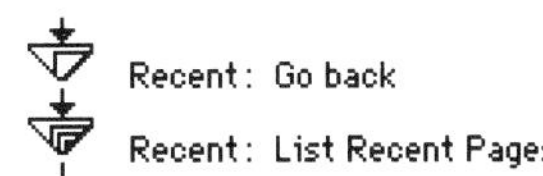

Go Back sends the user back sequentially through a list of recently executed Pages. The Pages may or may not be within the current Framework icon. If multiple frameworks exist, Go Back may return to Pages from other Frameworks. However, if only one framework exists, Go Back will eventually return to the first Page in the current framework.

List Recent Pages produces a navigation window that can be used to link directly to a Page (see what follows). Double-click on an icon's name to go directly to its icon.

To Understand How Go Back and List Recent Pages Work, Complete the Following Exercise:

- Place a Framework icon on the Course Flow Line. Label the icon "experiment".
- Attach three Display icons to the Framework icon. Label these icons "Language", "Math", and "Science".
- Type the words "Language", "Math", and "Science" into their respective Display icons.

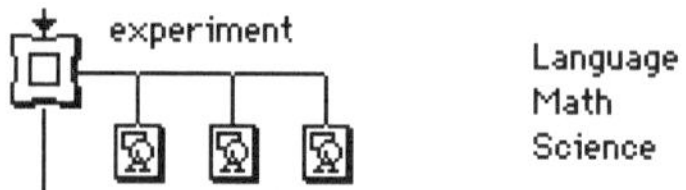

- Run the lesson. A Page with the word "Language" will appear.
- Click the Go-Back icon. Notice that nothing happens because you have not yet created a history that can be reviewed.
- Click the Go-Forward-one-Page icon. A page with the word "Math" will appear. Click it again and "Science" will appear.
- Click the Go-Back icon. The page containing "Math" will reappear. Click it again and the page containing "Language" will reappear. Now you are using the Go-Back button to revisit recently viewed Pages.
- Click the Recent-Pages icon. The following navigation window will appear:

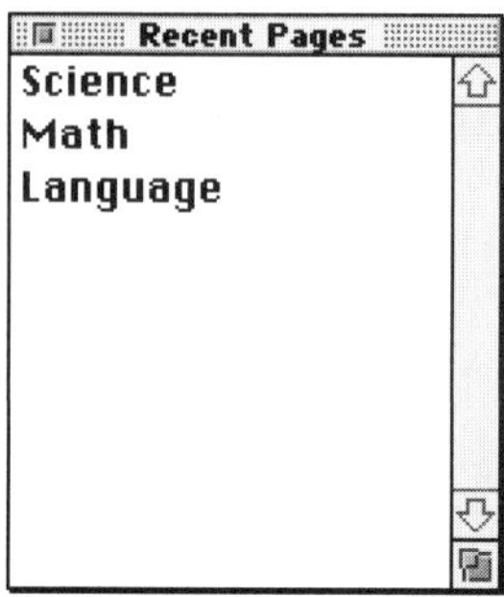

Notice that the window lists the names of the Pages you have viewed recently. You can navigate to a Page by double-clicking on its icon name in the window.

Note: List Recent Pages uses icon names to identify the path a user has taken. Consequently, it is important to name Pages meaningfully to help users navigate effectively.

Nearby

Selecting *Nearby* allows the designer to select from five options: *Previous, Next, First, Last,* or *Exit Framework/Return.* All five options refer to Pages within the current Framework icon.

Notice that the icons for each option differ slightly and provide visual clues to identify each icon's function. The icons look similar to the buttons on a VCR. All five options are included in the default Navigation Structure that is built-in to the Navigate icon.

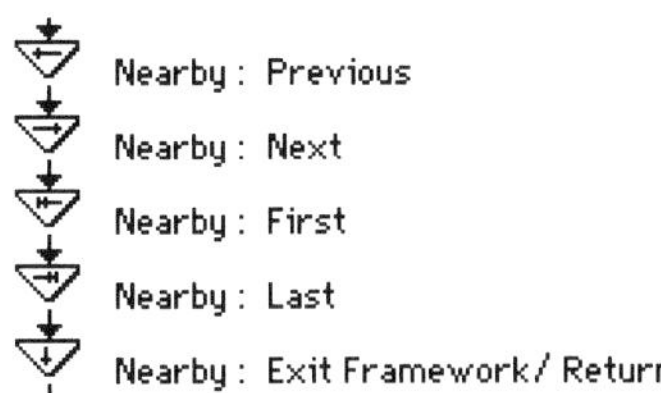

Nearby is only used for "local" navigation. *Nearby* options only allow the designer to select a Page from those attached to the current Framework icon. *Previous* recycles Pages in reverse order. If the user is currently on the first Page, *Previous* selects the last Page in the framework (i.e., if 26 adjacent Pages were labeled A, B, C,   X, Y, Z, then one possible outcome of selecting *Previous* repeatedly would be F, E, D, C, B, A, Z, Y, etc.).

Next presents Pages in order.   If the user is currently on the last Page, the list continues with the first Page in the framework (i.e., X, Y, Z, A, B, C, etc.).

First jumps back to the first Page in the current framework (i.e., to icon A). Last jumps forward to the last Page in the current framework (i.e., to icon Z).

As its name implies, *Exit Framework/Return* leaves the current framework and returns to the logic of the Course Flow Line or another Framework icon. This option is often critical. Without it, exiting a Framework icon may be impossible.

To Understand How Each of These Five Options Work, Complete the Following Exercise

- Place a Framework icon on the Course Flow Line. Label the icon "experiment"
- Attach three Display icons to the Framework icon. Label these icons "Language", "Math", and "Science".
- Enter the words "Language", "Math", and "Science" into their respective Display icons.

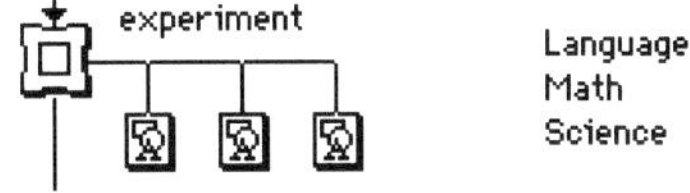

- Run the lesson. The page with the word "Language" will appear.
- Click the Previous icon ⬅ three time. Notice that "Science" appears (the item at the end of the list), followed by "Math", then "Language" again. Previous is accessing the Pages of the current Framework icon in reverse order.
- Run the lesson again. The page with the word "Language" will reappear.
- Click the Next Page icon ➡ three times. The following sequence will appear: "Math", "Science", and "Language". Next Page is accessing the Pages of the current Framework icon in order.
- Run the lesson again. The page with the word "Language" will reappear.

- Click the First icon. Nothing will happen because the lesson is already on the first icon. Click the Last icon. "Science" will appear. Click the First icon "Language" will re-appear.
- Click the Recent Pages icon. A navigation window will appear listing all recently visited Pages. Double-click on a Page's title to navigate directly to that Page.
- Run the lesson again. The page with the word "Language" will reappear.
- Click the Exit Framework/Return icon. The current framework will end.

Anywhere

Anywhere allows the designer to create links (from icons on the Course Flow Line or Pages in Frameworks) to Pages attached to any Framework icons in the lesson. In other words, *Anywhere* permits hyperlinks to be connected to a Page in the current file.

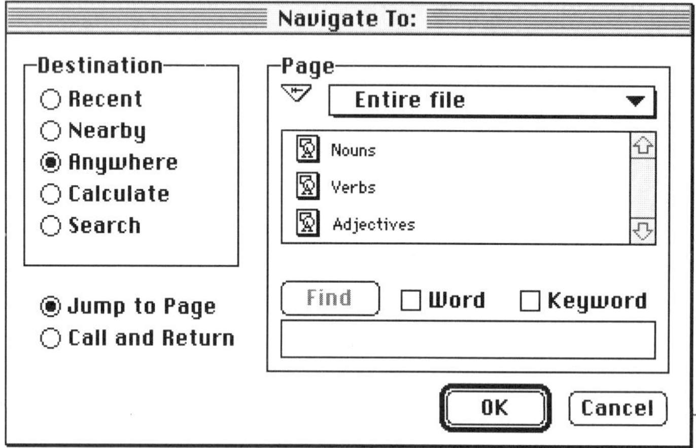

Making a link using *Anywhere* navigation requires the designer to select a destination Page from those listed. The Pages listed are grouped according to the title of the Framework icon to which they are attached. However, it is also possible to view a list of all the Pages that exist in the present file.

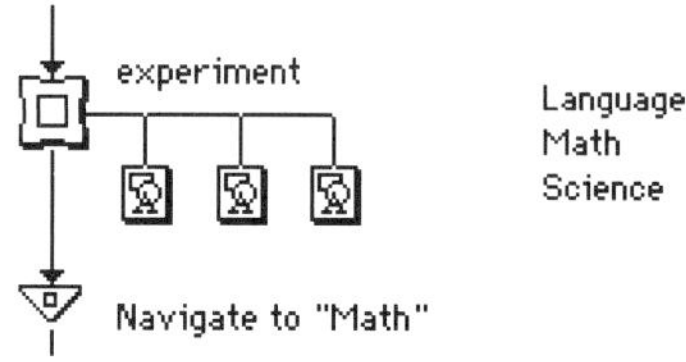

Calculate

The *Calculate* navigation link provides the most flexible navigation, but is the most complex to understand and use. Using *Calculate* requires that you understand Variables. Consequently, this section may be understood better after Chapter 13 on Variables has been completed.

The difference between *Calculate* and other navigation types is that *Calculate* allows the designer to create dynamic navigation. Standard use of the Navigate icon connects the user to a single Page in a Framework.

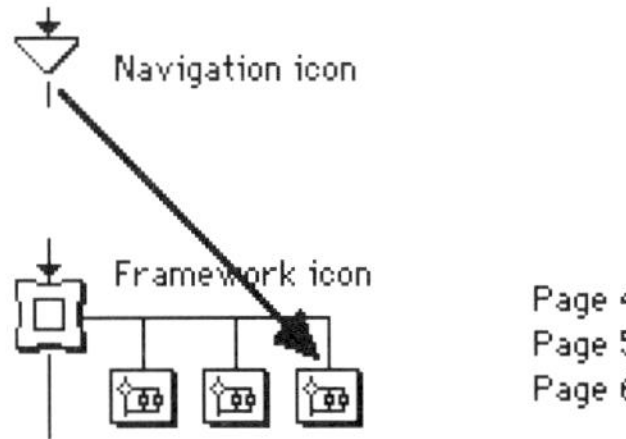

Standard link from a Navigate icon to a Page.

Creating a navigation link usually involves using the Navigate icon to make a single connection between a Navigate icon and a given Destination. For example, you might use a Navigate icon to connect to a Page titled "Page 6" in a framework. Once created, the Navigate icon cannot link to any icon other than the one to which a direct connection has been made. In effect, the Navigate icon and its destination page are *glued together*. However, by using *Calculate* to select a destination, together with an appropriately named variable, the designer can vary the destination to match the user's needs.

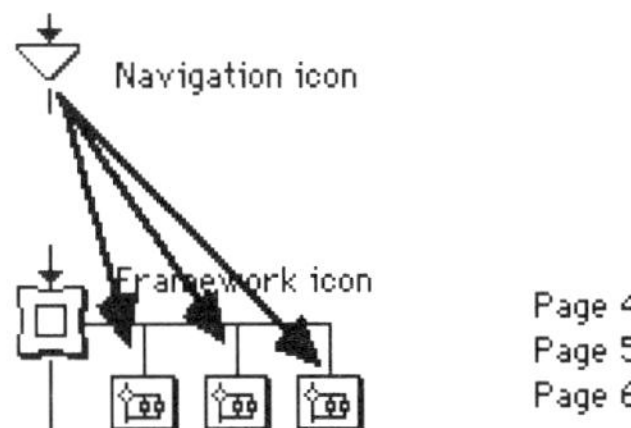

Link to a Navigate icon using *Calculate* to determine the destination.

Consider the following scenario. A designer wants to create a dynamic Help option in a lesson. By clicking on a word (or by using a pulldown menu), the user will connect to a help screen that contains contextually relevant information. That is, the help screen will be constantly updated to meet the user's ongoing needs.

One possible solution involves multiple Navigate icons. The designer could keep changing the navigation button as the user progresses through the lesson. However, this approach is "messy" because it involves using multiple Navigate icons.

Another solution involves using *Calculate* navigation. Using *Calculate* allows the designer to choose a destination that can change during a lesson. In other words, the Navigate icon can connect to many different Pages. Instead of connecting to a specific destination, *Calculate* connects to whatever destination is stored within a Variable. For example, the value stored in the variable may point to Page 4, or Page 5, or any other Page connected to a Framework.

Instead of connecting to a specific icon, the *Calculate* destination connects to an ID number stored in a Variable. Every icon has a unique ID number. Consequently, icons can be identified by their names or by their ID numbers. By storing a destination in a Variable and changing the value of the Variable, a Navigate icon can link to multiple Pages.

To find an icon's ID, highlight the icon and select Get Info from the Edit pulldown menu.

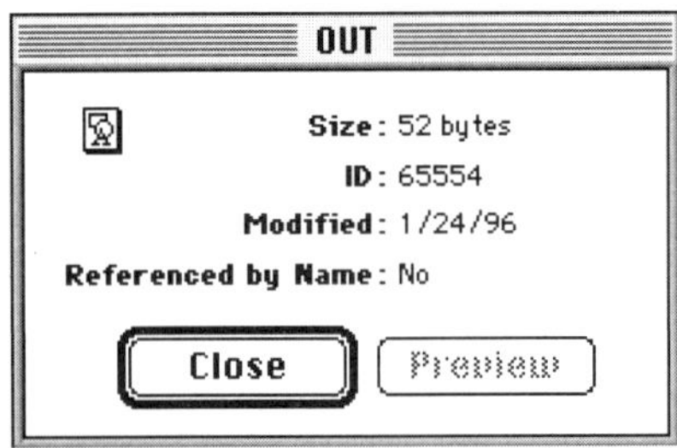

An information window containing important information about the highlighted icon, including the icon ID, will appear.

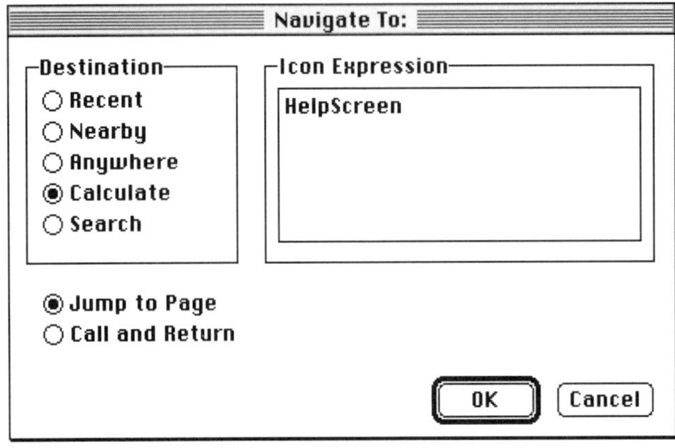

When you select *Calculate* as the destination, you enter a Variable into the window titled Icon Expression. This Variable stores the icon ID number and determines the destination Page. Rather than connecting to a specific Page, *Calculate* connects to the Page with the stored ID number. In the following illustration, *Calculate* connects to an ID number stored in a user-defined Variable titled HelpScreen.

Be Careful with the Calculate Destination!

The method you use to setup the *Calculate* destination is extremely important. As mentioned before, the *Calculate* destination links to a Page's ID number. On the surface, it appears to make sense to identify the ID numbers of the icons to which you want to link. A single Calculate destination could link to multiple Pages by changing the value of the Variable in the Icon Expression field to match the ID numbers of the destination Pages.

   Unfortunately, this apparent logic fails because the ID number assigned to a Page may change when the lesson file is Packaged! In other words, you may determine the ID number of a destination, only to find that Authorware changes this number, leaving you without a clearly defined destination. If this occurs, your lesson will not work properly.

   Outlined in what follows, is an approach that always works. The ID number of the destination Page is determined by using the Variable titled *IconID*. *IconID* returns the ID number of a named destination Page. Authorware never changes an icon's name. Consequently, you can use the *IconID* Variable to find an icon's ID by naming the Page you would like to link.

Calculations such as

HelpScreen=IconID@"Page 5"
or
HelpScreen=IconID@"Page 6"

vary the destination Page. Even though Authorware changes icon's ID numbers, this approach still works because the destination icon is identified by an icon name that will not change.

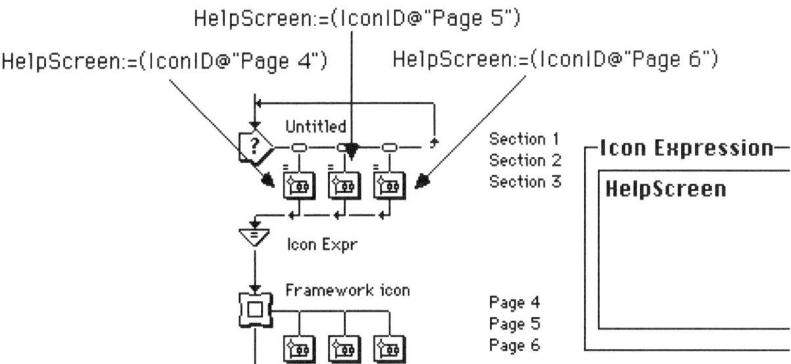

Search

Selecting *Search* causes a *Find* dialog box to appear. This box can be used by the user to hunt for Pages containing specific words or phrases. Authorware searches Pages for occurrences of the desired word(s) and returns a list of all matching Pages. The user can use the resulting list to navigate by double-clicking on a Page name.

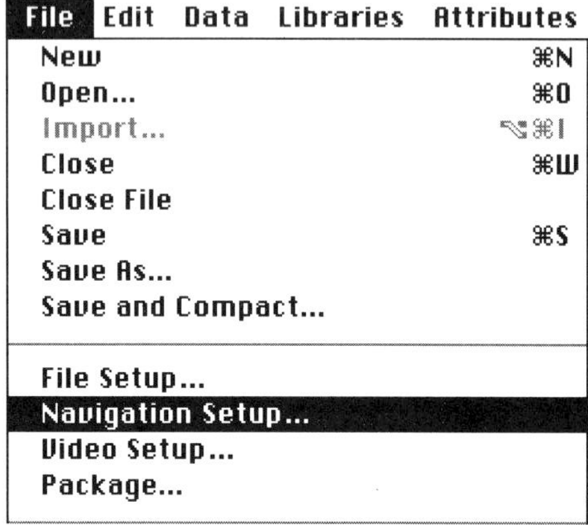

Note: The titles given to all buttons and windows for the Find dialog box can be edited.

Selecting Navigation Setup from the File pulldown menu produces the following editing window.

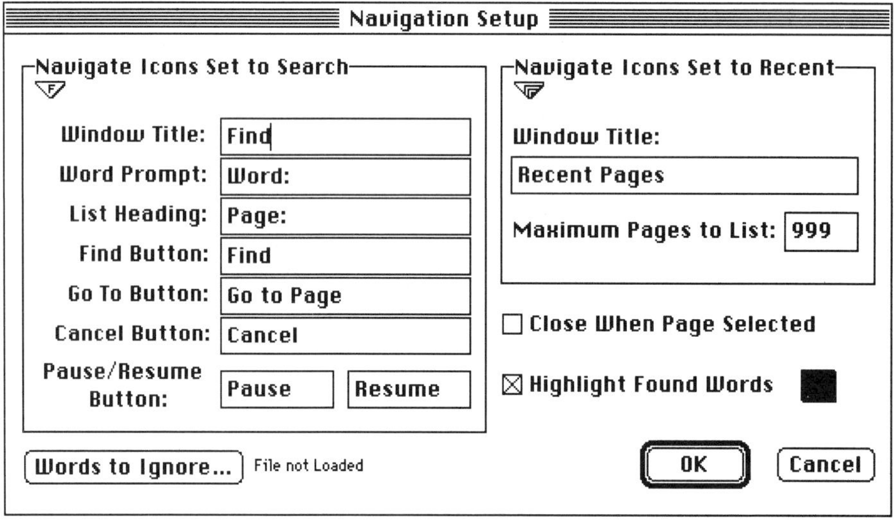

Other Types of Links

Navigate icons can also create links from any point on the Course Flow Line to a Page. In the following example, a Navigate icon creates a link to a Help screen. This type of link is different from others we have examined because the link is not initiated from a Page. However, the Destination icon is still (and must always be) another Page.

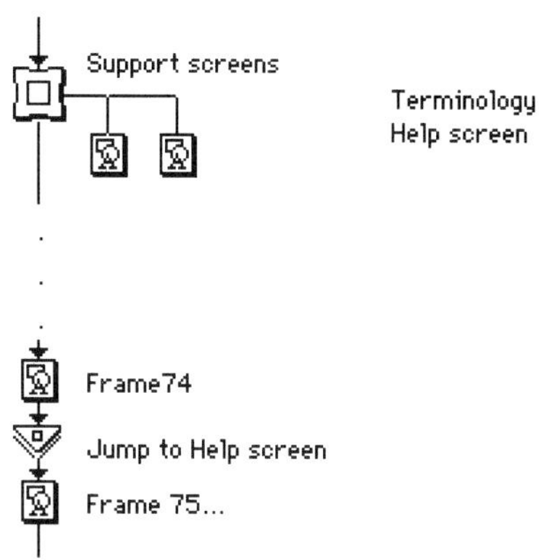

Call and Return

Sometimes you will want to link to a Page in another Framework and then return to where you came from. Three destination categories (Anywhere, Calculate, and Search) include the ability to connect to Pages attached to another Framework icon. Links may be one-way (called *Jump to Page*) or round-trip (*called Call and Return*).

Jump to Page links to a Page. Once connected, navigation is controlled by the new Framework. *Call and Return* also links to a Page, but returns to the original Page (or icon on the Course Flow Line) when it encounters an *Exit Framework/Return* navigation link. In effect, *Call and Return* works like a programming call to a subroutine.

Visual clues used to identify Call and Return are as follows:

Outlined (link set to Call and Return)

Not outlined (link set to Jump to Page)

Navigate icons that are "outlined" will return to the point from where they came when exiting a Framework.

To Understand How Jump to Page and Call and Return Work, Complete the Following Exercise

- Place a Framework icon on the Course Flow Line and label it Lesson. Add two Display icons as Pages and label each Page appropriately. Enter some text into each Display icon.
- Place a second Framework icon on the Course Flow Line and add three Display icons as Framework Pages. Label the Framework icon "experiment" and the Pages "Language", "Math", and "Science". Enter some simple identifying content into each Display icon.

- Create hyperlinks from the two Pages attached to the Framework icon titled "Lesson" to the three Pages attached to the framework titled "experiment". Select Anywhere as the destination and an appropriate destination Page for each link. In the following example a link will be established to the Page titled "Math".

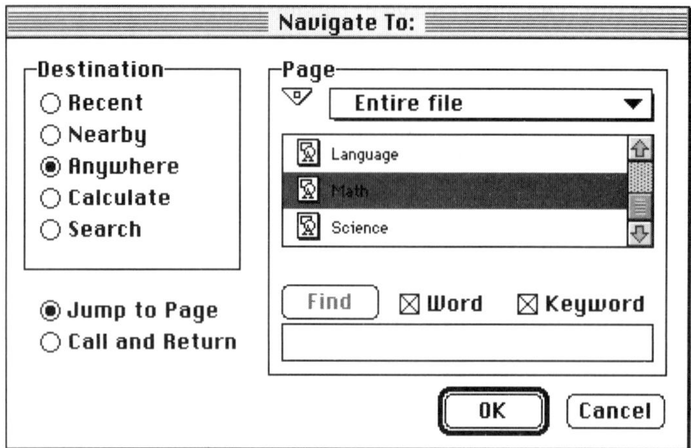

- Choose Jump to Page for the link. When you are done, your icons should resemble those outlined.

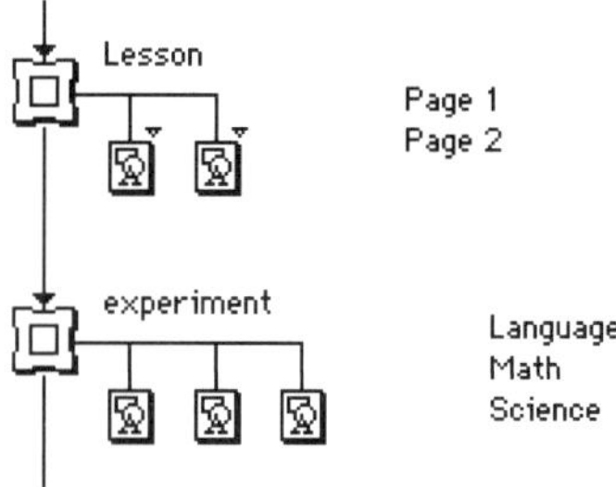

- Now Run the lesson and use the Navigation buttons to move between the Pages and to link from one framework icon to the other. Run the file several times and notice how links are created.

Erasing Pages

As you become more sophisticated as an Authorware designer, you will encounter different situations that require you to understand how Authorware erases information from the screen. *Jump to Page* and *Call and Return* use different erasing strategies when linking Pages. *Jump to Page* erases the contents of the current Page before displaying the new Page. This is very convenient because you do not have to worry about erasing or hiding unwanted information. In contrast, *Call and Return* leaves the contents of the original Page untouched. However, the advantage is that on returning to the original Page, the destination Page is erased.

Call and Return destinations can leave unwanted information on the screen. One technique to hide unwanted text or graphics involves creating a mask. A mask is an object (such as a rectangle) filled with white paint that covers unwanted displays. Once in place, the mask can be used as a fresh background on which new information can be presented. The following illustration shows a display with a mask that partially hides the screen. The mask can be enlarged and moved to ensure that no unwanted information shows. Also, lines on the mask are usually set to "invisible" in the Line palette.

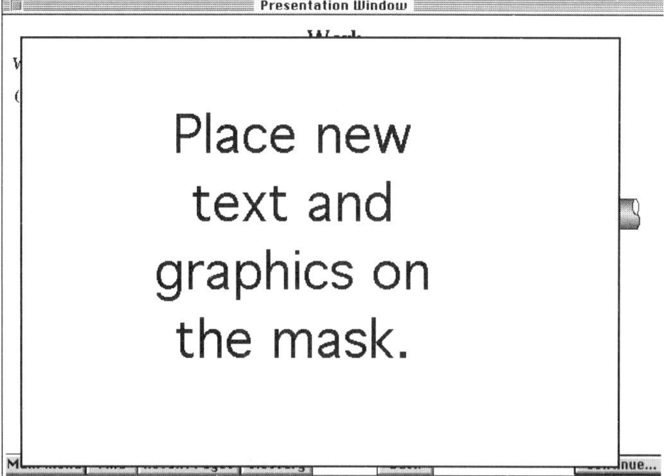

STUDY EXERCISES

1. Identify the destinations associated with each of the following Navigation types:

    Recent

    (A)

    (B)

    Nearby

    (A)

    (B)

    (C)

    (D)

    (E)

2. Explain the difference between *Jump to Page* and *Call and Return* navigation.

3. Create a lesson that includes at least two Framework icons and associated Pages. Establish Navigation links to Pages attached to the Framework icons using the *Anywhere* destination. Use the *Jump to Page* and *Call and return* options to experiment with their effects.

4. The following exercise is designed to help you to practice customizing your own Navigation Structures within a lesson. For each question, add three to four Pages to the Navigation Structure to test the Navigation buttons that you create.

    Create a Framework Structure that includes the following Navigation buttons:

    (a)   Page Forward and Page Back.

    (b)   Page Forward Recent Pages.

    (c)   Page Back and Last Page.

5. Create a Framework icon that includes three different Help screens. Using a Navigate icon with the destination set to Calculate, create a Help button that links to each of the Help screens at different points during the lesson.

13

Calculation Icons: Variables

CHAPTER OVERVIEW

In this chapter, you will learn about operations that can be performed in Calculation icons: storing information in Variables, performing transformations and other tasks with Functions, and writing comments to yourself or others.

Authorware's potential cannot be realized until Functions and Variables are understood. They make design flexible and many development problems can be by-passed through their creative use.

Many designers find this topic difficult to comprehend at first. The difficulty tends to be greatest for those who have never used a computer-programming language. However, with practice, most people prevail and learn to become much more effective designers.

This and the following chapter introduce Functions and Variables. Mastering their use involves many months, or even years, of practice. Most people find they become adapt at their use when they become involved with a real-life development task that requires designers to seek out tools that will resolve specific needs.

CHAPTER OBJECTIVES

By the end of this chapter, you will be able to

- Open the Calculation icon to use Variables and leave written comments.
- Understand differences among numeric, character, and logical Variables.
- Create your own Variables
- Type Variables into Display icons to display their contents.
- Type Variables into dialog boxes to control icons.

KEY TERMS

Calculation icon
Variables
System Variables
User Variables
Leaving comments

SUPPORT MATERIALS

On the CD-ROM disc, run **BEGIN.PKG** if you are a Macintosh user or **BEGIN.APP** if you are using a PC. When the file opens, click once on the title page to begin. Select the button titled **Chapter 13**, and watch the video about using Variables.

The folder on the CD-ROM titled MACDEMOS or PC_DEMOS contains several demonstration files that you can run and examine. The folder contains two versions of each file: a packaged file that you can run, and an unpackaged file containing the icons used to create the file. Run the file and examine how Variables can be used to control page numbering and other valuable lesson information.   Use the Text tool to examine each of the Variables on the screen.

Macintosh users:
Run the file CHP13.pkg to view its contents.
Open the data file CHP13.A3M to examine how the file was created.

PC users:
Run the file CHP13.APP to view its contents.
Open the data file CHP13.A3W to examine how the file was created.

Note: You must have a copy of Authorware on your computer to open the data files.

STUDY TOPICS

How Do I Enter Information Into a Calculation Icon?

There are two ways to enter information into a Calculation:
  (1).   By opening a Calculation icon on the Course Flow Line.
  (2).   By embedding a Calculation icon into an icon.

To open a Calculation icon, drag the icon on the Course Flow line and double-click on the icon.

Now, type your entry and Save before closing the Calculation icon window. If you close the icon before saving, you will be asked to save your entry or else you will lose any changes you may have made.

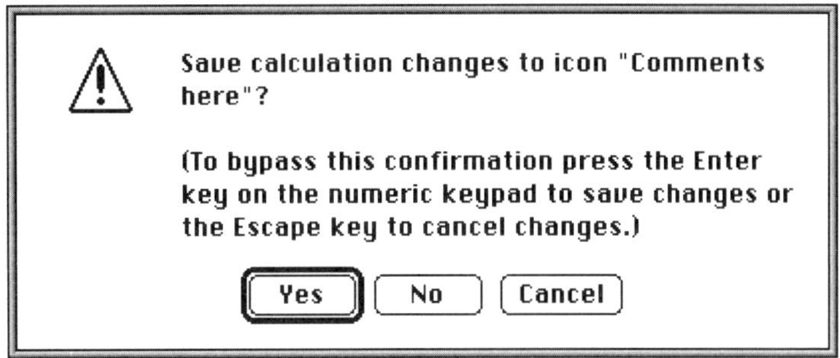

You can also embed a calculation into any other icon. This approach is useful when you want to ensure that an icon and a calculation are directly connected. Embedding a calculation into an icon is like making two icons into one.

Embedding calculations into other icons also helps to ensure that commands are executed in the correct sequence. Whenever an icon includes an embedded Calculation, the commands in the Calculation icon are performed before the contents of the icon are executed.

You can tell if an icon has an attached calculation simply by looking at the icon. Icons with calculations have an equals sign attached when they contain a calculation.

Example:

This Display icon includes an embedded calculation,

but this Display icon does not.

To embed a calculation into an icon, or to read the contents of an embedded calculation, highlight the icon and select Calculations from the Data pulldown menu. Enter text into the Calculation window that opens.

Leaving Comments

A Calculation icon can be used as a notepad. You can leave comments to yourself or other designers by typing two hyphens (i.e., – –) followed by the comment.

Comments are generally used in two ways. First, they are used to document complex processes that may be easily forgotten. Sometimes designers use several Variables and Functions in a single Calculation icon to resolve a problem. Comments help you to retrace your steps, especially when you have not worked on a file recently. Second, they help designers to communicate lesson details to each other.

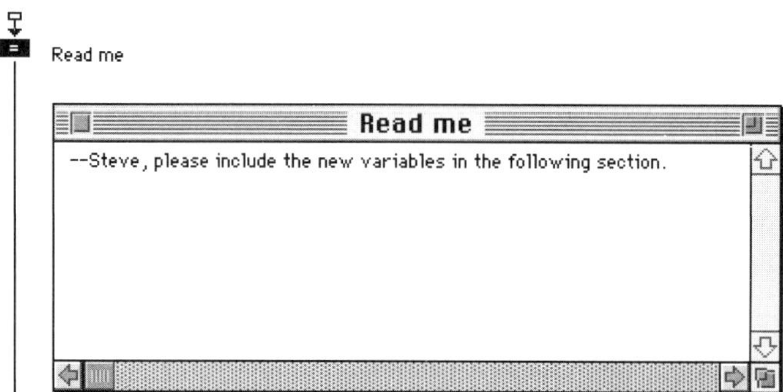

What Is a Variable?

Variables are like containers. However, whereas containers usually hold different types of objects, such as fuses, nails, and spaghetti, Variables contain information that may be useful in a lesson. For example, Variables may contain students' names, dates on which lessons were completed, students' achievement levels, and other information that may guide the design process.

Where Do I Use Variables?

Variables may be used in three locations:

- In Display icons
- In Calculation icons
- In dialog boxes

How Do I Use a Variable?

To use a Variable, either type the Variable's name where you want it to appear or place the cursor where you want the Variable and select Paste from the Show Variables window in the Data pull-down menu.

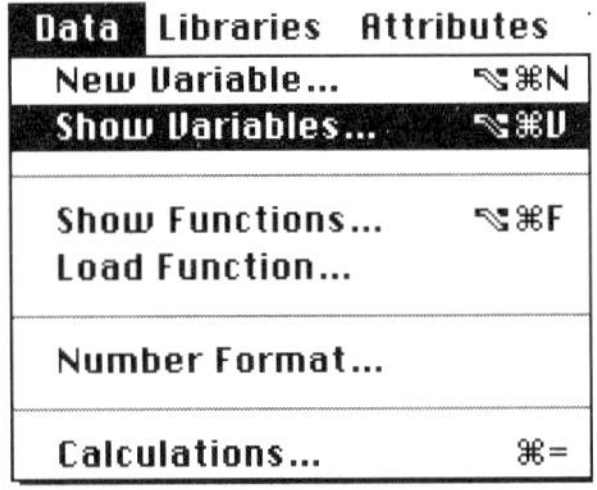

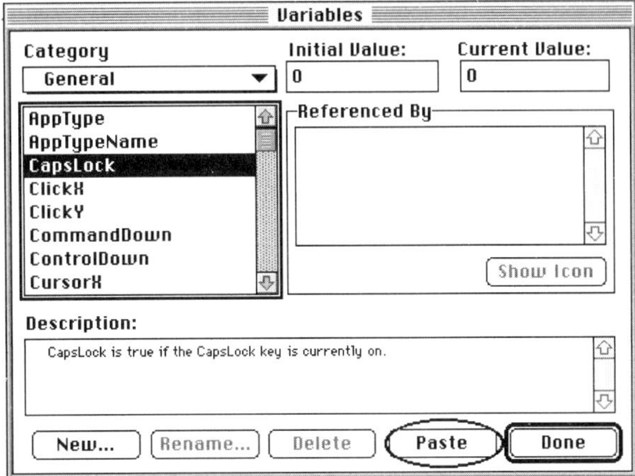

When Do I Use Variables?

Variables are used to perform three types of tasks:

- To display information on the screen.

  The contents of a Variable may be displayed on a screen by typing the Variable name within curly braces in a Display.

  Note: You MUST use { } and not [ ].

  Example: Type the following text into a Display icon. When you are done, choose the Selection tool with your mouse.

This produces the following display when the selection tool is chosen:

Today's date is 10/3/95.

- To trigger events.

  You may have noticed that some icons include a field titled Active If True.

Active If TRUE:

In the field you may compare a Variable to a condition. If the condition is true, the event is triggered.

Example: Imagine that you want a Help button to become active only when students have scored below 70%. If you type into the Active If True field

PercentCorrect<70

the option will be activated only when the value of the Variable PercentCorrect falls below 70.

- To track information; Variables can be used as counters.

  Example: To increment a student's score following a correct response, you could enter the following statement into a Calculation icon:

TotalCorrect:=TotalCorrect+1

This adds 1 to the old value of the system Variable TotalCorrect. So, if the student had previously answered 6 questions correctly, the total is updated to 7 following another correct response.

Types of Variables

Although recent versions of Authorware do not explicitly refer to different classes of Variables, it is important that you should understand that different classes do exist, that each class stores different types of information, and Authorware expects information to be entered in different ways.

Authorware uses three types of *Variables*: *numerical*, *character*, and *logical*. Numerical Variables contain numbers. For example, the mathematical constant Pi contains the value 3.1415926536. Character Variables contain text. For example, the words "Happy birthday!" could be stored in a Character Variable. Logical Variables contain the truth of a Variable, that is, either True or False. For example, the truth of the statement "Today is Tuesday" could be stored in a Logical Variable.

The difference between Numerical and Character Variables is especially important. Numerical

Variables can be manipulated with mathematical Functions. However, Character Variables contain only text and therefore cannot be manipulated mathematically. For example, if two Numeric Variables named First and Last contain the values 1 and 5, then

$$First + Last = 6$$

However, if First and Last were Character Variables containing the words "Happy" and "Sad", we could NOT add the Variables. Luckily, Authorware is rather forgiving and "senses" whether you are working with Numeric or Character Variables. In general, Authorware recognizes Character Variables by noting quotation marks around the contents of Variables. In the following example, the Variable *BestFriend* is a Character Variable because the information stored in the Variable is presented in quotation marks.

$$BestFriend:="Bill"$$

However, the statement

$$BestFriend:=21$$

is just as valid. In this case, however, BestFriend contains numeric data.

Note: The values 0, False, and Off are equivalent. Likewise, the values 1, True, and On are interchangeable.

System Variables

One of the Authorware's strengths is that numerous System Variables have been created for you. System Variables can be accessed through the Data pulldown menu.

Data	Libraries	Attributes
New Variable...		⌥⌘N
Show Variables...		⌥⌘V
Show Functions...		⌥⌘F
Load Function...		
Number Format...		
Calculations...		⌘=

System Variables are programmed to contain information that may be useful during a lesson. For example, the System Variable *PercentCorrect* contains an up-to-the-minute record of the student's performance during a lesson. System Variables save the designer considerable development time that would be needed to collect such information. However, if a Variable fails to perform a given task, the designer may need to create his or her own Variables. These Variables are known as User Variables.

The Variables window displays a list of System Variables. Click on a Variable to find out information relevant to that specific Variable. The following illustration shows the Variable titled *CursorX*. *CursorX* has an initial value of zero and a current value of 264. Based on information listed in the Description window, it is evident that the mouse is 264 pixels from the left edge of the monitor.

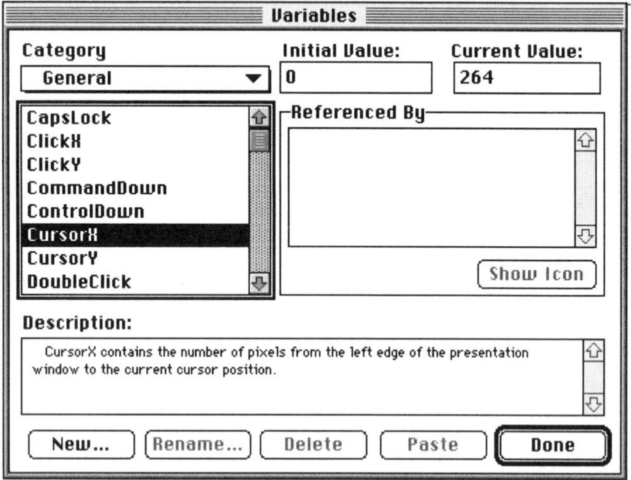

System Variables Categories

Learning to use Variables productively takes many months or even years of practice. Consequently, it is beyond the scope of this text to study Variables in depth. Instead, we will outline some of the more commonly used and important Variables.

System Variables are organized into categories for convenience. This helps to prevent searching the entire list to find one specific Variable. To see the list of categories, click-hold on the pulldown window beneath the label *Category*. You can view an alphabetized list of all the System Variables by selecting the "All" category.

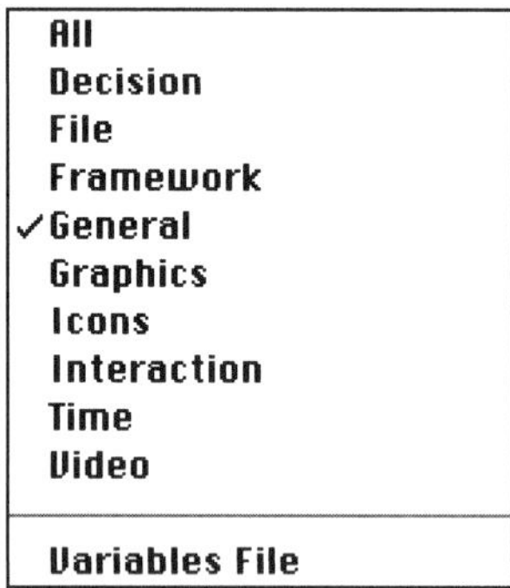

Decision Variables

Decision Variables store information about Decision Structures. The Variable *AllSelected* is a logical Variable that reports whether all the paths attached to a Decision icon have been selected at least once.

You could use *AllSelected* to check whether a user has examined every path in a Decision Structure. Users who have not examined every path might not be permitted to continue with the lesson.

File Variables

File Variables store information about file sizes and the location of specific files on hard or floppy diskettes. The Variable *FileLocation* is used to identify the location of the current lesson file. The location is important because it is common practice to store a database file containing lesson performance data in the same folder as the lesson file. *FileLocation* stores the path to the folder that contains the current Authorware file.

For example, if your hard drive is named Disk500 and your Authorware file titled "LessonFile" is stored in a folder named Lesson1, in a folder named Practice, then FileLocation will contain the following:

Disk500:Practice:Lesson1:

Notice that colons (except for the last one) are used to separate the names of folders. The final colon precedes the file name. On PCs, backslashes (/) perform similar tasks.

Framework Variables

Framework Variables store information about Framework Structures. The Variable *CurrentPageNum* contains the page number of the Page in the current Framework Structure. *PageCount* contains the total number of Pages in the current Framework.

Embedding the text

Page {CurrentPageNum} of {PageCount}

into a Display icon in a Framework icon entry Panel maintains a page-counting mechanism on the screen.

General Variables

The category General Variables provides an organizing structure to all Variables that do not have another home. As such, the types of data stored in this category tend to be quite diverse.

The Variable *Dragging* indicates whether an object in a Display icon is being dragged by the user. If you want to play a sound file while the user is moving an object on the screen, *Dragging* would let the system know whether or not the object was being moved.

Graphics Variables

Graphics Variables store information that is useful for placing graphics on screens. The Variable *Layer* contains the layer number assigned to an icon. For example, the Variable Layer@"Page5" contains the layer number assigned to the Display titled Page5. Remember that layers are assigned in the Effects dialog box.

Icon Variables

Icon Variables contain a wealth of information about different icons. The Variable ExecutingIconTitle is particularly useful in prototype testing and debugging. ExecutingIconTitle contains the title of the icon that is currently being used. Embedding this Variable into a Display allows the designer to enter text into a Display simply by modifying the icon's title.

Interaction Variables

Interaction Variables store information gathered while using Interaction icons. *EntryText* is probably the most commonly used Interaction Variable. Everything that a user types at a Text Entry interaction is stored temporarily in *EntryText*. For example, consider the following interaction:

Please type your full name.

When the user's name is typed into the computer, the text is stored in *EntryText* until another Text Entry interaction is answered. The Variable *EntryText* can be embedded into a Display icon or it can be compared to other Variables.

Time Variables

Time Variables contain information taken from the system clock on the user's computer or from dates that accompany files. For example, the Variable *Hour* contains the number that relates to the current hour (i.e., 0–23). At 11 p.m., *Hour* contains the value 23, and at midnight, *Hour* contains the value 0.

   Designers often embed Time Variables into Display icons. Typing the Variable *SessionTime* into a Display allows the user to view the amount of time invested in the present lesson.

Video Variables

Video Variables help to control digital movies and videodisc players. The Variable *VideoResponding* is a logical Variable that indicates whether a connection has been made between a video device and the computer. If the value stored in *VideoResponding* is true, a connection has been made. You could use *VideoResponding* to determine whether to start playing a videodisc.

User Variables

Although Authorware provides a diverse set of System Variables, you will often find that no Variable exists to meet your immediate needs. In such cases, it is necessary for you to create you own Variables known as User Variables.

How Do I Create a User Variable?

To create a User Variable:

- Under the Data pulldown menu, select New Variable. (The New Variable dialog box will appear.)

- Type a name for the new Variable (do not pick a name already assigned to a System Variable!). Try to select a meaningful name rather than a set of random characters.

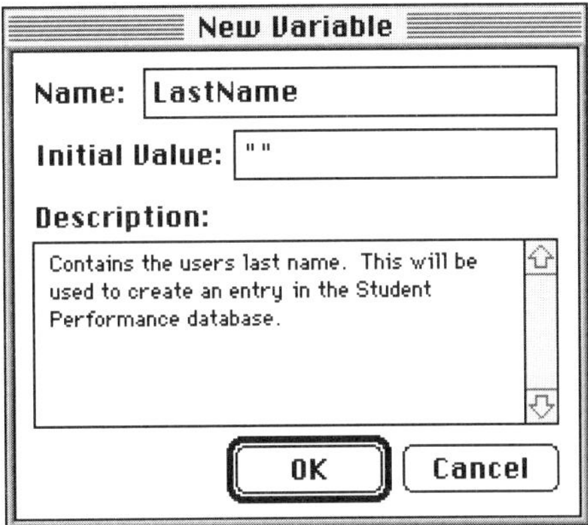

- State an initial value (i.e., a starting point for the Variable). The initial value in the Variable will remain until it is changed.   Remember that Character Variables are bordered with quotation marks. If you enter an initial value that is not a number and leave out the quotation marks, Authorware will assume you are trying to enter the name of another Variable.
- Document the Variable in the space provided. Provide sufficient information for another designer to be able to understand the purpose of the Variable.

Note: You do not have to create a new Variable before using it. Simply type the Variable in a Calculation icon, a dialog box, or a Display. Authorware will prompt you to define the Variable and will not continue with the lesson until the Variable is either defined or deleted.

Example 1

This example illustrates how the value of a Variable can be changed automatically.

- Type the Variable *FullTime* into a Display icon and run the lesson. Notice that *FullTime* does not change its value after it has been embedded into the Display, even though the time is constantly changing. However, Authorware has the capacity to update Variables as soon as their values change. In other words, Variables such as *FullTime* can change to reflect their new values.

To update the value of a Variable:

- Highlight or open the icon containing the Variable you want to update.
- Select Effects from the Attributes menu.

- Check the Update Displayed Variables box.

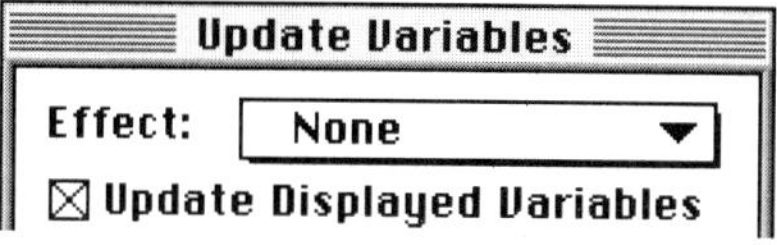

- Rerun the lesson.

What effect does this option have on the Variable? Notice how the time is now constantly updated. Also, the time remains on the screen until removed with an Erase icon.

Example 2

This example illustrates how the contents of one Variable can be transferred into another. The example illustrates how a System Variable named *FirstName* is automatically generated from the System Variable *UserName*. Remember that the Variable *EntryText* stores students' responses at Text-Entry interactions.

- Create an interaction with a Text-Entry response. Ask the user to enter his or her first and last names.

- Use a wildcard (*) to accept any entry. The text typed by the student will be stored in *EntryText*. The Map icon used for feedback in the following example is a "dummy" icon. It contains no information, but allows the designer to collect a response from the user.

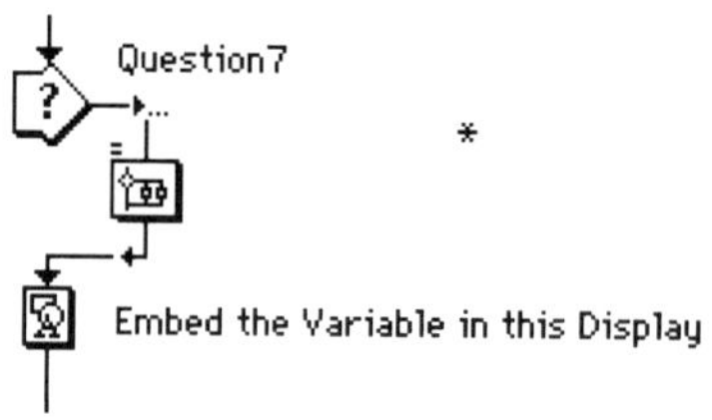

The calculation transfers the contents of *EntryText* into the Variable *UserName.*. The calculation contains the following:

UserName:=EntryText

- Type the Variables *UserName* and *FirstName* into a Display icon.
- Run the lesson to observe the result. Notice that the System Variable *FirstName* contains the user's first name even though you didn't put it there! *FirstName* is created automatically by Authorware. It contains the first word stored in the Variable *UserName*.

Example 3

This example illustrates how a User Variable can control whether a button appears or is hidden on the screen. Hiding buttons is important when users move from one screen to another. For example, in the following illustration, the designer might want to turn off each of the Navigation buttons when an option is selected, to prevent the buttons from cluttering the following screen.

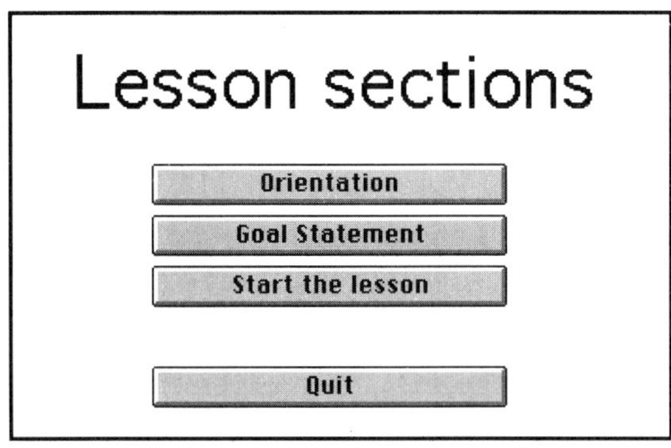

You can use a Variable to hide a button. The Variable can make the button inactive. The *Active If TRUE* field in the following illustration contains the User Variable *ShowButton*. The Variable operates like a switch. If *ShowButton* is true, the button shows, else it is hidden from view.

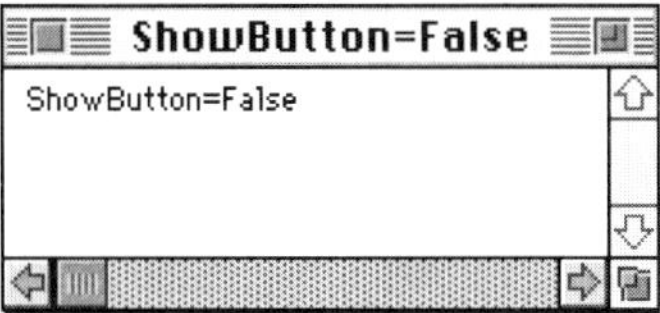

The value of the Variable is entered in a calculation. You could use the following Calculation icon in the entry Pane of a Framework icon to ensure the button is off.

This technique is powerful, because it allows you to make options available at different times during a lesson simply by changing the value of a Variable. Be very careful with calculations that turn buttons on/off. You need to be sure that you carefully plan and place calculations to ensure that buttons do not suddenly disappear when needed!

Special Features

The Assignment Operator

There is an important difference between the symbol = (i.e., an equals sign) and the := (i.e., the assignment operator). An equals sign is usually used to test the value of a Variable. For example, the calculation

$$\text{Test(Score=10)}$$

checks the value of Score.

However, the assignment operator is used to transfer information into a Variable. The calculation

$$\text{Score:=10}$$

places the value 10 into the Variable Score.

Luckily, Authorware recognizes the difference between the two cases and often replaces the equals sign with the assignment operator when necessary. Consequently, if in doubt, generally leave out the colon.

Resetting System Variables

Some Variables can be assigned values, but others cannot. For example, the system Variable *TotalCorrect* can be reset to 0 (or any other number). However, most system Variables are "read only." For example, the Variable Day, which contains the name of the current day of the week, takes its value from the system clock and consequently cannot be changed.

Reusing System Variables

Variables frequently change their values during lessons. However, Authorware never forgets the values assigned to some Variables. For example, the Variable *EntryText* changes its value every time a student answers a new Text Entry interaction. Luckily, although the value of *EntryText* changes, Authorware remembers old values of the Variable. To access the value of a Variable at a specific time during the lesson, use the following format: Variable@"IconName".

Example:

$$\text{EntryText@"question11"}$$

This example once again illustrates the importance of using unique icon name to avoid ambiguity.

Note: Not all Variables contain multiple values. Check the Authorware manual or the Variables dialog box for detailed information on each Variable.

STUDY EXERCISES

1. Look up the following Variables and provide a brief description of the types of information stored in each.

Variable Name	Description
ClickX	
Day	
DayName	
EntryText	
FileLocation	
FileName	
FirstName	

Variable Name	Description
Hour	
MachineName	
MemoryAvailable	
PathSelected	
PercentCorrect	
Sessions	
ShiftDown	
UserName	
WordCount	

2. Type the following text into Display icons to show the contents of the Variables:
    - Today's date is {Date}.
    - The present time {FullTime}.
    - The type of computer on which I am working is a {MachineName}.
    - The value of Pi is {Pi}.
    - I have been working on this lesson for {SessionTime} hours and minutes.

    Search through the list of System Variables and select five more Variables to embed in Displays. Read the description of each Variable in the Variables dialog box.

3. Authorware includes a System Variable to store students' names. The Variable is titled *UserName* and contains students first and last names. When *UserName* is used, Authorware automatically creates a new Variable that contains the user's first name. Not surprisingly, this Variable is titled *FirstName*!

    How can you obtain the student's first name?
    - Ask the user to type his or her first and last names as a Text Entry interaction.
    - Embed the following Calculation into a feedback icon:

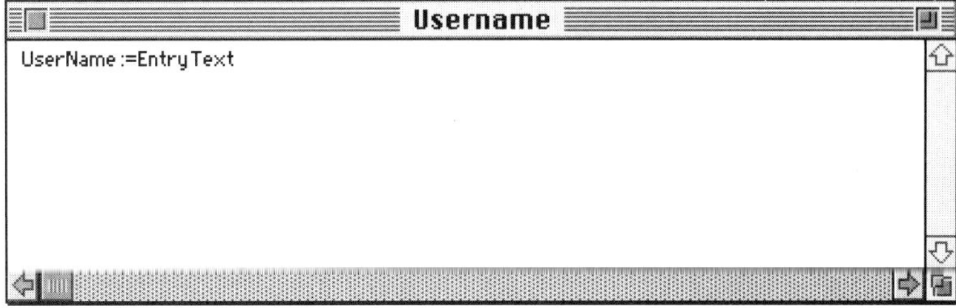

    Remember to Close and Save the changes to the Calculation icon.
    - Now type the following two Variables into a Display icon within curly braces that is {UserName} and {FirstName}.

5. User-defined Variables can be used to collect information during a lesson. User Variables are

particularly useful when the designer wants to collect information that is Not stored in System Variables. The following exercise 34e`    `1 employs User Variables to assist lesson navigation.

One of the greatest difficulties in computer-based lessons is navigating through information screens. Navigating through a book is much easier: just skim through the pages. To compensate, many designers include page number and indicate the total number of pages or screens in a unit (e.g., This is Page 3 of 7 pages).

The following exercise illustrates how to use User Variables to keep track of page numbers.

- Create a linear sequence of Display and Wait icons (approximately six screens). Title the screens Screen1–Screen6. (Although the information is not important, make sure that you include some content in each Display icon.)

- Create a New Variable titled Screencount. Set the Initial value of Screencount to the number of pages in the presentation.

- Create a new Variable titled Counter. Set the initial value of Counter to 0.

- Place a new Display icon titled Page Counter at the top of the Course Flow Line. Embed both Screencount and Counter into the Display icon at the border of the screen (i.e., Type the following: Page {Counter} of {Screencount}).

- While still in the Display titled Page Counter, select Effects from the Attributes menu and select Update Displayed Variables.

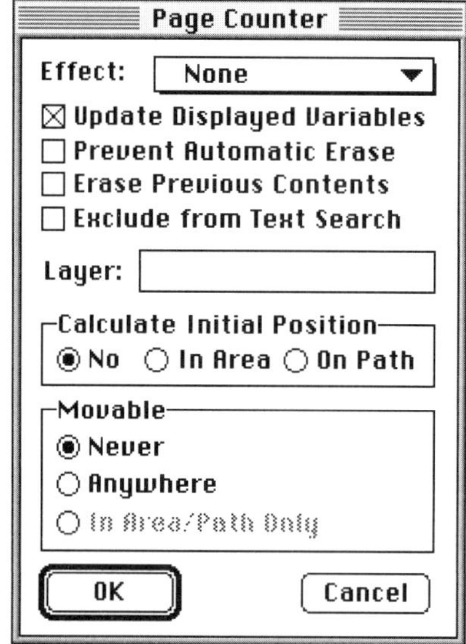

- Embed the following Calculations into Screen1, Screen2, and so on.

  Counter:=1

  Counter:=2

  Counter:=3, etc.

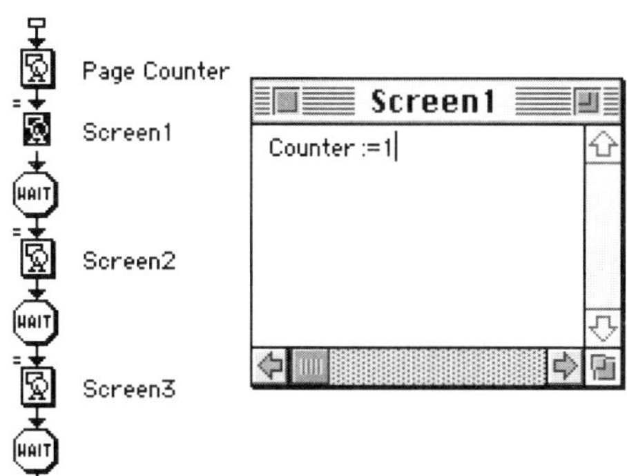

- Run the lesson and notice how the page numbers are updated.

6. Now repeat the preceding exercise using a counter to update the value of the Variable. This exercise employs the concept of incrementing Variables. In this exercise, page numbers are updated by increasing the value of the Variable Counter by 1 in each new Display, as opposed to including a specific value for the Variable. That is, the Variable Counter is updated without constantly entering the specific page number attributed to each screen frame.

- Use the same linear sequence of Display, Wait, and Erase icons used in the previous exercise.

- Replace the Calculation embedded into Display1, Display2, Display3, and so on, with the following:

$$Counter:=Counter+1$$

- Run the file and observe the result.

7. One way to make instruction more relevant involves using personal data to individualize questions. In the following exercise, you will use data collected during a lesson to personalize instruction.

Create a series of Text-Entry responses in which you ask the user to input personal information. For example, you might ask the user to name his or her favorite food, friends' name, sport, hobby and so on. Remember that information typed into the computer at Text-Entry interactions is stored in the Variable named *EntryText*. After collecting each entry, assign the contents of *EntryText* to User Variables. For example: Food:=EntryText; Friend:=EntryText; and so on. Now, create either a story or a series of questions that are "personalized" by including the information gained from the users.

14

Calculation Icons: Functions =

CHAPTER OVERVIEW

Consider the following scenarios:

(1). You ask a user to enter his or her full name into the computer. From this information, how could you separate the user's first name and last name?

(2). A user enters two numbers into a simulation to find the approximate area of a rectangle. The computer will multiply these numbers and print the result on the screen. However, you want to display only whole numbers. How can you remove any decimals from the result?

(3). In a backgammon game, the user will play against the computer. How can the computer generate random numbers to determine the values for the dice?

(4). You want to collect lesson information such as the names of users who have completed a lesson, the dates lessons were completed, and lesson scores. How can Variables be connected into a single Variable?

(5). Many lessons record students' performance and store the information into a data file. How can you record the information from the previous scenario in a text file on the computer?

(6). You may want to use and display the history of a student's progress. Such information is commonly stored in a datafile on the user's computer. How can you read the content of a data file into an Authorware Display.

(7). In a concept learning lesson, users must create maps that connect related ideas. How can you use Authorware to create a graphics program that will allow the user to create concept maps?

(8). Designers often transfer data files into lessons. These files can be disassembled and stored into many different Variables so the information can be used in the lesson. How can you transfer records from a text file into a lesson without having to use many Variables?

Creating files to achieve each of these scenarios involves understanding and using system Functions. In this chapter, we will examine how Functions work and illustrate their capabilities.

Functions are one of the most important and most difficult concepts to understand and use. To understand the full potential of Authorware's Functions, try to become involved in a development project. Solving real-world design problems will help you greatly to understand how Functions work.

CHAPTER OBJECTIVES

By the end of this chapter, you will be able to

- Understand the differences between Variables and Functions.
- Know how to use Functions.
- Know where to find on-line documentation about Functions.
- Apply system Functions to perform a range of tasks including

    --manipulating data

    --creating data files

    --concatenating Variables

    --collecting important lesson data

KEY TERMS

Functions
On-line documentation
Concatenation

SUPPORT MATERIALS

On the CD-ROM disc, run **BEGIN.PKG** if you are a Macintosh user or **BEGIN.APP** if you are using a PC. When the file opens, click once on the title page to begin. Select the button titled **Chapter 14**, and watch the video on using Functions in lessons.

The folder on the CD-ROM titled MACDEMOS or PC_DEMOS contains several demonstration files that you can run and examine. The folder contains two versions of each file: a packaged file that you can run and an unpackaged file containing the icons used to create the file. Run the file to see how Functions can generate sounds or create a simple graphics application.

Macintosh users:
Run the file CHP14.pkg to view its contents.
Open the data file CHP14.A3M to examine how the file was created.

PC users:
Run the file CHP14.APP to view its contents.
Open the data file CHP14.A3W to examine how the file was created.

Note: You must have a copy of Authorware on your computer to open the data files.

STUDY TOPICS

The following sections will

- Describe how Functions work.
- Explain how to use Functions.
- Illustrate a range of tasks that Functions can perform.

What Is a Function?

Many people confuse Variables and Functions. However, their roles are very different. In a nutshell, Variables are static, but Functions are dynamic. Whereas Variables simply store information, Functions perform tasks.

Functions are like tools. These tools perform a variety of operations that accelerate lesson development and allow designers to perform tasks that are not normally possible.   Just as a skilled carpenter carefully uses a range of tools to produce a professional product, effective Authorware designers use Functions to resolve development problems.

As Variables were organized into categories, Functions are arranged into one comprehensive list and 14 categories.

```
All
Character
File
Framework
✓ General
Graphics
Icons
Jump
Language
Math
Network
OLE
Platform
Time
Video
```

Sometimes Authorware does not have a Function to complete a specific task. In such cases, designers can create a new Function using programming languages like C and Pascal. Once created, these Functions can be loaded into Authorware where they become a permanent part of the application. Functions used in other software can sometimes be loaded into Authorware. To import a Function, select Load Function from the Data pulldown menu.

```
Data  Libraries  Attributes
New Variable...          ⌥⌘N
Show Variables...        ⌥⌘V

Show Functions...        ⌥⌘F
Load Function...

Number Format...

Calculations...             ⌘=
```

How Do I Use a Function?

Functions, like Variables, may be used in three locations:
- In Calculation icons
- In Display icons
- In dialog boxes

To use a Function, either type the Function's name or paste the Function from the Show Functions window in the Data pulldown menu.

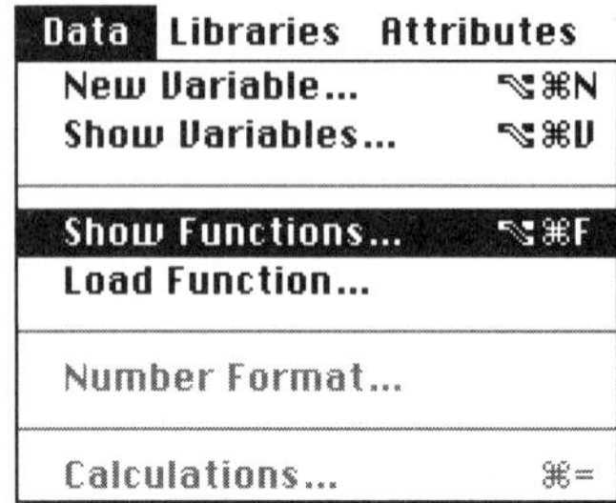

Clicking on the Function ASIN produces the following dialog box. Notice that the field titled *Referenced By* contains a single entry indicating that the Function has been used by one icon, titled "question2". Double-clicking on the label "question2" leads the designer to that icon on the Course Flow Line.

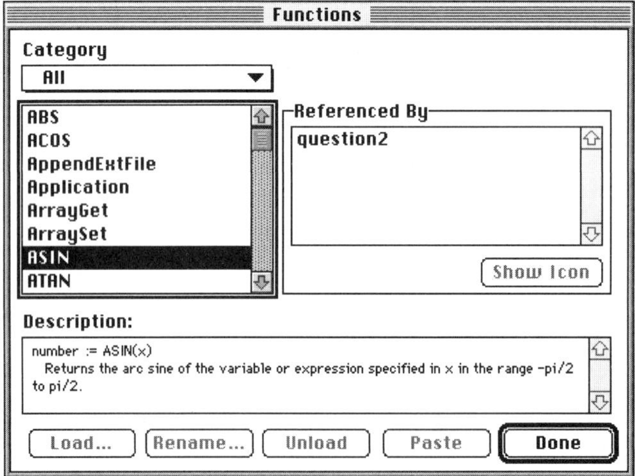

How Can I Learn More About Functions?

Every Function is described in the on-line documentation found in the Functions dialog box. Another approach to learn about Functions is to examine the files that accompany Authorware. Examine the Functions used in Calculation icons and dialog boxes in those files.

What Types of Tasks Can Functions Perform?

Functions can perform a broad range of tasks, too diverse to describe fully in this text. The following section will describe solutions to each of the problems posed at the beginning of this chapter. The problems have been chosen to illustrate Functions' breadth of use and to describe some of the more common tasks performed in course development.

Manipulating Data

Scenario 1: You ask a user to enter his or her full name into the computer. From this information, how could you separate the user's first name and last name?

Solution: The following illustrates how Functions can manipulate text. In the last chapter you used a System Variable named EntryText to store a user's name. The System Variable *FirstName* is automatically created by Authorware and contains the first word in *UserName*. You can use EntryText and the Function GetWord to determine the user's last name.

- Create a Text Entry interaction.
- Ask the user to type his or her first and last names into the computer.
- After the interaction, enter the following into a Calculation icon:

$$\text{LastName}{:=}\text{GetWord(2,EntryText)}$$

The Function *GetWord* extracts the second word from the Variable *EntryText*. The result of the transformation is placed into a User Variable titled *LastName*.   Remember that words in parentheses are assumed to be Variables unless the words are contained within double quotation marks (i.e., "").

Scenario 2:   A user enters two numbers into a simulation to find the approximate area of a rectangle. The computer will multiply these numbers and print the result on the screen. However, you want to display only whole numbers. How can you remove any decimals from the result?

Solution: The following activity illustrates how a Function can manipulate numbers.

- Create two Text Entry interactions titled "Question1" and "Question2".
- At each interaction, ask the user to type a number into the computer.
- Embed the following into a Calculation icon :

$$\text{Area}{:=}\text{EntryText@"Question1"*EntryText@"Question2"}$$
$$\text{Truncated}{:=}\text{INT(Area)}$$

- Place a Display icon on the flow line and type the following text:

$$\text{Your answer, truncated to the nearest whole}$$
$$\text{number, is \{Truncated\}.}$$

- The Function *INT* removes any decimals from the Variable *Area* and stores the result in the User Variable *Truncated*. Note that Truncated and Area are user-defined Variables.

Scenario 3:   In a backgammon game, the user will play against the computer. How can the computer generate random numbers to determine the values for the dice?

Solution: Authorware includes a random-number generator that will produce a random number between any two given values, in a specified step size. For example, the Function

$$\text{Random(0, 1, .01)}$$

produces random numbers between 0 and 1 in jumps of 1/100.

The product of a random-number generator must be transferred into another variable. For example,

$$\text{x}{:=}\text{Random(0, 1, .01)}$$

will transfer a single random number between 0 and 1, and measured in units of 1/100, into the User Variable *x*.

To produce numbers to use in a backgammon game, you need to generate two random numbers and transfer them into two User Variables (named x and y). The random numbers must be between 1 and 6 and must be whole numbers. The following calculation will produce the desired random numbers.

$$x:=Random(1,6,1)$$

$$y:=Random(1,6,1)$$

Now, you can embed the User Variables *x* and *y* into a Display icon, into a dialog box, or use them in another calculation.

Concatenation

Scenario 4: You want to collect lesson information such as the names of users who have completed a lesson, the dates lessons were completed, and lesson scores. How can Variables be connected into a single Variable?

Solution: Although storing information in Variables is a relatively straightforward task, arranging two or more Variables into a single Variable can be problematic. The technique used to combine two or more Variables into a single Variable is called Concatenation. The following examples illustrate how Variables can be connected through Concatenation.

Imagine that you have two User Variables, one named FirstWord and the other SecondWord. FirstWord contains the word "Happy". SecondWord contains the word "Birthday". You want to create a Variable (named *ConnectedText*) that contains the contents of FirstWord and SecondWord, separated by a space (i.e. "Happy Birthday"). Remember that text stored in Variables cannot be simply "added" together. In other words:

FirstWord + Space + SecondWord – Happy Birthday

The concatenation operator essentially glues together character Variables. It is indicated by a ^ [(i.e., a carat, (Shift-6)] between the Variables. Consequently, the solution to the question is:

ConnectedText:=FirstWord^" "^SecondWord^

Note that a space has been entered to separate the two Variables. Typing the Variable ConnectedText into a Display icon will produce the desired result.

From the original scenario, collecting lesson data into a Variable is achieved by concatenating several Variables. One solution is

StudentData:=LastName^TAB^FirstName^TAB^FullDate^TAB^TotalCorrect^Return

Note: Tabs and Carriage Returns have been used as separators. Tabs and Carriage Returns have important meaning in most database programs. Tabs enter data into a new field, and Carriage Returns create a new record.

Writing Data Files

Scenario 5: How can you record the information from the previous scenario in a text file on the computer?

Solution: The following activity creates a file on a hard or floppy disk. Before attempting this exercise, make sure that your current Authorware file has been saved onto a hard drive or a floppy disk: The activity uses the name of the disk and the folder where the lesson file is stored.

In the previous scenario, you stored lesson information into a Variable named *StudentData*. You will now store this information in a text (ASCII) file using the Function AppendExtFile. This

Function creates a text file in the specified location on the computer. If it already exists, the file is updated. In other words, the new information is added to the existing file.

The Function *AppendExtFile* uses the following syntax:

AppendExtFile("filename", string)

To use the Function, you must provide Authorware with two pieces of information:
filename: contains the location and name of the file that you will create or update,
string: contains the information that is to be stored inside the data file.

The filename includes the route to the folder where the file is stored and the name of the datafile. Remember that the Variable *FileLocation* contains the path to the folder when your lesson file is saved. For convenience, this is the same location where we will store the datafile. The string is usually a Variable containing organized lesson information.

In the following example, the Variable FileLocation and the filename (datafile.txt) have been concatenated using the concatenation operator (i.e., ^). The Variable containing data is titled *LessonData*.

Type the following into a Calculation icon *Exactly* as follows without additional characters or spaces:

LessonData:="lots of good stuff"
AppendExtFile(FileLocation^"datafile.txt",*LessonData*)

Close the Calculation icon and Run the file. After running the file, look inside the folder on your computer that contains your saved Authorware file. Notice that a new file titled "Datafile.txt" now exists. This file can be opened in a word processor. Open the file and look at its contents. The file should contain the words "lots of good stuff".

To solve the problem presented in the scenario, type the following into a calculation (assuming that the Variable StudentData contains some information):

AppendExtFile(FileLocation^"datafile.txt",StudentData)

Each time Authorware encounters this statement, another entry is added to the file datafile.txt. In this way, a database of student performance can be established. The file can be opened in a word processor, database, or spreadsheet program.

Reading an External Data File

Scenario 6:   You may want to use and display the history of a student's progress. Such information is commonly stored in a datafile on the user's computer. How can you read the content of a data file into an Authorware Display.

Solution: The following activity will read data from an external text file into Authorware.

- First, use a word processor to create a text file named "Data" containing a message. Remember to save the file in Text Only format. Place this file on your hard drive in a folder titled *Information*.

- In Authorware, create a User Variable titled *Message*.

- Use the *ReadExtFile* Function to read the contents of the file titled Data.

  Type the following into a Calculation icon:

  Message:=ReadExtFile("*your hard drive's name*: Information:Data")

- Now embed Message into a Display icon as follows:

  The content of the data file is {Message}.

- Run the File. The text that you typed into the word processor now appears on the computer screen. If it does not appear, place the data file into the folder on your computer where your current Authorware file is stored and replace the Function in the Calculation icon with

  Message:=ReadExtFile(FileLocation^"Data")

Generating Graphics

Scenario 7:   How can you use Authorware to create a graphics program?

Solution: Authorware Functions allow you to create graphics. You can combine Hot-Spot interactions with Functions to create a graphics palette that can be used to create concept maps that outline relationships between important lesson ideas. Users could draw ovals around related ideas or identify connections with straight lines.

  The following illustration describes how to set up graphics tools for users. The Interaction creates a hot spot on the screen. The Function DrawLine(1) is responsible for creating a drawing tool. The user draws a line by clicking and dragging the mouse anywhere within the hot spot. Remember to resize the hotspot in the Interaction display to provide the user with enough space to draw the shape.

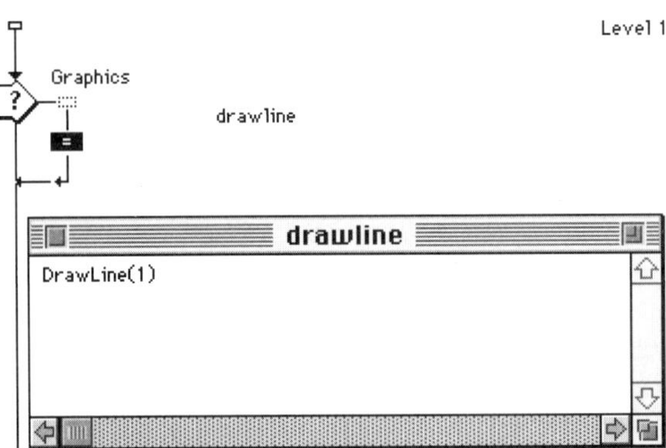

You can create a tool palette by combining multiple drawing Functions and an interface that switches on the drawing tools. In the following illustration, the Interaction icon titled Interface allows the user to select from three drawing tools, a line, a circle, and a box. Each tool is controlled using appropriately named User Variables in the Active if True box in the Hot-Spot response options. For example, the options for the hot spot titled *line=true* are set as follows.

Each hotspot in the interface also switches on the tool to be used. The tool is switched on with a Variable. For example, the hot spot titled *line=true* contains the calculation:

line=true

Switching on the tool allows the user to draw the shape in the drawing area. After using the tool, a User Variable switches off the tool, as illustrated.

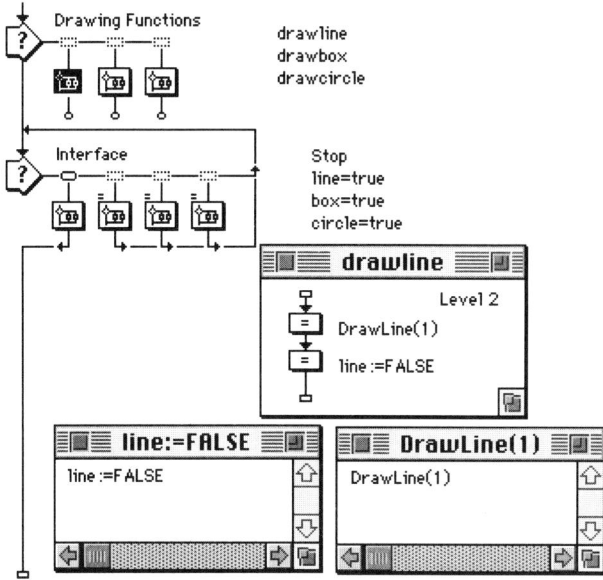

Data Transfer

Scenario 8:   How can you transfer records from a text file into a lesson without having to use many Variables?

Solution: An Array is an organized framework for storing large quantities of indexed data. The Array contains 2,501 cells numbered 0 through 2,500. Each cell can hold virtually an unlimited supply of information. Importantly, because each cell is numbered, it is possible to systematically store and retrieve information from the Array.

Functions are used to place information into or to retrieve information from a cell. The Function ArraySet() places information into the Array. The Function ArrayGet() retrieves information from the Array. For example,

ArraySet(251,StudentData)

places the contents of the User Variable StudentData into cell 251 in the Array

ArraySet(777, "Completed")

places the word *Completed* into cell 777.

Question1:=ArrayGet(1234) places the contents of cell 1234 into the Variable Question1.

To read several records from a text file into an Array:

Before beginning this exercise, place a text file titled datafile.txt into the folder containing your current Authorware file. The text file should contain at least 10 lines of text.

1. Type the following into a Calculation icon titled Calculation1:

$$Data:=ReadExtFile(FileLocation^{\wedge}\text{"datafile.txt"})$$

$$Records:=LineCount(Data)$$

- The Function ReadExtFile transfers the contents of the datafile into a User Variable titled *Data*.
- The number of records (or lines) in the Variable *Data* is counted by the Function *LineCount* and the result stored in the User Variable *Records*.

2. Type the following into a Calculation icon titled Calculation2:

$$ReadData:=GetLine(Data,1)$$

$$ArraySet(Line,ReadData)$$

$$Line:=Line+1$$

$$Data:= DeleteLine(Data, 1)$$

- The Function GetLine transfers the first line of text from *Data* into the User Variable *ReadData*.
- The Function *ArraySet* transfers the contents of the Variable *ReadData* into the first cell (cell 0) of the Array. (*Line* is a User Variable created with an initial value of 0.)
- The statement Line:=Line+1 increments the value of the Variable *Line* to move to the next line in the Array.
- The statement Data:=DeleteLine(Data, 1) cuts the first line from the Variable *ReadData*.

3. Place a Decision icon on the Course Flow Line. Repeat the Decision icon "Records" times.

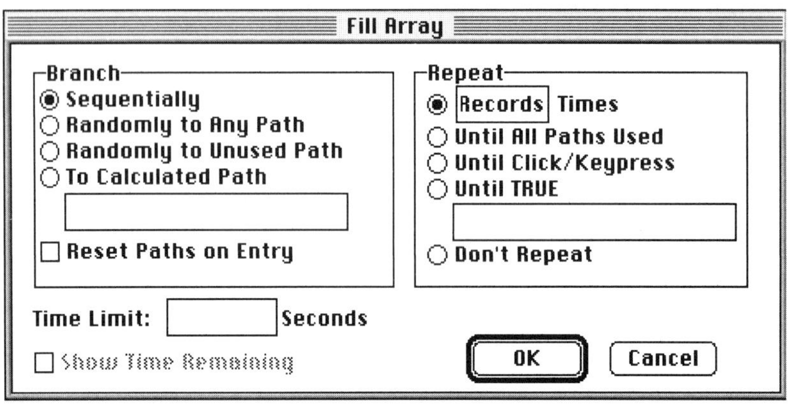

4. Attach Calculation2 to the Decision Framework.

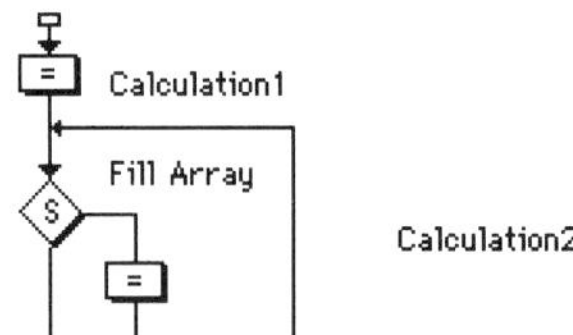

5. Running the file will place the contents of the text file into the Array. To see the contents of the Array, it is necessary to use the *ArrayGet* Function to transfer the contents of the cells from the Array into Variables. The following calculation transfers the content of the Array into three User Variables: *Cell1*, *Cell2*, and *Cell3*. Finally, the Variables must be embedded into a Display to show their contents.

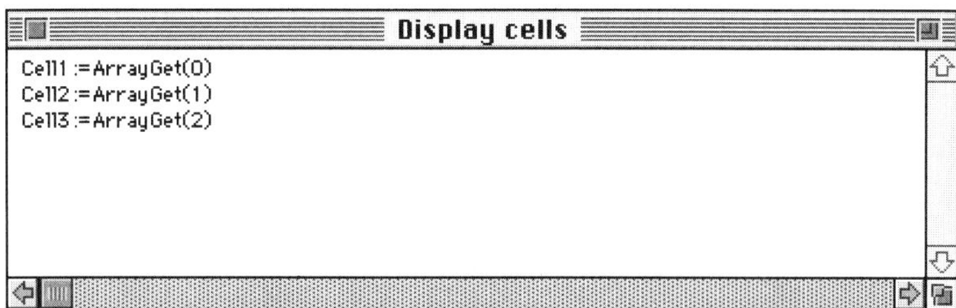

Arrays are very important in advanced courseware design. They are often used to store data sets in what is sometimes called "data-driven design." Data-driven design involves creating templates that use Variables to display lesson content in Display icons, instead of typing content directly into Display icons.

Data are transferred from a data file into cells in the Array. Functions are used to transfer information from the Array into the Variables. This technique can improve design efficiency greatly, because a single template can be used to create multiple lessons. When using a data-driven design approach, changing lesson content involves creating a new data file or editing an existing file in a word processor as opposed to developing an entirely new lesson file in Authorware.

STUDY EXERCISES

1. Create a new File and embed the following Functions into separate icons Calculation icons. Examine each Function separately.

    (a)   Beep()

    (b)   Box(3,50,50,100,100)

    (c)   Place two Calculation icons on the Course Flow Line and a Wait icon between them.

    In the first Calculation icon type: ShowTitleBar(Off)

    In the second Calculation icon type: ShowTitleBar(On)

    Now Run the file. What do you notice happening?

2. Create a lesson that asks the user for his or her last name. At the end of the lesson, create a data file using the given name to title the file. Inside the file record the time that the student took to complete the lesson.

3. (a)   Use the Function titled Random to simulate the role of a single die.

    (b)   Repeat the exercise to simulate the sum obtained from rolling two dice.

4. Create a generic bank of feedback items that includes statements such as "Great", "Well done", "That's Right", and so on. Create a minilesson and randomly generate such feedback. Try to do the same for incorrect feedback.

Note: You can also use alternate keys with Hot Spot and Button responses. These alternate keys can be used to activate Perpetual responses. That is, within the perpetual response, you can accept a given keypress to act as a Hot Spot or Button response. Then you can use the Function PressKey() in a Calculation icon to send a message to the computer that a given key has been pressed [(e.g., PressKey ("a")].

5.   Use Functions to create a Tic-Tac-Toe (also known as Noughts-and-Crosses) game against the computer. This is the child's game where players must connect circles or crosses onto a grid. Players alternate and the winner is the first to connect three like objects in a straight line.

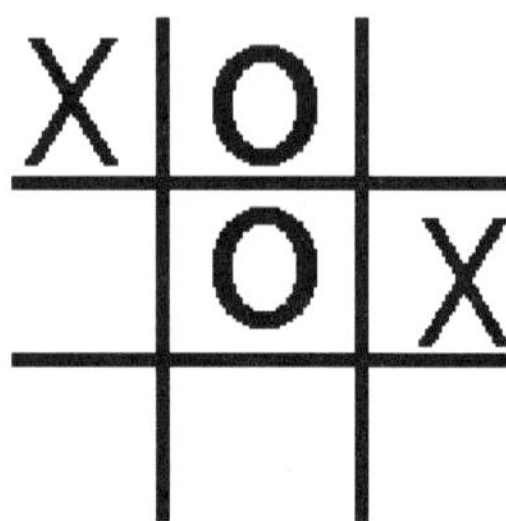

6.   Use Functions to create a simple game such as hangman or a crossword puzzle.

7.   Use Functions to create your own graphics application. The application should allow the user to select from three different tools, a rectangle, an oval, or a line. Also, the user should be able to select different line-thicknesses for the tools, different colors for the outlines of each tools, and a range of colors for the fills.

To complete this activity you will need to use the following Functions:
*   DrawLine
*   DrawCircle
*   DrawBox
*   RGB
*   SetFill
*   SetFrame
*   SetLine

Packaging Files 

CHAPTER OVERVIEW

The final step in the development process is to convert your lesson file into a stand-alone application. This process is known as course packaging. In this chapter, you will examine the options that must be set and additional files that sometimes have to be distributed with Packaged files.

CHAPTER OBJECTIVES

By the end of this chapter, you will be able to

- Transform your lesson into a stand-alone application.

- Understand the options that accompany file packaging.

- Distribute supplemental support files that are needed to ensure smooth lesson performance.

KEY TERMS

- Packaging a file

- Packaging a Library

- Including fonts

- Runtime software

- RunA3M

- Driver files

SUPPORT MATERIALS

On the CD-ROM disc, run **BEGIN.PKG** if you are a Macintosh user or **BEGIN.APP** if you are using a PC. When the file opens, click once on the title page to begin. Select the button titled **Chapter 15**, and watch the video to see how packaged files are created.

STUDY TOPICS

The files that you have been creating can be opened only on machines that have the Authorware application stored on the computer's hard drive. This causes problems when you want to distribute your lessons. Even if you could be sure that Authorware was installed on all the machines that were to be used, you wouldn't want users to change the lesson content and you would need to find a way to prevent users from accessing the Design Window. You can solve these problems by packaging your files. Packaged files will run on any computer regardless of whether Authorware is present. Also, Packaged files are not editable and do not allow access to the Course Flow Line.

Before packaging a file you should consider how several options in the File Setup pulldown menu may affect your final product. These options control how information is displayed in the finished lesson. See chapter 5 for these options.

To Package a course, select Package from the File menu.

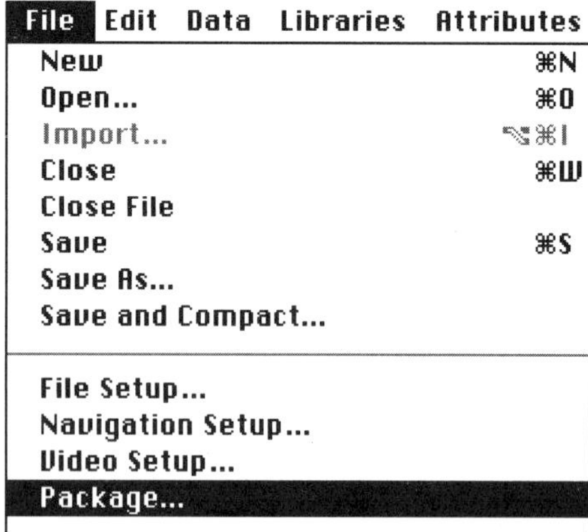

The following window will appear:

You must decide whether to package the file with or without Runtime software. Although all Authorware files must be packaged if they are to be standalone applications, not all files need to be Packaged with Runtime. Packaging with Runtime embeds RunA3M software into the Packaged file. Packaging without Runtime creates a compiled file that is no longer editable, but may not run as a standalone application on a computer. You can run a file that has been Packaged without Runtime if a copy of the RunA3M software is placed onto each computer. Packaging with Runtime software guarantees the packaged file will run.

It may help to think of RunA3M as a battery. Without the battery, Authorware files are powerless to run. However, a single battery is capable of running several Authorware files. Each file may be given its own battery or multiple files on the same computer may share a battery. Sharing saves batteries.

When multiple Packaged files are distributed on a CD-ROM or over a network, only one copy of RunA3M is needed to run all the files. Each Packaged file shares the Runtime software. Sharing RunA3M saves disk space.

If your lesson includes only a single Authorware file, it is typical to add Runtime into the Packaged file. However, if your lesson uses multiple Authorware files, including RunA3M in every file greatly increases the amount of space needed to store the files. Each time you include RunA3M in a lesson file, the file increases in size by approximately 900 K. Consequently, when packaging several related files, you will package Without Runtime.

You need to identify the computers that will be used to run the Packaged file. You can choose to package RunTime software for Power Macs, which takes advantage of the special processing capabilities possible with these systems, or you can package for standard Macintoshes. Alternatively, choose to package for all Macintoshes if you want to create just one application that will work on all Macintosh computers. Packaging For All Macintosh Models creates a file containing both Runtime files and increases the file size by approximately 1.8 MB.

If you Package without Runtime, you must include a copy of the Runtime software on each computer (or the disk containing lesson files) to be able to run the lessons. The figure below illustrates three files packaged without Runtime. These files share one copy of RunA3M. The following figure illustrates a single Authorware file packaged with Runtime.

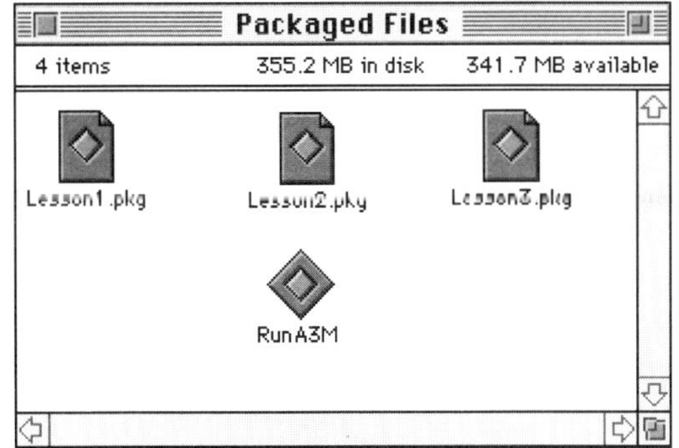

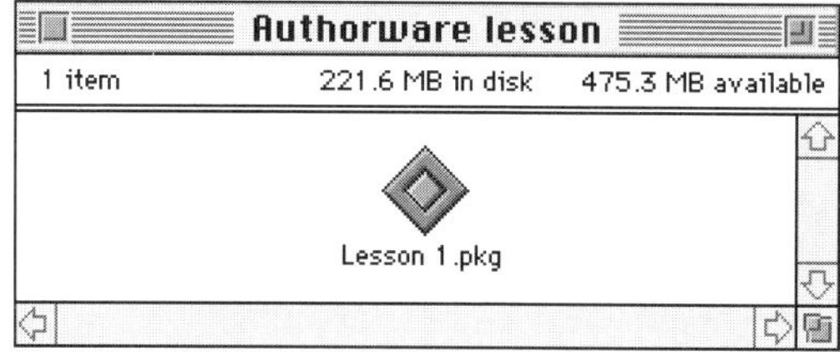

You must also consider four other options while packaging:

- Resolving broken links.

  This is important when using Libraries. When changes are made to Library files, for example when an icon is cut from a Library, Authorware must reestablish connections between icons in Libraries and icons on the Course Flow Line to ensure that content is properly displayed. In general, select this option unless you are sure that no changes have been made to the Library file or if a Library file is not used.

- Packaging libraries internally.

  Libraries can be packaged within a lesson file or independently. Independently packaged files must be included in the same folder as the Packaged lesson files. Using a Library during development automatically prompts Authorware to produce the following dialog box during the packaging process.

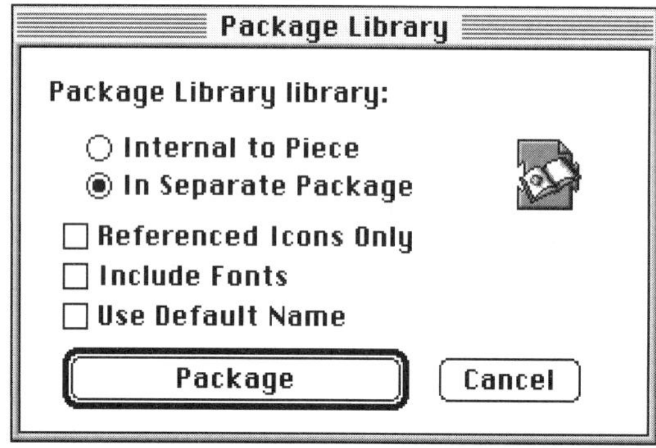

Your primary decision is whether to Package the Library within the lesson file or as a separate file. The decision, as with the decision to package files with or without Runtime, depends on how many lessons reference the Library. In the same way that you can package the Runtime software, RunA3M, within each packaged lesson file or enclose a single copy with multiple packaged Authorware files, you can package a Library within a packaged file or place a single Library in the folder that contains multiple packaged files. You can save storage space when distributing multiple lesson files by adding a single packaged Library file into the folder with the packaged lesson files.

If you have only one lesson file, then Package the Library internally. However, if you have several lesson files that share a Library then include the Library as a separate file. The following figure illustrates a file packaged with a separate Runtime file and a separate packaged library file.

- Including fonts helps to ensure that information will appear during the lesson just as it was designed. It is often difficult, or impossible, to ensure that users will have on their computers the same fonts and font sizes as those used by the designer to create a lesson. For example, a lesson might include instructions written in 18-point Avant Garde font. If the Avant Garde font is missing from the target computer, Authorware substitutes a font in its place. This often results in screens looking very different from the way they were originally designed.

  Including fonts helps to overcome this problem and is especially important when you are using any special characters in a lesson. Including fonts adds the fonts to the lesson file, ensuring that displays will appear as intended. However, including fonts increases the size of your final packaged file. In some cases, packaging fonts only marginally increase file size; however, in others, increases are significant.

- Using default names when packaging.

  Selecting this option causes Authorware to name the Packaged file with the given file name plus the suffix .pkg. For example, if your lesson file is named Tutorial, Authorware will name the Packaged file Tutorial.pkg. Be very careful with your name choice. Do not choose the same name for the Packaged file as the lesson name. This will erase the original file.

Distributing Files

After packaging a lesson, you will probably transfer the packaged files to a storage medium to facilitate distribution. This usually involves transferring your lesson to a floppy disk, a CD-ROM, or a transportable disk such as a Syquest or Bernoulli cartridge.

You may need to distribute some additional files with your Packaged lesson. You must include additional files if any of the following cases exist.

- Files were packaged without Runtime
- Files were packaged without a Library
- Lesson uses QuickTime or Director movies
- Lesson uses a Videodisc player or VCR

If you Packaged your file without Runtime software, you must include a copy of RunA3M in the folder that contains the Packaged lesson and/or Library files. Similarly, if one or more Library files were not included with a Packaged file, they too, must be included in the folder that contains the Packaged lesson. The following figure illustrates two packaged files together with a separate Runtime file.

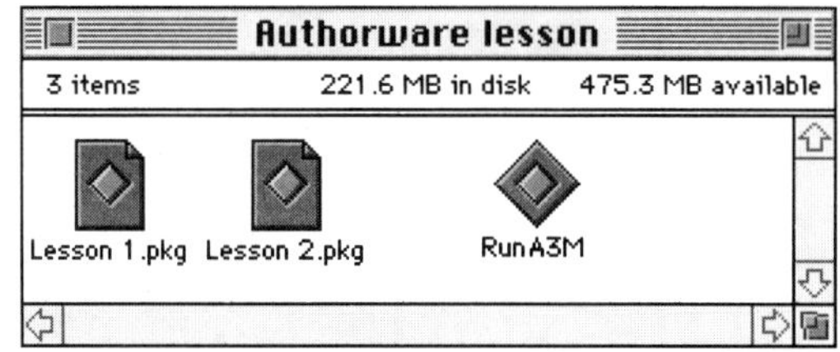

In addition to including runtime software and Library files with your Packaged lesson, additional files may be needed to ensure your lesson runs smoothly. You must include driver files whenever you use QuickTime or Director Movie files in your lesson. Driver files must be included whenever your lesson interfaces with a videodisc/tape player or a video digitizing board. For example, if your Packaged lesson uses both QuickTime movies and a Panasonic LDV-6000 videodisc player, two files titled *QuickTime™ Overlay* and *Pioneer LDV-6000* must be placed into the folder containing the Packaged lesson file. The driver files can be found on disks supplied with the Authorware application. The following figure illustrates a single packaged file that uses QuickTime files and accesses a Pioneer videodisc.

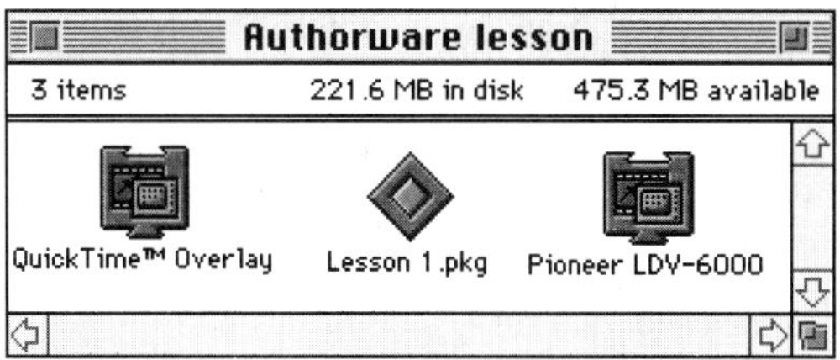

STUDY EXERCISES

1. Create a mini lesson that you will use to experiment with packaging options.
   - Package a lesson with RunA3M and run the Packaged file.
   - Reopen the unpackaged lesson file. Open the File Setup window and experiment with the options. Repackage and run the lesson file to observe the changes.
   - Create and use a Library. Package the lesson file and embed the Library in the Packaged file.

2. Create a mini lesson that includes a QuickTime digital movie. Package the file and place the packaged file into an otherwise empty folder. Run the Packaged file. What do you notice about the movie?

   Place a copy of the *QuickTime™ Overlay* file into the folder and rerun the packaged lesson. What happens to the movie now? Why is the *QuickTime™ Overlay* file important?

Shockwave for Authorware 

CHAPTER OVERVIEW

Although local networks and the Internet can be used to transport Packaged Authorware files from one location to another, until recently, Authorware files could not be opened directly over networks. In the past, through a process known as file transfer protocol (better known as FTP), files could be transported from one computer to another over a network. However, this approach did not allow files to be delivered on demand via a Web browser such as Netscape Navigator. Instead, quite sophisticated computer skills were needed by the end user to be able to access and run packaged files.

Shockwave for Authorware allows Authorware files to be delivered directly over networks and run through Netscape Navigator. Delivering a file via a network (known as Shocking a file) involves processing a packaged file through a software application named Afterburner. Afterburner prepares the Authorware site for network delivery, allowing users to connect directly to an Authorware file from a local network or a site on the World Wide Web (WWW).

CHAPTER OBJECTIVES

After completing this chapter you will be able to
- Shock a packaged file for delivery via a network.
- Load the necessary Plug-in software onto your computer to run Shocked files.
- Test the Shocked file from your computer.
- Configure a World Wide Web server to deliver Shocked files.
- Understand the capabilities of Authorware's networking Functions.

KEY TERMS

Internet
Netscape
Web browser

Shockwave
Intranet
File transfer protocol (FTP)
Uniform Resource Locator (URL)

SUPPORT MATERIALS

On the CD-ROM disc, run **BEGIN.PKG** if you are a Macintosh user or **BEGIN.APP** if you are using a PC. When the file opens, click once on the title page to begin. Select the button titled **Chapter 16**, and watch the video on preparing files for network delivery.

STUDY TOPICS

Authorware 3.5 allows developers to combine network capabilities with Authorware lessons. Until recently, Authorware lessons could be only distributed by using various delivery media (i.e., floppy disks, CD-ROMs, downloading from a network, etc.) to place copies of lessons onto users' machines. With the development of Shockwave for Authorware, multiple users can now receive lessons via the Internet or a local network, users can be directed to other network locations such as sites on the WWW, and data from lessons can be returned for central processing.

Shockwave has the potential to solve many existing educational and training needs. Consider the following scenarios:

Scenario 1: A company's human resources department regularly delivers updated training to employees on a CD. Copies of the CD are mailed to the employees, in several locations, who then load the training from the CDs onto their desktop computers. Apart from the development costs, distribution expenses include creating and mailing the CDs. By using Shockwave, the training department no longer distributes training on CDs. Instead, a singled Shocked version of the training is uploaded to a server and employees now run the lessons directly via the Internet.

Scenario 2: Students at a university must take a test. The test is delivered in paper form and students submit answers on mark-sense forms that can be scanned by a machine. Using Shockwave, students now log-on to a computer to take the test, and answers are scored and recorded into a database file.

Scenario 3: Shockwave also presents some futuristic capabilities for curriculum development. A biologist working for a pharmaceutical company comes across a problem in her work that she does not, but needs to, understand. Typically, she would go to the library to find information on the question. Such an approach would probably work well. However, going to the library involves leaving the workplace, finding the necessary information, and processing the information sufficiently well to be able to understand the information.

Alternatively, the biologist could use an expert system that quizzes her on what she needs to know as well and what she does not presently know. Once this information has been collected, Authorware could deliver an instructional module on the topic and ensure that she reaches an acceptable mastery level, without ever having to leave her laboratory.

Scenario 4: Another benefit of using Shockwave is that transitory information can be easily updated. Consider the simple example of a phone book. Typically, phone books are updated annually at great expense. In the future, a user working in a Shocked Authorware file could be connected with an on-line database that quickly returns the requested information from a database stored locally or on the Internet.

Shocking an Authorware File

The process of creating a file that can be delivered over a network involves three phases. First, a packaged file must be prepared for network delivery. This process is known as Shocking a file. Second, the designer must ensure that each machine on which the Shocked file is to run contains the necessary software. That is, the necessary Plug-in files must be loaded onto the computer. Finally, the computer that will store the Shocked files must be properly configured to deliver the files and a Home page must be written in HTML to create a link to the Shocked file.

The application *Afterburner* converts packaged Authorware files into Shocked files that can be delivered over local networks or the Internet. Afterburner compresses and dissects files into smaller chunks that can be delivered quickly and efficiently. Afterburner also creates a management file that controls which chunks will be delivered, when the files should be sent to the user, as well as the names of any additional files (such as Director movies) that might be needed.

To shock an Authorware file:

- Package the file without Runtime. The Runtime software that is needed to run the packaged file will already exist on the end user's computer. We will deal with this later.

- Run the Afterburner application. The Macintosh version is titled *Afterburner-MacFat-AW*.

- From the File pulldown menu select Afterburn.

File	
Open...	⌘O
Afterburn...	**⌘A**
Flatten...	⌘F
Quit	⌘Q

- Choose a file to Shock and a destination folder in which the processed files will be placed. This step establishes the location where the Shocked files will be stored and the name of the Map file. In the following illustration, a packaged file titled *lesson1.pkg* has been selected. The title *lesson1.aam* for the Map file is to be given automatically and is taken from the name of the packaged file.

- After selecting the Save button, the Segment Settings dialog box appears. Segmenting a packaged files creates two types of file: segment files and a map file. Each segment file contains a slice of the packaged lesson. The map files remembers how the slices fit together.

  The Segment Settings dialog box contains two fields. The Segment Prefix field is used to name the segments. The field contains four characters that are used to name each of the file segments that will be produced by Afterburner. You can use the default settings or use your own four-character prefix.

  Each segment is named with the prefix and four digits starting with 0000. Consequently, the second segment of the present example will be named less0001. Each segment also has the suffix *.aas*. Consequently, the complete title of the second segment will be *less0001.aas* The map file, which is an editable text file, has the suffix *.aam*.

  The Segment Size controls the byte size of each lesson subset. Shocked files are delivered in segments over networks as each segment is needed. Smaller segments are transmitted faster than larger segments, but require more frequent delivery. The default segment size is 16,000 bytes.

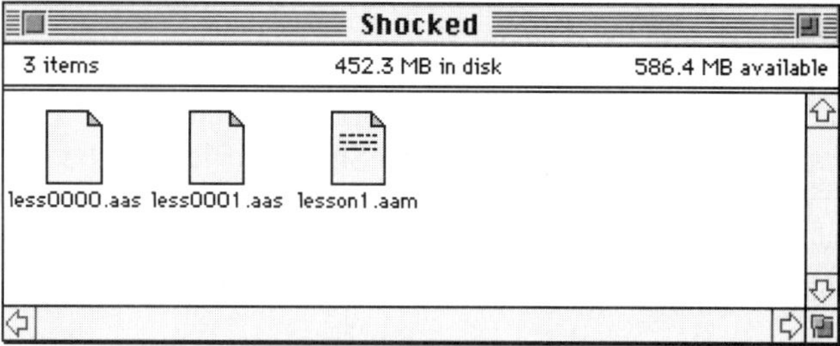

- After selecting OK, Afterburner creates the segment files and a map file that manages each of the segments. The following illustration shows two segments (less0000.aas and less0001.aas) and a map file (lesson1.aam), although in reality most lessons are made up of many more segments.

Loading Plug-in Software Onto Your Computer

To run a Shocked Authorware in Netscape Navigator, it is necessary to load special files known as Plug-ins into your Web browser. You must be using Netscape 2.0 or a more recent version of Netscape to be able to load the Plug-ins. The Plug-ins necessary to run Shocked Authorware files are presently available from Macromedia at the U R L :

`http://www.macromedia.com`

Plug-ins must be placed into the Plug-ins folder of your Web Browser on your hard drive. The illustrations that follow show a folder containing Netscape Navigator 2.01 together with the Plug-ins folder. The following illustration shows the contents of the Plug-ins folder including a default Plug-in and the two Plug-ins needed to run Shocked Authorware files on a Macintosh Power PC.

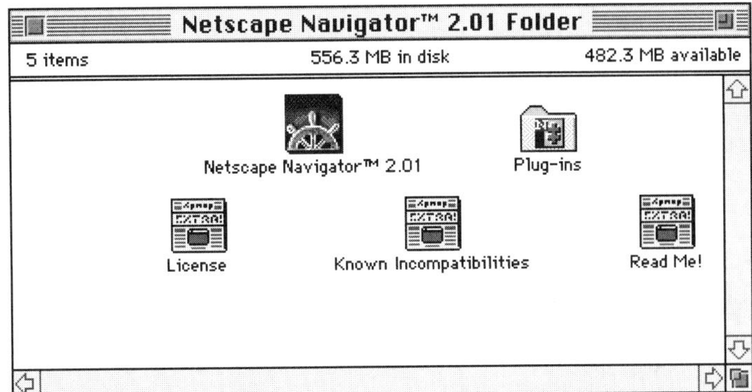

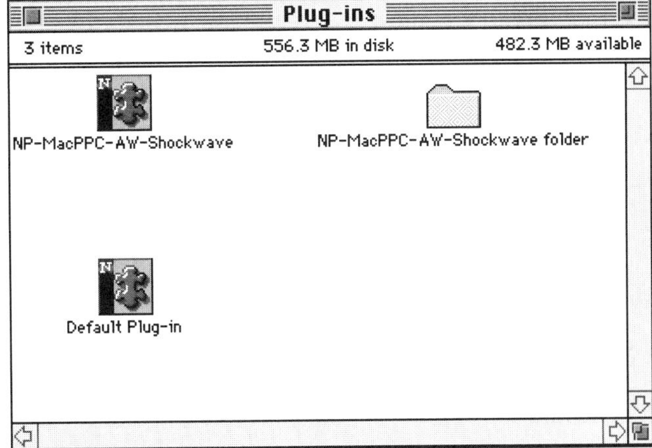

Testing Shocked Files

The folder containing the Shocked files will be placed onto a file server for delivery. Before placing your Shocked file on a server, you should test the file on your own computer. Select Open File in Netscape and open the appropriate file. You will open a map file with the .aam suffix. In the following illustration a Map file for the application titled *lesson1* is opened. The Map file determines the order in which the segments will be delivered.

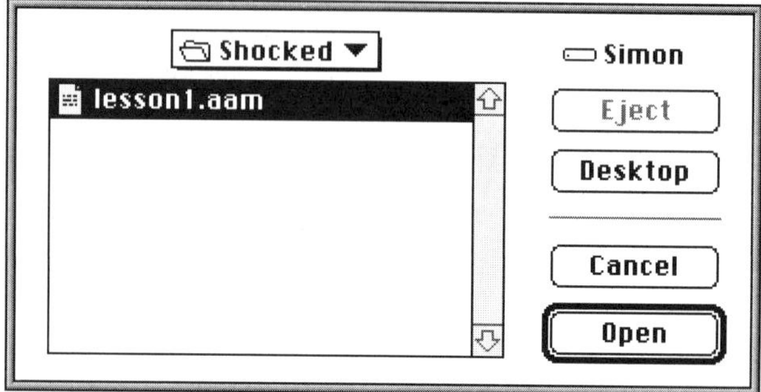

When you are sure the files are working properly, transport the entire folder to the server. However, before accessing the Shocked file from the server, the server must first be *configured*.

Configuring the Server

The server you are using to deliver Web pages must be configured to deliver Shocked Authorware files. The method you use to configure a server will vary according to the server type. To configure a Macintosh HTTP server, you must add the following lines to the MacHTTP.config file. The file can be found in the same folder as the default Web page for the server.

```
BINARY .AAM TEXT * application/x-authorware-map
BINARY .AAS TEXT * application/x-authorware-seg
BINARY .AAB TEXT * application/x-authorware-bin
```

Information on how to configure other types of servers is available from the MacroMedia web site listed above.

Writing the Web Page

When the Shocked files have been loaded onto a server for network delivery, you must write a home page that includes a link to the file. Running a Shocked file requires you to use the HTML tag EMBED. The EMBED tag tells the Web browser to play a Shocked file in the specified location.

The instruction is as follows:

```
<EMBED SRC="lessonname.aam" WIDTH=640 HEIGHT=480 WINDOW=onTop>
```

The WIDTH and HEIGHT commands specify the size of the window (measured in pixels) in which the Shocked file will be displayed. The WINDOW command controls the type of window used for the file. Macintosh users may select onTop or onTopMinimize.

The following illustration shows a file and folder as they would appear on the server. The file titled default.html contains a link to another page containing the EMBED command. The folder titled Shocked contains the Shocked lesson segments (less0000.aas, less0000.aas, and less0000.aas), the map file (lesson1.aam) and the file containing the EMBED tag (shockedfile.html).

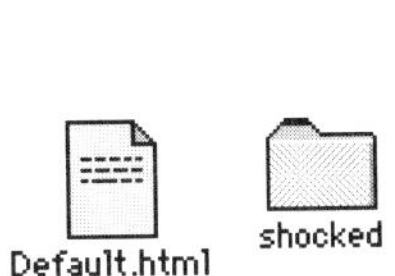

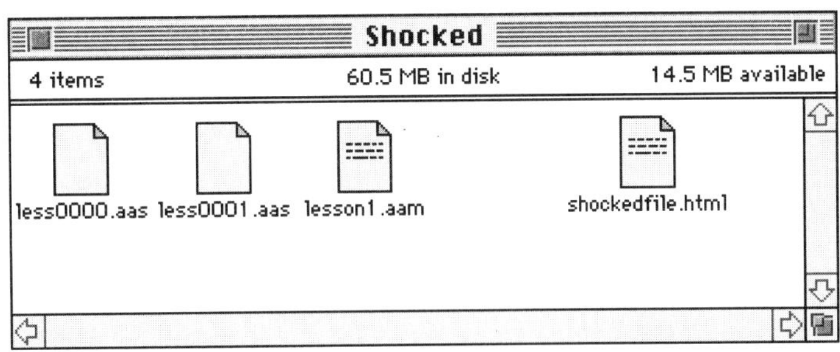

The following lists the HTML code to specify the link from the Home page to the file that includes the EMBED tag. After writing the HTML code, test the commands on your server.

File name: default.html

```
<HTML>
<HEAD>

<TITLE>Link to a Shocked File</TITLE>

</HEAD>
<BODY>
```

An example of a `<A HREF="Shocked/shockedfile.html">Shocked</A>` Authorware file.

```
</BODY>
</HTML>
```

File name: shockedfile.html

```
<HTML>
<HEAD>

<TITLE>Shocked File</TITLE>

</HEAD>
<BODY>

<EMBED SRC="lesson1.aam" WIDTH=640 HEIGHT=480 WINDOW=onTop>

</BODY>
</HTML>
```

Networking Functions

Two important networking Functions can be used to link to a Web page or to bring information from the Web into an Authorware file. You can use Authorware to connect the user directly to a Web Page. The Function *GoToNetPage* sends the user to the given Uniform Resource Locator (URL). URL is the term given to an Internet address where information is stored.

GoToNetPage gives the designer a tool to update lesson content. By connecting to Web pages, you can keep users current with up-to-the minute information.

Example:

Typing the following into a Calculation icon sends the user to the Macromedia home page.

GoToNetPage("http://www.macromedia.com")

As well as sending users to Web sites, you can download and use files stored on the Internet. The Function *NetDownload* transfers a file at the specified Web site into a Variable.

Example:

Typing the following into a Calculation icon

Latest:= NetDownload("http://www.university.edu/statslesson.txt")

transfers the file *statslesson.txt* onto the users' computer. Using the Function ReadExtFile, you can now transfer the contents of the datafile into a named User Variable. The information can be presented in Display icons, placed into dialog boxes, or used in any other way that data can be used in Authorware. As mentioned in Chapter 14, data downloaded from file servers can be used also for data-driven design. Designers can create lesson shells and lesson content can be accessed from files delivered over the Web.

STUDY EXERCISES

1. Take one of your lesson files that is packaged without Runtime software and prepare it for network delivery. Remember to
   - Shock the file
   - Store the Shocked files on a file server
   - Configure the server
   - Write a Web page to access the Shocked file
   - Load the necessary Plug-ins into Netscape's Plug-ins folder

   Before loading onto a file server, test the files on your computer.

2. Create a Shocked file that directs the user to information stored at various locations on the WWW. You will need to ensure that the users have Internet access for this activity to work.

End User License Agreement

PLEASE READ THIS DOCUMENT CAREFULLY BEFORE BREAKING THE SEAL ON THE DISK ENVELOPE. AMONG OTHER THINGS, THIS AGREEMENT LICENSES THE ENCLOSED SOFTWARE TO YOU AND CONTAINS WARRANTY AND LIABILITY DISCLAIMERS.

BY BREAKING THE SEAL ON THE DISK ENVELOPE, YOU ARE AGREEING TO BECOME BOUND BY THE TERMS OF THIS AGREEMENT. IF YOU DO NOT AGREE TO THE TERMS OF THIS AGREEMENT, DO NOT BREAK THE SEAL. PROMPTLY RETURN THIS PACKAGE, WITH THE UNOPENED ENVELOPE, TO THE PLACE WHERE YOU OBTAINED IT FOR A FULL REFUND.

1. Definitions

(a) "Company" shall refer to Prentice-Hall, Inc.
(b) "Software" means the software program included in the enclosed package, and all related updates supplied by the Company.
(c) "Company Product" means the Software and the related documentation, instructions, user's guides, tutorials, models and multimedia content (such as animation, sound and graphics), and all related updates supplied by the Company.
(d) "End-User Product" means the executable output file generated by you using the Software for use by a third party. Examples of End-User Products include animations, courseware, presentations, demonstration disks, interactive multimedia material, interactive entertainment products, and the like.

2. License

This agreement allows you to:
(a) Use the Software on a single computer of the type identified on the package, and load the Software in that computer's temporary memory and hard drive.
(b) Make one copy of the Software in machine-readable form solely for backup purposes. You must reproduce on any such copy all copyright notices and any other proprietary or confidentiality legends that are on the original copy of the Software.
(c) Transfer the Software and all rights under this Agreement to another party together with a copy of this Agreement, provided the transferee reads and accepts the terms and conditions of this agreement, and provided further you do not retain the original or any other copy of the Software.
(d) Make copies of the End-User Product and distribute those copies: (i) for use by personnel who are employed by you; or (ii) for use by third parties, provided that the copies are distributed free of direct or indirect charges to those third parties.

3. Supplementary Licenses

Certain rights are not granted under this Agreement, but may be available under a separate agreement with Prentice-Hall. In each case, if you would like to enter into one of the Supplementary Licenses listed below, please contact the contact person listed below.
(a) Site License: This Agreement does not authorize copying of the Software except onto a single hard drive and for backup. If you wish to make copies of the Software for use with additional CPUs owned by you, you must contact the person identified in paragraph 14 and request permission. The Company may, in its discretion, enter into a Site License with you.
(b) Distribution License: This Agreement does not authorize you to copy and distribute the End-User Product except as set forth in Section 2, above. If you wish to otherwise distribute an End-User Product, you must contact the contact person identified in paragraph 14 and request permission. The Company may, in its discretion, enter into a License Agreement with you.

4. Restrictions

The Software contains trade secrets and in order to protect them you may not decompile, reverse engineer, disassemble or otherwise reduce the Software to a human-perceivable form. YOU MAY NOT MODIFY, ADAPT, TRANSLATE, RENT, LEASE, LOAN, RESELL FOR PROFIT, DISTRIBUTE, OR CREATE DERIVATIVE WORKS BASED UPON THE SOFTWARE OR ANY PART THEREOF.

5. Ownership

The foregoing license grants give you extensive but limited rights to use the Company Product and the Software. Although you own the disk or other medium on which the Company Product and the Software is recorded, you do not become the owner of, and the Company retains title to, the Software and the Company Product, and all copies thereof. All rights not specifically granted in this agreement are reserved by the Company.

6. Limited Warranties

(a) The Company warrants that, for a period of ninety (90) days from the date of delivery (as evidenced by a copy of your receipt)(the "Warranty Period"), (i) the Software will perform in substantial conformance with the documentation supplied as part of the Product; and (ii) that the media on which the Software is furnished will be free from defects in materials and workmanship under normal use. EXCEPT AS SET FORTH IN THE FOREGOING LIMITED WARRANTY, THE PRODUCT IS PROVIDED "AS IS" WITHOUT WARRANTY OF ANY KIND, EITHER EXPRESS OR IMPLIED. THE COMPANY DOES NOT WARRANT THAT THE FUNCTIONS CONTAINED IN THE SOFTWARE AND THE COMPANY PRODUCT WILL MEET YOUR REQUIREMENTS OR THAT THE OPERATIONS OF THE SOFTWARE WILL BE UNINTERRUPTED OR ERROR FREE. THE COMPANY DISCLAIMS ALL OTHER WARRANTIES, EITHER EXPRESS OR IMPLIED, INCLUDING THE WARRANTIES OF MERCHANTABILITY, FITNESS FOR A PARTICULAR PURPOSE, AND NONINFRINGEMENT OF THIRD PARTY RIGHTS IF APPLICABLE LAW IMPLIES ANY WARRANTIES WITH RESPECT TO THE PRODUCT. ALL SUCH WARRANTIES ARE LIMITED IN DURATION TO NINETY (90) DAYS FROM THE DATE OF DELIVERY.
(b) NO ORAL OR WRITTEN INFORMATION OR ADVICE

GIVEN BY THE COMPANY, ITS DEALERS, DISTRIBUTORS, AGENTS, OR EMPLOYEES SHALL CREATE A WARRANTY OR IN ANY WAY INCREASE THE SCOPE OF THIS WARRANTY, AND YOU MAY NOT RELY ON ANY SUCH INFORMATION OR ADVICE UNLESS IN A WRITING SIGNED BY AN AUTHORIZED OFFICER OF THE COMPANY.
(c) SOME STATES DO NOT ALLOW THE EXCLUSION OF IMPLIED WARRANTIES, SO THE ABOVE EXCLUSION MAY NOT APPLY TO YOU. THIS WARRANTY GIVES YOU SPECIFIC LEGAL RIGHTS AND YOU MAY ALSO HAVE OTHER LEGAL RIGHTS WHICH VARY FROM STATE TO STATE.

7. Exclusive Remedies

(a) If the Software does not perform in substantial conformance with its documentation during the Warranty Period, please return the Software to the place from where you acquired this software, with a copy of your receipt and a description of the nature of the nonconformance. The Company will use reasonable commercial efforts to supply you with a replacement copy of the Software or work-around that reasonably conforms to the documentation. The Company shall have no responsibility with respect to Software that has been altered in any way or where the nonconformance arises out of the use of the Software in conjunction with software or hardware not supplied by the Company.
(b) If the media on which the Software is furnished proves defective during the Warranty Period, please return the media to the address in paragraph 14 with a copy of your receipt and a description of the defect. The Company shall have no responsibility with respect to any copy if the media was damaged by accident, abuse or misapplication.
(c) As an alternative to replacement as described above, and as your exclusive remedy in the event of a breach of the limited warranty, the Company may refund to you your purchase price for the Product.

8. Limitations of Damages

(a) THE COMPANY SHALL NOT BE LIABLE FOR ANY INDIRECT, SPECIAL, INCIDENTAL OR CONSEQUENTIAL DAMAGES (INCLUDING DAMAGES FOR LOSS OF BUSINESS, LOSS OF PROFITS, OR THE LIKE) WHETHER BASED ON BREACH OF CONTRACT, TORT (INCLUDING NEGLIGENCE), PRODUCT LIABILITY OR OTHERWISE, EVEN IF THE COMPANY OR ITS REPRESENTATIVES HAVE BEEN ADVISED OF THE POSSIBILITY OF SUCH DAMAGES AND EVEN IF A REMEDY SET FORTH HEREIN IS FOUND TO HAVE FAILED OF ITS ESSENTIAL PURPOSE.
(b) THE COMPANY'S TOTAL LIABILITY TO YOU FOR ACTUAL DAMAGES FOR ANY CAUSE WHATSOEVER WILL BE LIMITED TO THE AMOUNT PAID BY YOU FOR THE SOFTWARE THAT CAUSED SUCH DAMAGES.
(c) SOME STATES DO NOT ALLOW THE LIMITATION OR EXCLUSION OF LIABILITY FOR INCIDENTAL OR CONSEQUENTIAL DAMAGES, SO THE ABOVE LIMITATION OR EXCLUSION MAY NOT APPLY TO YOU.

9. Basis of Bargain

The limited warranty exclusive remedies, and limited liability set forth above, are fundamental elements of the basis of the bargain between the Company and you. The Company would not be able to provide the Software or the Company Product on an economic basis without such limitations.

10. Termination

This agreement is effective until terminated. You may terminate this agreement at any time by destroying the Product together with any permitted copies. This Agreement shall terminate automatically upon your breach of your obligations under this Agreement. Upon termination you must destroy the original Company Product together with any copies in your control.

11. Export Control

The Software is subject to the export control laws of the United States. You agree and certify that neither the software nor any direct product thereof is being or will be shipped, transferred or re-exported directly or indirectly into any country prohibited by the United States Export Administration Act and the regulations thereunder, or will be used for any purposes prohibited by same.

12. Government End-Users

If this product is acquired by or on behalf of a unit or agency of the United States Government, this provision applies. The Software
(a) was developed at private expense, is existing computer software, and no part of it was developed with government funds,
(b) is a trade secret of the Company for all purposes of the Freedom of Information Act,
(c) is "restricted computer software" submitted with restricted rights in accordance with subparagraphs (a) through (d) of the Commercial Computer Software - Restricted Rights clause at 52-227-19 and its successors,
(d) in all respects is proprietary data belonging solely to the Company, and
(e) is unpublished and all rights are reserved under the copyright laws of the United States.

13. General

This Agreement shall be governed by and interpreted in accordance with the internal laws of the State of New York, as applicable to contracts made and fully performed therein. This Agreement contains the final, complete, and exclusive agreement between the parties with respect to the subject matter hereof and supersedes all prior or contemporaneous agreements or understandings, whether oral or written. If any provision of this agreement shall be held by a court of competent jurisdiction to be contrary to law or otherwise unenforceable, that provision will be enforced to the maximum extent permissible and the remaining provisions will remain in full force and effect. Sections 6 and 7 shall survive termination of this Agreement.

14. Inquiries

All questions concerning the Product and this agreement shall be directed to: Prentice-Hall, Inc., One Lake Street, Upper Saddle River, NJ 07458, Attention New Media Department